THE INNER TEMPLE OF WITCHCRAFT

ABOUT THE AUTHOR

Christopher Penczak (New Hampshire) teaches classes throughout New England on witchcraft, meditation, reiki, crystals, and shamanic journey. He is the author of *City Magick* and *Spirit Allies*, and writes for several local and national metaphysical magazines.

THE INNER TEMPLE OF WITCHCRAFT

MAGICK, MEDITATION
AND
PSYCHIC DEVELOPMENT

CHRISTOPHER PENCZAK

Llewellyn Publications
Woodbury, Minnesota

First Edition
Tenth Printing, 2012

Book design by Donna Burch
Cover background © 2002 Studio Backgrounds by PhotoDisc
Cover design by Lisa Novak
Editing by Andrea Neff
Interior Illustrations © 2002 by Mary Ann Zapalac on pages 21, 32, figure on page 80, 150, figures on pages 200–201, figure on page 206, figure on page 208, figure on page 211, tree on page 227, 250, 253
Interior Illustrations by the Llewellyn art department on pages 47, 65, 75, 80, 102, 123, 127, 138, 145–146, 164, 166, 171, 179, 189, 200–201, 206, 208, 211, 227, 229, 312–313

Library of Congress Cataloging-in-Publication Data
Penczak, Christopher.
    The inner temple of witchcraft : magick, meditation, and psychic development / Christopher Penczak—1st ed.
        p.   cm
    Includes bibliographical references and index.
    ISBN 13: 978-0-7387-0276-6
    ISBN 10: 0-7387-0276-5
    1. Witchcraft. 2. Magic. 3. Psychic ability. I. Title

    BF1566 P465 2002
    133.4'3—dc21   2002030059

Llewellyn Publications
A Division of Llewellyn Worldwide Ltd.
2143 Wooddale Drive
Woodbury, MN 55125-2989
www.llewellyn.com
Llewellyn is a registered trademark of Llewellyn Worldwide Ltd.

 Printed in the United States of America on recycled paper

Other Books by Christopher Penczak

City Magick: Urban Spells, Rituals and Shamanism
(Samuel Weiser, Inc., 2001)

Spirit Allies: Meet Your Team from the Other Side
(Samuel Weiser, Inc., 2002)

Gay Witchcraft: Empowering the Tribe
(Samuel Weiser, Inc., 2003)

The Outer Temple of Witchcraft: Circles, Spells and Rituals
(Llewellyn Publications, 2004)

The Witch's Shield: Protection Magick and Psychic Self-Defense
(Llewellyn Publications, 2004)

Magick of Reiki: Focused Energy for Healing, Ritual & Spiritual Development
(Llewellyn Publications, 2004)

Sons of the Goddess: A Young Man's Guide to Wicca
(Llewellyn Publications, 2005)

The Temple of Shamanic Witchcraft: Shadows, Spirits, and the Healing Journey
(Llewellyn Publications, 2005)

Instant Magick: Ancient Wisdom, Modern Spellcraft
(Llewellyn Publications, 2006)

Magia Blanca al instante: Descubre el poder de tu intencion y tu palabra
(Llewellyn Espanol, 2006)

The Mystic Foundation
(Llewellyn Publications, 2006)

Ascension Magick: Ritual, Myth & Healing for the New Aeon
(Llewellyn Publications, 2007)

The Temple of High Witchcraft: Ceremonies, Spheres and the Witches' Qabalah
(Llewellyn Publications, 2007)

DEDICATION

To my parents, Steve, Laura, Christina, Jessica, Jen, Bridget, Kat, and all my teachers.
Thank you for setting me on this path.

CONTENTS

List of Exercises . . . ix
List of Figures . . . xi
Introduction: What Is the Inner Temple? . . . 1

CHAPTER ONE
Ask a Witch . . . 7

CHAPTER TWO
Digging for the Roots . . . 17

CHAPTER THREE
Flavors of Witchcraft . . . 41

CHAPTER FOUR
The Witch's Path . . . 59

CHAPTER FIVE
Lesson One—The Magickal Mind . . . 71

CHAPTER SIX
Lesson Two—Meditation . . . 93

CHAPTER SEVEN
Lesson Three—The Magick of Science . . . 119

CHAPTER EIGHT
Lesson Four—The Science of Magick . . . 129

CHAPTER NINE
Lesson Five—The Art of Defense . . . 167

CHAPTER TEN
Lesson Six—The Power of Light . . . 181

CHAPTER ELEVEN
Lesson Seven—Energy Anatomy . . . 193

CHAPTER TWELVE
Lesson Eight—Journey Work . . . 221

CHAPTER THIRTEEN
Lesson Nine—Spirit Work . . . 237

CHAPTER FOURTEEN
Lesson Ten—The Inner Temple . . . 259

CHAPTER FIFTEEN
Lesson Eleven—Healing . . . 273

CHAPTER SIXTEEN
Lesson Twelve—Born Again . . . 291

CHAPTER SEVENTEEN
Lesson Thirteen—Initiation . . . 305

Appendix: Self-Test . . . 323
Bibliography . . . 329
Index . . . 333

LIST OF EXERCISES

Exercise 1—Intention Ritual . . . 69

Exercise 2—Feeling Energy . . . 81

Exercise 3—Ball of Energy . . . 82

Exercise 4—Feeling the Aura . . . 83

Exercise 5—Pushing and Pulling Energy . . . 84

Exercise 6—Earth Walking . . . 85

Exercise 7—Total Relaxation . . . 96

Exercise 8—Candle Meditation . . . 97

Exercise 9—Counting Down to a Meditative State . . . 99

Exercise 10—Basic Visualization . . . 102

Exercise 11—Affirmations . . . 107

Exercise 12—Programming Your Trigger . . . 114

Exercise 13—Mental Projection . . . 134

Exercise 14—Correspondences . . . 141

Exercise 15—Vibrational Statements . . . 144

Exercise 16—Polarity of the Earth and Sky . . . 148

Exercise 17—Heartbeat Control . . . 152

Exercise 18—Sun and Moon . . . 154

Exercise 19—Tree Meditation . . . 157

Exercise 20—Protection Shield . . . 176

Exercise 21—Showers of Light . . . 182

Exercise 22—Sending Light . . . 190

Exercise 23—Aura Gazing . . . 195

Exercise 24—Aura Clearing . . . 202

Exercise 25—Chakra Opening and Balancing . . . 215

Exercise 26—Psychic Travel . . . 232

Exercise 27—Pendulum . . . 249

Exercise 28—Muscle Testing . . . 252

Exercise 29—Automatic Writing . . . 255

Exercise 30—Clairaudience—Conscious Channeling . . . 256

Exercise 31—Visiting the Inner Temple . . . 266

Exercise 32—Psychic Scanning . . . 279

Exercise 33—Healing Case . . . 286

Exercise 34—Past-Life Exploration . . . 300

LIST OF FIGURES

Figure 1—Early Goddess Images . . . 21

Figure 2—Timeline . . . 32–33

Figure 3—Wheel of the Year . . . 47

Figure 4—Witch's Pyramid . . . 65

Figure 5—The Three Minds . . . 75

Figure 6—The Four Energies . . . 80

Figure 7—Shapes . . . 102

Figure 8A—Recording a Holographic Image . . . 123

Figure 8B—Projecting a Holographic Image . . . 123

Figure 9—Vesica Pisces . . . 127

Figure 10—Atom and Solar System . . . 138

Figure 11—Yin-Yang . . . 145

Figure 12—Polarity Wheels . . . 146

Figure 13—Scales . . . 150

Figure 14—Pentacle . . . 164

Figure 15—Triskelion and Triple Knot Images . . . 166

Figure 16—Banishing Pentagram . . . 171

Figure 17—Protection Symbols: Pentacle, Cross, Ankh, Eye, Hexagram, Seal of Solomon . . . 174

Figure 18—Protective Rings . . . 179

Figure 19—Banishing and Invoking Pentagrams . . . 189

Figure 20A—Damaged Aura . . . 200

Figure 20B—Healthy Aura . . . 201

Figure 21—The Seven Chakras . . . 206

Figure 22—Kundalini Rising, Caduceus, DNA . . . 208

Figure 23—Layers of the Aura . . . 211

Figure 24—Symbols of Balance . . . 216

Figure 25—Kabalah . . . 224

Figure 26—World Tree . . . 227

Figure 27—Planes of Reality . . . 229

Figure 28—Pendulums . . . 250

Figure 29—Muscle Testing Hand Positions . . . 253

Figure 30—Chakra Chart . . . 276–277

Figure 31—Healing Light . . . 284

Figure 32—Traditional Degree Symbols . . . 312

Figure 33—My Personal Degree Symbols . . . 313

"Know thyself."
Temple of Delphi, Greece

WHAT IS THE INNER TEMPLE
OF WITCHCRAFT?

I never thought I would be teaching classes on witchcraft, much less making it the focus of my life. But here I am, now writing books on it, too. When I started out, I was not even looking to get involved in witchcraft. A long-time friend introduced me to the topic, and I thought she was kidding. I made bad *Wizard of Oz* jokes simply because I had never heard of a person calling herself a witch and being serious, even reverent. This was quite a few years ago and the notion has gained a bit more media attention since then. My friend is a very intelligent person, whose opinion I respect, so I asked her all sorts of questions. We discussed European history and art influenced by the pre-Christian cultures. We explored philosophy and symbols. Since we both have a love of art, she truly got my attention by showing me Egyptian symbols, such as the eye of Horus and the ankh.

The more we talked, the more I thought this witchcraft thing might be something I would be interested in pursuing. I had come from twelve years of Catholic school, and although at one time I felt a spiritual connection to something, I was no longer sure what it was, since I did not feel a connection to the Catholic Church. I could not agree with many of their views, so I released that spiritual connection with some guilt and anger. When my friend told me about the craft and how it stressed individual and personal connections, I was intrigued. Perhaps it was what I was always seeking, but never knew the option existed.

The final piece that started me on this path was my first ritual. I was invited to a Full Moon ritual and given the opportunity to do a spell. I wasn't sure I believed in it, but I thought, "Why not try?" Another friend of mine was having a difficult pregnancy. She did not get the prenatal care she needed, and doctors thought she and the child were both in danger. Making matters worse, she had a difficult relationship with her divorced parents, and, as a senior in high school, hid the pregnancy until the last few weeks. Although I don't remember the exact wording, my spell basically intended that she and the baby come out healthy with as little pain as possible, if this is for their highest good. Later I found out they were both healthy, and I was happy. Then I discovered that her labor lasted less than two hours and was almost pain free. I was shocked and thought back to the spell. I'm sure she had many people praying for her, but at that point I thought that spells and witchcraft were more real than I had previously believed.

Soon I started studying witchcraft with a well-known local teacher. My mother and my best friend came along, half out of interest, and half out of fear that I was joining a cult. The experience was life-changing. The most important aspect of the course was the empowerment. We learned basic meditation techniques to open to our intuitive and psychic powers. By the end, we had completed several different exercises with a certain amount of real-world verification. The skeptic in me loved this, because it was like a scientific experiment. In a short time, I learned to do things that I believed were truly impossible. Now I was doing the impossible! This empowering tradition stressed the ethics of witchcraft regarding personal responsibility. I truly understood that I was responsible for my own life and my own happiness. Before this class, I had bouts of depression and anger, but always thought it was someone else's fault, not my own. Through this process, I learned how I made my own reality and that I better start taking responsibility for it because no one else will. Empowerment and responsibility are the heart, and true lesson, of magick.

In the next few years, I finished college and pursued my music as both a performer and businessman. I got my life in order and accepted myself and my own personal power. I studied witchcraft and related topics such as shamanism, tarot, healing, and runes to further my education, but my practice of witchcraft was a very personal, private affair. Gradually I grew more relaxed and came "out of the broom closet," as many witches like to say.

A group of friends really noticed the changes in me and became interested in witchcraft. My small coven invited them to rituals and celebrations. These newly interested friends would ask me to do spells for them, but I declined. I'd rather do a spell with them and teach them the skill than have them rely on me. They asked to learn some meditations and healing work. Soon my friends asked me to set up a formal class. I agreed, and that forced me to rediscover the most important aspects of witchcraft.

My life-changing event was my discovery of personal power and responsibility. It was about finding the sacred within myself, my center, my peaceful core. We each have a sacred space within us, a part of us. This sacred space is a temple, a temple to our inner power, our intuition, and our connection with the divine. Discovery of psychic powers, spells, and meditation are all things that lead us to the temple. They help us find the road within and walk our path to the inner temple.

For me, witchcraft is the building of sacred space, in myself, my life, and my environment; I decided to make that the focus of the class. I wanted to help others find their own sacred space, their own inner temple. The information and exercises would build up to that experience. I owe a great deal of thanks to all my teachers for giving me the tools necessary to do this work. I am also thankful for those first friends and students who set me on this path.

The class went well, and like the old telephone commercial, "They told two friends, who told two friends, and so on . . ." I started getting calls from strangers to teach the class. At that point in my life, I was still working in the music industry and didn't have much time to devote to teaching witchcraft. As strange as this may sound to those unfamiliar with spiritual journeys, I had a visionary experience. In meditation, my patron, the Celtic crow goddess Macha, came to me and told me to teach more. After some debate, I finally promised I would teach if she could get me more time. It was an easy promise to make, because I knew my schedule was full. A few weeks later, forgetting about the promise, the situation at work deteriorated and I was laid off. While meditating for guidance, the only advice I received was, "Now you can teach."

I did teach after knocking on numerous office doors that would not open for me. I couldn't get a job answering telephones, but when I put up a flyer for witchcraft classes, my phone rang off the hook. Evidently people needed to find their inner temples.

I refined the material of my course Witchcraft One: Building the Inner Temple, and subsequently designed four additional courses. Each one is based on one of the five elements: fire, earth, water, air, and spirit. Witchcraft One is based on the element of fire, for fire helps you feel your own personal power. Fire is the light of guidance, purifying, yet protecting. The experiences and exercises of the course are the basis of this book.

After teaching full-time for a few years, I discovered that many people really want to study witchcraft, but they have difficulty laying the foundation. Such people jump right to love or money spells, and have some success following a spell by rote from a book, without understanding why it works. They jump into the material needs of the tradition before laying the groundwork for both an intellectual understanding and a spiritual experience. Anyone can do a spell, but not everyone experiences a life-changing event. *The Inner Temple of Witchcraft* lays that foundation.

This course is unlike many traditional Witchcraft 101 books. I will not focus on rituals, altar building, circle casting, and how to celebrate the Wheel of the Year. Those are the tools of the priestess and priest. I've found that students who have not experienced energy and psychic abilities, the foundation stones of magick, have a less profound experience with ritual. They do not understand the subtle mechanics and opportunities interwoven with it. Symbols and ceremonies not understood and personally experienced have a danger of becoming dogma rather than spiritual expression. When students dive right into traditional spell work, they don't understand their inherent abilities and lack a perspective of the long history of witchcraft.

This book begins by covering some basic definitions of witchcraft, and then guides you into the ancient history up to the modern traditions of the craft, to help you find the path that suits you best. The rest of the book is divided into thirteen lessons, with practical exercises and homework for a year-and-a-day course of study. Topics include meditation, instant magick, ancient philosophy, modern science, protection, light, energy anatomy, astral travel, spirit guides, and healing, culminating in a self-initiation ritual. Some of the exercises ask that you find a partner, so be on the lookout for a friend to help you in these studies. Having a partner can keep you focused, and it is also great fun to have a peer with whom to share your experiences.

Once you have created this foundation of light and guidance, the tools of the priestess and priest are learned with a deeper appreciation and understanding. The second book of this series, *The Outer Temple of Witchcraft*, will be a detailed course for this level of study.

I have discovered that people who take this course generally fall into three categories, and all three are welcome. Sometimes it is best to know what your own motivations are. The first group are those who are really interested in witchcraft and other neopagan traditions and seek an experience or training to help them on the path.

Second are those who come with an open mind and later discover that the material really resonates within them. I was in this category. I didn't want to become a witch until I had already become one. I only had to claim the name.

The last group are those who are interested in building a spiritual foundation, a meditative or psychic practice, but do not go on to pursue witchcraft. A few even harbor a stigma associated with the word "witch" and ask me why I call the classes "witchcraft" instead of "New Age" or "psychic development." Many traditions of the New Age come from the history of the witch and healer, and this information is the foundation of witchcraft.

Members of the last group sometimes go on to become healers, psychics, mediums, shamanic practitioners, and magicians. Some do not follow any specific tradition, but take the foundation stones of the inner temple and build their own house. In essence, that is what we all do with such material. I come from quite an eclectic tradition and encourage others to follow their heart and use what resonates with them. Understand the basics, but use what speaks to you. Some choose not to reclaim the word *witch* because they do not resonate with it. That's fine. I think the teachings of the craft have something to offer all of us, whether we use the word or not, as we enter the

"New Age." Many like myself feel it is important to bring the word witch into the twenty-first century without the stigma attached to it. Modern witches must live by example to show people that our traditions are loving, healing, and spiritual.

I would like to thank many people without whom this book would not be possible. I would particularly like to thank my first students who pushed me into teaching at the Goddess' prompting, provoked me with questions and challenges to refine the material, and allowed me to use their stories as examples in my work. I thank my first teachers in the craft for opening this world to me, and I thank Laurie Cabot for her classes based in the science tradition of witchcraft and her demand that all magick must start with self-esteem and self-love. Without that, my life wouldn't have so completely changed. I thank my friends, family, and coven for their support. I thank Ginella, Scott, Amanda, Lena, and Patti. I thank Nicole for her input and suggestions, and I thank the many authors, teachers, and healers who have built the foundation of modern witchcraft and mysticism.

Blessed be,

Christopher Penczak

Ask a Witch

What is a witch? What is witchcraft? These two questions don't have easy answers. The word *witch* is a very emotionally charged word, bringing up conflicting images across the centuries. It is hard to understand which image, if any, is correct.

For most of the Western world, the word *witch* evokes the villain of many fairy tales. We watch the old hag giving the poisoned apple, brewing harmful potions, eating children, and casting curses. At Halloween, stores sell decorations of witches, old ugly women with green faces and pointed hats riding around on broomsticks. Although these are familiar portraits, they are not the first. Because of humanity's fear of that which is different and mysterious, the witch was resigned to the world of children's stories, to make the folk stories of witchcraft impotent from the realm of make-believe. If only children believed in witches, then the power of the witch would no longer be a reality, but a fantasy. Unfortunately, fictionalizing witchcraft was not the only way humankind dealt with its fear.

If you turn back a few hundred years, you can see the word *witch* all across the records of one of Europe's greatest holocausts, the witch trials. Men and women were persecuted and killed for being different. Some call it the Burning Times, because many were put to death by fire, burnt at the stake. Typically, history books gloss over this particular bit of history, but it is every bit a part of us, as relevant to our modern cultures as wars of conquest.

At the top of the list of victims were those accused of practicing witchcraft. The ruling powers of the time had their own ideas about witchcraft, spreading stories of black masses, sacrifice, and contracts in blood signing souls over to the Devil. These stories are the roots of the children's fairy tales. The vast majority of the condemned were not practicing "true" witchcraft. Some held the teachings of the wise women and cunning men of the tribes, a knowledge of healing herbs, remedies, midwiving, and simple charms. We call such skills old wives' tales, but they have endured because there is truth to them. We don't know how many of the accused and condemned were actually practicing what is now called the Old Religion, the way of the witch.

If you turn back even further, to cultures whose histories were not often written down, you find a different kind of witch. This witch was not shrouded in the darkness of fear and fairy tales, but in the darkness and light of the Goddess. This witch was revered as a healer, teacher, leader, and wise one. The image of the witch inspired the same reverence that a priest or minister does now in modern culture, for the ancestors of modern witchcraft were the priestesses and priests, the seers and advisors living a spiritual life by tuning into the forces of nature, the tides of the seasons, and the cycles of the Moon. They held a kinship with the plants and animals and, in essence, all life. Their teaching and histories were kept in the oral tradition, holding the myths and magick of the culture.

Modern witches focus on this particular root in the witchcraft tree. Those claiming the name and title of witch are truly reclaiming and building on the image of the witch from these ancient days. If you really want to know what the words *witch* and *witchcraft* mean as we move into the next century, look at the growing movement of modern witches.

If you ask a witch what he or she means by the word, you will get as many definitions as there are witches. And yes, witches can be both women and men. I'm a man and identify myself as a witch. Male witches are not called warlocks. The word *warlock* can be traced from Scottish, Old English, Germanic, and Indo-European roots and is now generally regarded to mean "deceiver" or "oath breaker" to those involved in the craft. Such a title was probably associated with witchcraft by those who wanted to defame the practice.

When I began my journey into this wonderful world, I was taught that the root of the word *wic*, or *wicca*, means "wise," for witches were the keepers of the wisdom, evolving into the images of wise women and wizardly men. Another definition was "to bend and shape," meaning those who practiced witchcraft could bend and shape the natural forces to do their bidding, to make magick. The word *witch* is actually considered to be Anglo-Saxon in origin, and some feel that only those who are practicing European traditions, or more specifically Celtic, Saxon, or Germanic traditions, have the right to claim the title witch. The etymology of the word can possibly be traced back to Sanskrit and the earliest Indo-European languages, although this could be a popular folk etymology used by many modern witches. The Middle English word *wicche* is traced back to the Old English *wiccan*, meaning "to practice witchcraft." Male and female witches were distinguished through the words *wicca* and *wicce*, respectively. In Middle High German, *wicken* means "to bewitch or divine the future." In Old German, the word is traced to *wih*, meaning "holy." From the Old German to Old Norman, we have the word *ve*, meaning "temple." Notice an interesting shift from the W sound to the V sound, but notice the similar shape of the letters. The letter *double U* actually looks more like *double V* in our alphabet. In French, the letter is called *doublevay*. The further back you go, the further away you get from the stereotypical witch and to a word of sacredness and spirituality. Now you are getting to the true meaning of witch.

In modern English, *witch* is used to refer to both men and women. *Wicca* refers to the modern revival of witchcraft. After the witch trials and persecutions, what remained of the teaching went underground. Other teachings were lost forever, but the practices were revived and the surviving traditions came to light in the twentieth century. In several modern traditions, *witchcraft* refers to the practice and art of the craft, such as spells, while the religion is known as *Wicca*. Though you can make a strong distinction between the definitions of *witch* and *Wiccan*, or *Witchcraft* and *Wicca*, most practitioners accept both words and identities. If you are not sure what to call someone, ask them or see how they refer to themselves.

The Science

One of the first definitions I learned from my early teachers, trained in the Cabot tradition, was "Witchcraft is an art, science, and religion." A witch is one who "lives the art, science, and religion of witchcraft." You might find this definition strange, as did I, because it brings together some seemingly conflicting ideas. This definition shocked me, because I considered myself a man of science. I was studying chemistry and probably would have pursued it if my experience with magick hadn't inspired me to pursue my more creative side. At the time, I was very much a "prove it to me" kind of guy, giving no one an inch unless they could back up their statements. And I found in my witchy friend someone who could. She explained to me the theories behind spells and psychic powers. I wasn't sure I agreed, but it did intrigue me enough to not dismiss it as "New Age kookiness." Then my friend introduced me to one of the most advanced scientific ideas I had encountered at the time, quantum physics. I didn't understand how physics and witchcraft were related until she drew corollaries between ancient philosophies and modern, cutting-edge science. From her viewpoint, she was waiting for modern science to catch up to the ancient truths. The more I learn, the more I am inclined to agree.

For the longest time, I ignored the other facets of the definition of witchcraft, namely art and religion. I focused on the science of the craft. I looked at witchcraft as an experiment. The experiment yielded wonderful results, but I resisted the other meanings of the tradition. Regardless, they led me to explore myself and my spirituality.

The Art

Witchcraft is an art. It is a system based on the cycles of life. Life is change, plain and simple. Change encourages new expressions of the same patterns and energies. Change encourages creativity. Even though two witches can say the same exact words of a spell, each does it differently, each brings his or her own personal nuances, intentions, and inflections. More often than not, witches would probably write their own spells, creating a personal tradition. Each witch works with the same principles based on the science of witchcraft, but they express it quite differently, elevating the craft to a very beautiful art form. The poetry of magick can bring a tear to the eye and evoke our highest emotions. Song, chant, drumming, instruments, poetry, and drama are used in ritual. Whatever the creative expression, no one can doubt that witchcraft is a form of art once they experience it.

THE SPIRITUALITY

Lastly in our threefold definition, witchcraft is a religion. In fact, it is called the Old Religion, for many trace their tradition's roots back to the early Mother Earth goddess cults of the Paleolithic era. Since I have been teaching witchcraft I felt the need to change the definition slightly to "science, art, and spirituality." The word *religion* can conjure up some discomfort in those who are seeking witchcraft as an alternative to the more dogmatic religions. Spirituality, to me, carries a gentler connotation to the original meaning of religion. When I say witchcraft is a spirituality, I mean it is a spiritual path. You walk it for nourishment of the soul, to commune with the life force of the universe, and to thereby better know your own life. Misunderstandings surround those new to the path because of television, movies, and other stories. People do not realize that witchcraft is a daily commitment to renew yourself in the cycles of the Earth, to synchronize yourself with the powers of life. It is a path to enlightenment. Living life as a witch is no easy task.

Certain spiritual aspects of witchcraft set it apart from other traditions. First, it is a nature-based spiritual practice. Divinity in all things is recognized, from the land, water, and sky, to plants, animals, and people. All material things are seen as an expression of life, as the divine. Witches are often involved in environmental reforms and animal-rights groups because of this belief.

Witches are polytheistic, meaning we worship more than one deity. We recognize the spirit of life running through all things, but believe it expresses itself through a multitude of faces. I like to think of it as looking at a giant, brilliantly cut diamond with many facets shining, each an expression of the one diamond.

Witches focus on divinity in the form of male and female energies, gods and goddesses. The prime focus of many traditions is the Great Mother, the primal creative goddess as embodied by the planet Earth. The Goddess is also seen in the Moon, the night, and the oceans. She is portrayed in the modern craft as the Triple Goddess, one who is three in her aspects of Maiden, Mother, and Crone. These faces correspond with the changes in the Moon and seasons. The Goddess' energy is vast, portrayed as loving, kind, and life giving at certain times, while dark, warrior-like, and vengeful at others.

Her consort, the God and Good Father, has been depicted as the sky, the Sun, and vegetation, or as the animal lord. Like the Goddess, the male aspect of divinity has many faces. He is warrior and protector, king and judge. The God can reveal the secrets of magick and illumination or surround you with darkness to force you to face yourself. The God is usually dual in nature, in the form of the Lord of Light and the Lord of Darkness, though some of his images cannot be put into these categories. He presides over the year as the life giver in the fertile months and the life taker in the waning year.

From these two beings spring all the deities of myth. Groups of goddesses and gods from a particular culture, called pantheons, were created. The pantheon we are most familiar with in the West is the Greek, taught in classical mythology classes and found in many modern reinterpretations. The Greek and the later Roman pantheons were not the only ones, nor the first. The ancient Egyptians, Sumerians, Celts, Norse, Africans, and Hindus all had their own pantheons. Each had some type of mother goddess and father god. Then the subtle differences became more distinct. Each had deities to preside over different realms of the earthly domain. One was for the oceans, and another for the sky. Gods and goddesses would rule the Underworld, the sky kingdom, agriculture, animals, healing, the Moon, the Sun, stars, travel, poetry, and divination.

In psychological terms, we call these common visions *archetypes*. Archetypes are primal images that can be found across many different cultures. They exist in our collective consciousness. Psychologist Carl Jung popularized the term *archetype*, but they existed far before his identification. Each culture had individual names for an archetype, as represented by a different goddess or god. Each culture wove stories and myths involving this being, but the basic concept is the same. To those who work with the archetypes, they are living, conscious energies, beings of great power. Modern witches understand the concept of archetypes, but know these powers through personal, spiritual experiences. The common belief is that archetypes are primal beings of an almost unknowable nature, but they express themselves through god forms, the individual descriptions and personalities of the gods of myth. The god forms act like a mask. The primal mother archetype exists without borders, but she expresses herself as Gaia in the Greek tradition, Danu in the Celtic tradition, Isis to the Egyptians, and Pachamama to the Incans.

Most mainstream religions, particularly the Judeo-Christian traditions, are monotheistic, acknowledging only one god: theirs. Some feel these traditions focused on the masculine vibration of the divine and saw it as the one and only source of life. In our diamond analogy, they are looking at the brilliance of the whole diamond, but are blinded to look at the individual facets. Or they are fascinated by one facet of the diamond, one god, and exclude all else. The spiritual ancestors of modern witches were in a position that seems unique to us today. Because of their polytheistic nature, they could recognize the gods of another tribe, land, or culture as different expressions of their own gods. They could see the diamond as a whole as well as the individual facets. As we look to the Great Spirit at the center of the diamond, witches remember that we, too, are facets of the diamond. Like the trees, oceans, and animals, we are expressions of the divine, the Goddess, God, and Great Spirit.

The Healer

Another great definition of *witch* is "healer." In the ancient cultures, people went to the priestesses and priests for healing. At the time, healing encompassed much more than our modern medical profession. Modern medicine is wonderful in many ways, but in these ancient times, healing was a process involving the mind, emotions, and spirit as well as the body. In short, healing was an energetic process. We are now coming full circle with the rise in popularity of holistic and alternative treatments. A healer was one to counsel, advise, and minister to the spiritual balance of the individual or tribe, as well as do ritual, divination, and hands-on healing. You will probably find many witches now involved in the healing arts, traditional or otherwise, because helping others is such an important part of the practice of witchcraft.

The Walker

The last definition of the word *witch* that I will present to you goes hand in hand with the healing arts. It is also my favorite identity. A witch is "a walker between the worlds." This was the first hint I got at the rich shamanic tradition found within the teachings of witchcraft.

Due to a revival of interest in Native American practices, many people associate the word *shaman* with the medicine man of a tribal people. That is true. Shamans are spiritual leaders, but that is not the entire picture. The term originated in Siberia, but has been applied to native practices throughout the Americas and more loosely to practices across the world. The shaman believes in nonphysical, spiritual realms and learns to send his or her spirit to such realms. In these worlds, one can retrieve information and healing energy, and commune with spirits. The shaman ministers to his or her people through this ability, to effect healing of the mind, body, and spirit.

Witches, too, believe in nonphysical realms. They believe in the physical and a multitude of spiritual dimensions. Witches hone their abilities to pierce the veil and travel to these dimensions, where they speak with goddesses, gods, and spirits. Like the shamans, they are expected to remain grounded in the material world with responsibilities to their people, yet keep one foot ever ready to enter the spiritual world. They are bridges between the worlds, seeking to bring their people into greater partnership with the divine. The native people in Siberia and the Americas remained more tribal and retained a certain amount of reverence for these shamans, even in the modern era. As the European people became less tribal, they stamped out their very own shamanic traditions, the practices of the witch. That fear of spiritual power, of the unknown, of mysteries in a culture with a growing patriarchy, turned the image of the witch from a priestess and healer into a monster of the night.

The Weaver

To me, the words *witch* and *witchcraft* are wonderfully all-encompassing terms. They evoke a sense of humanity's mystical past and a hope for the future. Whenever someone, as an individual or as a culture, sought to understand spirit through the cycles of life, honored the divine as being both masculine and feminine, recognized the Earth and sky, quieted themselves enough to hear the soft inner whisper, and took an active partnership with nature, they were practicing witchcraft. Not everyone would agree with that; many tribal traditions would not ever call themselves witches, but it is my personal feeling that such traditions are all practicing the same craft, regardless of the name, place, or time. It is only through an unfortunate period of history that the words *witch* and *witchcraft* became maligned. Without this slander, I think the word *witch* would be translated into more languages as "healer," "teacher," "shaman," and "wise one," rather than "curse bringer." Witches weave all these threads together in the modern traditions.

The most important aspect of this tradition is the individual's sovereignty. Each practitioner is his or her own priest or priestess. Teachers, elders, and healers are respected and can help you on the path, but ultimately witchcraft is about your own personal, individual relationship with the divine. Through such training you have the ability to perform your own spiritual rituals and seek guidance. To my friends still in the world of Catholicism, I explain that we are not only our own priests, but also our own popes. We have the last word on what is correct and good for us, as well as the responsibility of living with those decisions.

I had lunch with a student and friend who told me she was "finally okay with the *W* word." She was drawn to take my classes, cast spells and circles, and basically perform all the rites of a witch, but always had difficulty with that word. She is a great healer, using conventional massage therapy with both reiki and shamanism. She had been giving psychic readings before she had any formal training in the area. She didn't claim the word *witch* as her own, and that was fine with me. It's not for everybody. But she seemed so bothered by the fact, and she didn't know why. We speculated about past-life persecution for being a witch, but she didn't explore it further. She came to the conclusion that she didn't want to be limited by the word *witch*. There are so many things to do and explore that she did not want to settle for being "just a witch" when she could try everything. I could understand her sentiment, but I never thought of myself as "just a witch."

Almost a year later, we had lunch and she told me she was coming to terms with the word *witch* and, in my opinion, the true meaning of the word. Even if we learn all these definitions, sometimes our own preconceived notions and prejudices and those of society do not allow the real meaning to absorb into our psyche. In some ways she saw the role of witch as something that could pigeonhole her into an expected role and tradition, without any freedom or change to it. There is a stereotype even in the pagan world that a witch has to wear black all the time, love dark gothic music, and take things very seriously. Hopefully that stereotype is dissolving away, with all the others. To me, witchcraft has given me a frame of reference to experience the world by being open to all possibilities. It has also taught me to look at things practically, to remain grounded in timeless philosophy while still open to modern interpretations. The eclectic witch borrows from many cultures. These cultures do not necessarily have to be Celtic or even European to be a part of the modern craft, even though some traditionalists feel that witchcraft is exclusively Celtic. We come from a tradition filled with the mysteries of the past, but now witchcraft generally encourages one to find the path that works for the individual. All our other "hats"—healer, therapist, herbalist, shaman, mother, brother, priest, priestess, environmentalist, counselor, researcher, writer, psychic, and teacher—all fit nicely under the "hat" of witch, for witches are all these things, too. Nothing is prevented or forbidden. The path of the witch is truly the path of knowledge and, more importantly, wisdom. It changes and adapts as new information is discovered. Witchcraft is a living religion.

As you can see, the witch has many faces and wears many hats, both woman and man, old and young. The witch is a symbol of darkness and fear to many still, but is really a patron of wisdom and magick. Each practitioner in turn has a personal meaning. If this is all brand new to you and you feel the call of the art, science, and spirituality of the Goddess and God, you will be called on to answer these questions: What is witchcraft? What is a witch? And most importantly, what does it mean to become a witch? If you want to explore the foundations of the inner temple, you are already walking the path of the witch, so ask yourself how *you* would define the word *witch*.

Digging for the Roots

History is written by the victors. Whenever cultures clash, the dominant force is the one left to record the events of the past for future generations. Those defeated leave behind physical artifacts, and even folk tales and myth, but their way of life is lost in the march of time. Whenever you are digging through the roots of history, be aware of this fact. Although actual events are objective, a viewpoint of those events is subjective, depending on your previous beliefs. If you read about the American Revolution, written by an American, the text would be biased in favor of the American heroes, with the British as the villains. If you read about the same events from a British author, the objective facts, dates, and locations would be the same, but the tone would be very different. The same could be said for most conflicts in history, and the more subtle cultural revolutions that are not as well documented. Every culture has its own point of view. Even when a writer is aware of such a bias, it can be difficult to separate from such a key element of one's personal identity.

When we are digging for the roots of witchcraft, we must keep in mind that the practitioners of the craft were seldom the victors over the last two thousand years, so our common history is colored. Much of their point of view has been lost to us. As historians, anthropologists, scholars, teachers, and students, we can reclaim and recon-struct, but we can never really know the truth.

The facts of witchcraft and ancient spiritual traditions are shrouded in mystery and misunderstanding because they were almost completely vanquished by the conquer-ing forces of Europe. Everyone telling the story has a bias. Traditional researchers do not want to challenge what they "know" to be fact and dismiss any theories to the con-trary. Those excited by the prospect of ancient religions can let their modern enthusi-asm cloud their less biased analytical skills. People involved in modern pagan religions have a strong bias as well. Practitioners and teachers like myself have a vested interest in showing the beneficial aspects of witchcraft throughout history, while discrediting the misconceptions surrounding it.

For many years, I wanted to know exactly what happened. I wanted information on the ancient rituals and practices. I needed to know exactly where my witch roots came from, and how my spiritual ancestors practiced. And I was disappointed. There is no definitive history accepted by everyone. No one could tell me the ancient rituals and stories, unchanged.

I now welcome the multitude of well-thought-out, researched views, but I am no longer attached to the idea that any one history is more correct than any other. The lit-eral facts of our history may never be known beyond a shadow of a doubt, and they do not need to be. Our history has changed so much in the last hundred years, but such new revelations do not change how I practice witchcraft today. My practice changes as I grow and evolve. I am open to personal revelations as well as historical in-formation. My foundation is based on those who have come before me, and that foun-dation is as solid as I need it to be.

Many of the early books and stories used as a foundation by Wiccans have been somewhat discredited by later scholars, but that does not mean the wisdom of the cul-ture they drew from is discredited. It only means that we are still looking at their truths. Think of such works as poetic histories, if not literal ones, and be inspired by the words of those who came before you.

For modern witches, the history of the craft is told orally, as the story of a people's journey over time. Our history is a living story. We are a part of it. We are writing our own chapter now. Our children will continue the story, and hopefully it will never go so far underground that it will be lost again.

THE STONE AGE

For me, the roots of the great tree of witchcraft stretch deep into history, to our earliest ancestors. In the Paleolithic era, the early Stone Age, human societies were hunters and gatherers, nomadic people continuously following the source of food. Most modern people think of the Paleolithic times as the age of barbaric cavemen, but these tribes were probably more sophisticated than we give them credit for. In those societies, the men usually hunted for food, while the women stayed with the tribe, caring for the family. Women were logically considered the lifeblood of the tribe, and cherished, since women gave birth to the children. Men were more "expendable" in terms of survival, since one man could impregnate many women. Scholars speculate that the role of man in pregnancy was not even understood in Stone Age times. In this harsh life, children were vital to continuing the tribe. This gave rise to the belief that many of these societies were matriarchal, meaning they were led by women. These societies were more right-brained, focusing on pictures, feelings, and instinct.

Religiously, cave painting and other artifacts indicate a level of spiritual belief. We believe that these early people saw the divine in nature, animated by nature spirits or gods. The Earth was the mother of life, providing the vegetation needed to survive, while her consort was an animal lord, providing the animals needed by the people. Stone Age people were polytheists, believing in more than one god. Other spirits possibly animated the sky, storms, mountains, rivers, and fire.

Certain members of the tribes noticed that they had abilities that set them apart from their kin, and some developed these abilities further. Women and men who were either too old or too injured to hunt lived lives that allowed them the opportunity to expand these abilities. Notice that our surviving archetypes of these people are the wise old women and men, and often such sages are called wounded healers, their injuries helping them understand the nature of healing. These individuals developed their natural rapport with the spirits, developing psychic talents, knowledge of herbs and other healing skills, and becoming the wise ones of the tribe. They became the religious leaders, petitioning the elements and leading hunters to the herds. They conducted ceremonies and celebrations. They were the magick makers. Such people did not necessarily use the word *witch* or *witchcraft*, but in essence, this was their practice. They were akin to the Native American shamans, but we do not have a proper name for the shamans' ancient European, African, or Middle Eastern brethren. To me, they were witches in every sense of the word. Anytime a people honored both Mother and Father aspects of the divine, revered nature, and shaped the forces of the world for healing and change, they were practicing witchcraft. No one culture owns the tenets of witchcraft. They are universal.

As women were so critical to the development of witchcraft, the Goddess played a pivotal role in its development, then and now. Humanity's earliest works of art and religion are based on Goddess figures, images that we now believe represent the Great Mother. In the earliest creation myths, the Mother was often the prime source of creation, self-fertilizing and single-handedly manifesting reality from the void. Similar images are found all over the world, depicting She of a Thousand Names, the mother of witchcraft (figure 1).

The Changing Age

Goddess-oriented scholars suspect that this culture dominated until the rise of the patriarchal religions, near the time of Abraham, the first prophet of Yahweh. From that point on, the pendulum swung in the opposite direction, and the goddess cultures in Europe, Africa, and the Middle East slowly lost their foothold in our world, to the point that we now doubt their existence at all, since they seem so different from our "normal" conceptions of religion and reality. We now sit on the cusp of a new shift, with the potential to strike a balance between the two and synthesize the best of each, achieving a state of harmony.

Aleister Crowley, modern magician and scholar, divided the ages into three categories, based on Egyptian myth. The current age we are leaving is the Age of Osiris, marked by sacrificial gods such as Osiris, Dionysus, and even Jesus. The previous age was the Age of Isis, when the goddess cultures dominated. We affectionately call it the "cradle of civilization." We are entering the next great age, the Age of Horus, the child of Isis and Osiris, the young god who possessed the powers of both Mother and Father. Although I don't agree with everything Crowley said or did, I think this metaphor is quite appropriate. The Age of Aquarius, or New Age, is another name for the current shift.

Venus of Willenorf
30,000 B.C.E.

Venus of Lespugue
25,000 B.C.E.

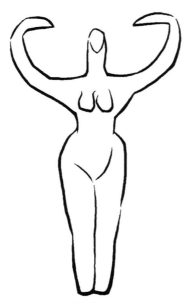

Nathor,
Nile River Goddess
4000 B.C.E.

Ishtar / Inanna / Astarte
of Babylon
2000 B.C.E.

Figure 1: *Early Goddess Images*

As we continue through the middle, or Mesolithic, Stone Age, and the new, or Neolithic, Stone Age, which occurred at different points in different locations across the world, weather patterns changed and food became more available. Nomadic tribes settled down and learned the arts of agriculture. Crude stone tools become more sophisticated. Pottery and other arts expanded. Agricultural settlements continued to grow, and what modern people call "civilization" developed. The ancient lands of Egypt, Sumeria, and Greece became beacons for the new agricultural revolution. The American and Asian settlements developed into the ancient cities and sophisticated cultures. Monuments were built, and, with the advent of writing, histories were recorded.

As larger groups of people gathered together, the number of healers and magick workers in each community increased. Solitary and small groups of practitioners organized into orders of priests and priestesses. Personal experiences and tribal wisdom evolved into cultural mythologies. Such wise ones continued to counsel and heal, often working for the rulers of the emerging empires. As religion played an important part in the secular world, these brotherhoods and sisterhoods held a great deal of clout in society. The orders developed sophisticated religious and magickal systems, establishing mystery schools to educate and initiate the seeker. They continued to act as intermediaries, but spirituality still contained a very personal spark and flair to it. Worship of the deities was a daily event conducted by both priests and the general populace.

The similarities of gods, rituals, and teachings from culture to culture is now evident from our twenty-first-century perspective, inspiring some to see a central root culture influencing them all, possibly the ancient anecdotal myths of Atlantis or Lemuria, but no definitive evidence exists for such a connection. Quite possibly each society was tapping into the same fundamental archetypal energies of that time, and each expressed them a bit differently.

From this era we draw on the familiar pantheons of classical mythology. The godforms of the Middle East migrated into the pantheons of Greece and later Rome. Toward the beginning of this period, there was a strong goddess reverence, harkening back to the earlier Paleolithic tribes. As living conditions improved, the pendulum of social trends swung toward a patriarchy, as evidenced by the change in many myths. Powerful goddess myths were retold with new twists, often disempowering many of the goddesses. In her book *When God Was a Woman*, Merlin Stone does an excellent yet controversial job tracing this transformation of deity.

PAGAN EUROPE

When these ancient civilizations were thriving, the less structured tribes of Europe, north of the Mediterranean Sea, were developing their own customs and magick that were no less powerful, but less formalized and documented than others. The Celtic people were migrating west, across Europe, and eventually came in contact with the Greeks and Romans.

The ancient Celts were very complex and culturally different from the "civilized" cultures of the time. Scholars believe they came from a common Indo-European root with the Hindu culture. One band moved west across Europe and another moved east to populate India. Common points of language, myth, and art support this theory. Look at Celtic knot work and Indian art with geometric patterns. The Celtic version is softer and rounded, but they are similar. Celtic stories of the dark goddess figure the Caillech survive today, striking a similar phonetic and magickal resonance with the dark Hindu goddess Kali. The Celts were warriors, but had an unusual code of ethics compared to Greco-Roman society. They did not conquer for resources, or to subjugate people, but as a sign of prowess, and were as likely to fight among themselves as against "outsiders." They did not push their own ideology, and quite often incorporated much of the myth, culture, and wisdom of the people they conquered into the Celtic worldview. Such absorptions, along with the lack of a written language, account for the somewhat disjointed mythos of the Celts when compared to the Greeks, Romans, or Egyptians.

The Druids were the religious leaders of the Celts. The generally accepted meaning of the word *Druid* is "to know the oak." Oak trees are symbols of life and death, and the Druids had knowledge of the spirit world, magick, and nature. They conducted ceremonies, counseled kings, and performed healing. They settled disputes, not bound by the identity of individual Celtic tribes. They were both honored and feared for their role, seen not as gods, but as the sacred interpreters of the gods' will. My first teachers of the craft taught me that the roots of witchcraft came from the legacy of the Druids, who were both male and female, though most historical accounts portray them as exclusively male.

As the Celts come from a warrior culture, scholars dispute the dominance of the goddess in the Druids' theology, seeing them as being primarily concerned with solar figures and animal lords. Many goddess myths play an important part in surviving Celtic culture, but we are uncertain where those myths came from: the Druids themselves, or the cultures the Celts conquered. I feel the sacredness of nature, of the forest, of life, and of death are very goddess oriented, and the Druids saw the benefits of both aspects of the divine. The dark warrior goddesses reach back to the heart of the Celtic people.

The Celts eventually based themselves in Gaul, which encompasses modern-day France, and some migrated to the British Isles, involving themselves with the inhabitants of the isles, the Picts. The Pict society harkened back to the Stone Age era. It is likely that the Picts and Celts influenced each other. Because of their shorter stature, the Picts are sometimes theorized to be the genesis of the "little people," the faery folk in Celtic myth.

At the time of the Celtic settlement in Gaul, the Roman Empire was in full swing. Empires are only prosperous while they continue to expand, and Julius Caesar set out to conquer Gaul and the tribes living there. He met resistance, but was eventually successful. The people were "Romanized" and the empire ultimately included parts of Britain. The Romans at the time were still polytheistic, and a general mingling of myths occurred between these cultures. The witchcraft of the Romans and the Etruscans from northern Italy could have intermingled with the magick of the Druids.

Caesar was a scholar of his time, recording his encounters with the Celtic people and the Druids. Unfortunately, the few written accounts of the Druidic priests come from Caesar. Though I do not disparage Julius Caesar's scholarly abilities, we must bear in mind his personal biases. Here we have a leader of an empire conquering a people through military might. The Druids were the organizing force between Celtic tribes. Though the tribes held a similar identity, there was no hierarchy to the leaders, but everyone would listen to the word of the Druids. If Caesar extolled the virtues of the Druids and the Celts to his people, they might have questioned his decision to subjugate them. If he painted a darker portrait, there would be no chance of public outcry. Caesar spoke of human sacrifice performed by the Druids. Such claims may or may not be true, but you must remember that we live in a world where many states and countries still have the death penalty. What is accepted in one culture, place, and time may not be accepted in another.

The Druids, on the other hand, have no surviving documentation written from their own point of view. The Druidic tradition was oral, involving at least nineteen years of intensive study and memorization, a period of the great lunar cycle, what the Greeks called the Meton cycle. Druids had in-depth knowledge of magick, medicine, poetry, music, history, mythology, astrology, and astronomy, but did not commit their knowledge to paper. Writing was seen as sacrilegious. If the information was important or sacred, one did not write it down. To write something down meant it was a minor thing, unimportant, and not worth committing to memory. Part of the Druids' training was bardic, meaning they learned the oral traditions, stories, myths, and songs. While it appears that the Druids were wiped out, they most likely went into hiding, as the bards and storytellers of the people, keeping the culture alive through its art. Others gave up the mantle of priest or priestess and became healers. They lived on the outskirts of civilization, keeping the ways of nature and offering their services when they could.

Similar to the Celts in many ways, yet fundamentally different, were the Teutonic tribes of northern Europe, eventually becoming the German and Nordic tribes. The word *Teuton* is now a synonym for German, but at the time, it encompassed a larger group of people. These tribes honored the shifts in the Sun as the equinoxes and solstices, performed intricate magick, particularly that of the runes, and had a complex mythological, religious, and shamanic tradition. They had some contact with the Celtic tribes, and made their way into Gaul. The Germanic tribes also did battle with the Roman Empire. The Teutons are not credited with the rebirth of Wicca as much as the Celts, but their practices definitely played a part in the revival, particularly as their myths mingled with the Celts and Saxons in later periods.

The Rise of Christianity

During this time, a new religion took root, heralded from the Middle East. The name of this new faith was Christianity, based on the teachings of Jesus of Nazareth, also known as Jesus Christ. He preached a faith of unconditional love while he performed miracles of healing. After Jesus' death, a new religion sprung up around him, based on the testaments of his apostles. The teachings of certain sects within this early church, particularly those of Gnostic Christianity, were quite mystical and personal traditions.

Reincarnation, healing, and trance work were part of the religion. Later, the teachings other than Gnostic were codified into one Church, with a strict dogma and much less personal mysticism.

A small number of modern witches feel Jesus was fundamentally a witch in action, if not in name, traveling with twelve apostles plus himself, creating the traditional number of a coven, and doing acts of magick. He is also seen as an expression of the sacrificed-god archetype, found many places in the world, such as the Egyptian god Osiris, the Greek Dionysus, and the Celtic sacrificed king. In Christian mythology, Jesus Christ resurrected himself after death, and was associated with vegetation, most notably grapes and wine, like Dionysus. Ironically, the early Christians were persecuted by the western Roman Empire, giving us the popular image of the Christians being thrown to the lions. The Romans thought they were cannibals, eating flesh and drinking blood.

Soon after the rise of Christianity, the Roman Empire underwent a fundamental shift. The Edict of Milan in 313 C.E. made Christianity the official religion of the Empire. Churches were constructed over the temples of the old pagan gods. Pagan practices were systematically denounced and outlawed. The horned gods of the Celts, known as Cernunnos or Herne, and the Greco-Roman horned satyr god Pan, were fused with the Hebrew myths of Lucifer, the fallen angel, and Satan, the tester of faith. Together they became the Devil, the source of evil, temptation, and sin in Christian doctrine. The word Devil comes from a corruption of a Greek word, as does *demon.* Devil is from *diabolos,* meaning "accuser," and demon from *daimon,* translating to "divine power," referring to an intermediary spirit between humans and the gods, much like an angel.

Pagan rituals were absorbed into the Christian calendar to speed conversion. Any unsavory aspects of the holidays, such as dancing with animal masks, were legally banned, though many pagan elements linger to this day. The craft of the witch was often divided by the public into "good," or white, witchcraft, being of benefit to the greater society, like the cunning folk with cures and divinations, and "evil," or black, witchcraft, practiced by those seeking to harm individuals or the greater community. Black magickal practices were legislated against by the local governments and Roman law, while white witchcraft was somewhat welcomed, or at least tolerated; but eventually, the line between the two types of witchcraft blurred in the eyes of the law.

Interestingly enough, in many cases, asking a white witch to place a curse on someone who purposely had done wrong, such as a thief or murderer, was not considered an evil act, though most contemporary witches would abhor such a request. Modern witches would also not usually divide themselves into categories of white and black. Such labels have a smack of inherent racism, assuming black to be bad and white to be good. It also dishonors the loving and healing dark goddesses so popular in the current practice of the craft.

Although *witch* is the commonly recorded English word for these practitioners, drawing on the Anglo-Saxon entomology, magickal practitioners were known by many other names and titles, including magician, magus, wizard, warlock, and sorcerer. Each has a different connotation regarding powers, morality, and gender of the practitioner, depending on the area and time period when used. For example, the word *sorcerer* has a wide range of meanings. In Europe, it often denoted an evil practitioner, stemming from the Eastern school of thinking where sorcery is a base art. A sorcerer gets trapped in the accumulation of power without seeking enlightenment. In South America, a sorcerer is a holy man, a shaman and spiritual warrior held in high regard. In Africa, medicine men were considered witch doctors, perhaps because they offered healing and protection from the spells of "evil" witches.

The important thing to remember about these various names and terms is that the actual word *witch* is fundamentally European, and was introduced into other cultures as an equivalent translation to a word from that culture's words. As European influence became more dominant, the indigenous culture's words fell into disuse and were commonly replaced in the general vocabulary. Christian Europeans told many of the indigenous people they conquered that a witch is a practitioner of evil, but the Christians believed that all forms of magick that were not done by a priest were evil, coming from the Devil. Unfortunately, many native people took the word *witch* to mean "evildoer," rather than equate it with their own shamans and healers. To this day, many practitioners of the Native American traditions shudder when Wiccans refer to themselves as witches.

Christians looking for an excuse to condemn witchcraft will quote the Bible, "Suffer not a witch to live," from Exodus 22:17. This passage has been translated many times. In older versions of Exodus, the meaning was "Thou shall not suffer a sorceress to live." In this particular setting, a sorceress referred to a poisoner, a murderer. The original meaning was "suffer not a murderer to live," which eventually got confused with the word *witch*, causing misunderstandings to this day. Ancient Hebrews did not outlaw the practice of magick. In fact, the rabbis were practitioners in the tradition of King Solomon, keeping knowledge of the Kabalah, their mystical teachings. I think most people would agree that being a witch does not mean one is a murderer. Unfortunately, many old Inquisitors had no problem assuming that the two go hand in hand.

The Holy Roman Empire and the Burning Times

The western Roman Empire declined greatly in power over the fifth and sixth centuries, until it was in complete disarray. By 500 C.E., the Romans left the British Isles in a state of confusion, fending off Saxon invaders. Here we have the generally accepted time period of King Arthur's Camelot, though the historical setting differs greatly from our romanticized literary version. The Celtic Christian Church existed, but was highly influenced by pagan traditions.

In 800 C.E., the Holy Roman Empire was established when Pope Leo III crowned Charlemagne "Emperor of the Romans." As the original western Roman Empire fell, the Catholic Church, led by the pope, was the one institution that remained stable and in power over this time. The Church's power was threatening to the eastern Byzantine Empire and the marauding Lombards. The Church looked to the Frankish kings for protection, and through the recently converted pagans, built a Christian empire. Although many converted to Christianity, some did not, and kept their ways private and secret in the countryside. The practices of the old faith were generally discouraged by the dominant Church, even those of "white" witches, whom some Christians considered more harmful than the "black" ones, because they were thought to be doing "the Devil's work" and passing it off as healing.

The Inquisitions were originally intended to seek out and punish heretics. Anything that contradicted official Church doctrine was considered heresy. Originally, witchcraft and sorcery laws were considered civil concerns, punishable by fines or imprisonment. Through the Inquisitions, all forms of witchcraft, which by its very nature is a form of worship unsanctioned by the Church, were defined as heresy, punishable by death. Ironically, the root of the word *heresy* comes from the Greek word *hairesis*, meaning "free choice."

Now we enter the witch's holocaust, the Burning Times, a term coined by modern witches for the extended period of witch trials and executions in Europe and the American colonies. The phrase refers to the popular method of execution by burning at the stake, though hanging and drowning were common, too.

Starting in the fifteenth century, various people, usually enemies of the Church or political figures, were accused of witchcraft, and tried and sentenced to death. The trials did not end until the eighteenth century, roughly the life of the Holy Roman Empire, and in total, the death count will never be known, but has been conservatively estimated from several thousand to as many as nine million. The more reasonable estimates are closer to 200,000. In any regard, the Burning Times was the first, and often forgotten, holocaust in Western history.

In short, all those who did not agree with the Church, including those practicing old pagan folk magick, Jews, healers, and other "heretics," were accused of renouncing the one true God and making a pact with the Devil. As Christianity branched out into sects, they accused each other of Devil worship. With the discovery of the New World, Native Americans were tagged with this label.

Assumed to be part of the pact with the Devil were acts of magickal violence against the common folk. If anything unfortunate occurred, one looked for a witch in the village, and often the finger was pointed at the person causing the most trouble, or liked the least by the local citizens. Wise women, herbalists, and midwives were included, because they challenged the power of the budding medical community. If you heal and do not practice medicine, then you must be working for the Devil. If you do magick for the Church, it is a miracle. If you do not work for the Church, it is the work of the Devil, which became synonymous with witchcraft. The hysteria of witchcraft was a convenient way to get rid of those with their own personal power and strong opinions in the society, as well as the elderly who were perceived as burdens to the struggling communities. The majority of the accused were not likely practitioners of witchcraft at all. At most, they had held on to folk magick. Townspeople would often accuse unwanted neighbors of practicing witchcraft in order to get rid of them.

The hysteria rose in fervor at this particular point in history because of economic downturns, poor social conditions, growing disease, and threats to the Church's power base from religious sects and theological schisms. The main force of Europe, the Christian Church, may have been blamed for these conditions. This institution needed a scapegoat on the outside: blame these problems on the power of the evil witches.

Although not the first act of persecution, the publication of the *Malleus Maleficarum* served to fan the flames of these murders. This manual, called the Hammer of the Witches, or Witch's Hammer, served as a supposed description of the witch's practices, how to hunt them, capture them, and elicit confessions using tests and tortures that few people could ever hope to resist. None of the material was based on actual pagan practices, but on Christian doctrine and flights of the authors' imagination and misogyny, although there is some speculation that the material was used by others as a manual to practice "witchcraft," including the Black Mass, a mockery and corruption of the Catholic mass. Here are the roots of Satanism, not witchcraft. Contemporary witches see this form of "Satanic witchcraft" as having nothing to do with the true spiritual roots of the craft. The practices of witches, from various cultures to the Anglo-Saxon roots of the word *Wicca*, predated Christianity. To believe in the Devil, one must first believe in the tenets of Christianity. The Devil held no place in the pre-Christian pagan myths because ancient pagans did not recognize a source of ultimate evil. They recognized the forces of creation manifested in nature. Modern traditions of Satanism vary greatly, from those inspired by bad horror movies to those with sophisticated magickal philosophies. Some call themselves Satanists, but don't even believe in an entity named Satan. These Satanist and Satanic witches have nothing to do with the healing roots of pagan witchcraft. All types of people claim to be witches, but not all of them claim the same beliefs and history.

For safety's sake, anyone connected to the ancient pagan practices and arts of folk magick went underground with the knowledge, sharing it with a few, and passing it along family lines, because blood relatives were the only people who could be trusted. For ease of disguise, practices were cloaked in everyday actions and household tools. The broom, the knife, the spoon, and the cauldron all made their way into the magickal arts. Everyone had these objects, so you could not be accused of witchcraft for simply owning them.

Witches were not the only ones persecuted at this time. Anyone practicing a faith or lifestyle in a different manner was persecuted. Homosexuals were persecuted along with witches. The derogatory term "flaming faggot," which refers to a gay person, originated in the Burning Times, citing execution through fire. The word *faggot* originally referred to kindling.

In 1492, Spain forced all Jews to choose between leaving the country, converting to Christianity, or execution. Some left, while others converted or seemingly appeared to convert. The Jewish people are the keepers of the Kabalah, a system of mysticism and magick. They found allies among the countryside witches, and possibly shared magickal secrets. Modern practitioners of the Kabalah greatly influenced the re-emergence of Wicca in the twentieth century.

Pope Alexander proclaimed an Act against witchcraft in 1502, followed by similar measures by Henry VIII in 1542 and Elizabeth I in 1563. Various laws and proclamations were passed in Europe and England throughout the time of persecution. Witch hunts in England and subsequently in America focused less on the antireligious act of heresy and more on the civil crime of witchcraft. The material of the *Malleus Maleficarum* was later absorbed by the Protestant witch hunters in England, but the country had ample material from their own demonologists. Matthew Hopkins proclaimed himself Witch Finder General in England, inspiring many other witch hunters. Some speculate that witches migrated to the American colonies to escape persecution, but the hysteria soon followed in the form of the infamous Salem witchcraft trials.

In Salem, Massachusetts, now a neopagan mecca, a hysteria of witchcraft led by the accusations of a few teenage girls fascinated with the occult lead to the death of thirty-six people and the imprisonment of over 150 men and women in this Puritan community in 1692–93. This episode in America's history is considered part of the Burning Times, but no one was burned at the stake in Salem. Many were hung on Gallows Hill, and present-day pagan community members of Salem, Massachusetts, celebrate rituals on the site believed to be Gallows Hill, to remember those who died in the name of witchcraft. Most likely the victims of the Salem trials did not practice witchcraft, but were targets of malice by their accusers. Although a few subsequent witchcraft trials took place in America after the end of the Salem trials in 1693, none yielded an execution. The end of the hysteria was a turning point for the Burning Times. The transformation to capitalism, the Industrial Revolution, advances in science, and a general social criticism and disgust for the tortures in this newly evolving modern world helped end such unfounded hysteria.

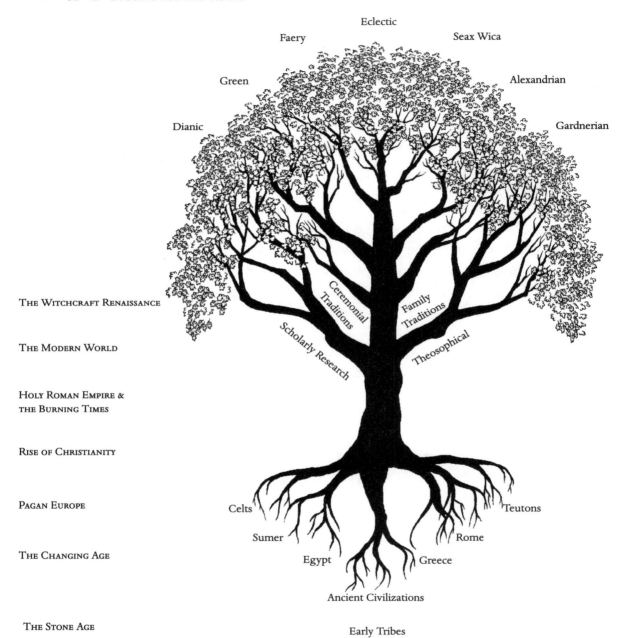

THE WITCHCRAFT RENAISSANCE

THE MODERN WORLD

HOLY ROMAN EMPIRE &
THE BURNING TIMES

RISE OF CHRISTIANITY

PAGAN EUROPE

THE CHANGING AGE

THE STONE AGE

Figure 2: Timeline

1972 C.E. U.S. IRS recognizes witchcraft as a religion and grants tax-exempt status to the Church and School of Wicca.

1966 C.E. Goddess-oriented archeological discoveries from the Neolithic period.

1954 C.E. *Witchcraft Today* by Gerald Gardner is published.

1953 C.E. Gardner forms his own coven.

1951 C.E. England's Witchcraft Act is repealed.

1939 C.E. Gerald Gardner initiated into witchcraft.

1921 C.E. *The Witch Cult in Western Europe* by Dr. Margaret Murray is published.

1899 C.E. *Aradia: Gospel of the Witches* by Charles Godfrey Leland is published.

1898 C.E. Aleister Crowley joins Golden Dawn.

1890 C.E. Sir James George Frazer publishes *The Golden Bough*.

1888 C.E. Founding of the Golden Dawn.

1875 C.E. Founding of the Theosophical Society.

1834 C.E. Suppression of the Spanish Inquisition.

1735 C.E. King George's Witchcraft Act of 1735.

1693 C.E. Salem witchcraft trials end.

1692 C.E. Salem, Massachusetts witchcraft trials begin.

1645 C.E. Matthew Hopkins proclaims himself Witch Finder General.

1563 C.E. Elizabeth I's Act Against Witchcraft.

1542 C.E. Henry the VIII's Act Against Witchcraft.

1502 C.E. Pope Alexander's Act Against Witchcraft.

1492 C.E. Spain forces Jews to convert to Christianity.

1486 C.E. Publication of *Malleus Maleficarum*.

1478 C.E. Beginning of the Spanish Inquisition.

1400 C.E. Approximate start of the Burning Times.

1313 C.E. Supposed birth of Aradia, daughter of Diana.

1231 C.E. Beginning of the medieval Inquisition.

800 C.E. Holy Roman Empire is founded.

500 C.E. Romans leave British Isles.

476 C.E. General date for the fall of the Roman Empire.

447 C.E. The Council of Toledo defines the Devil as the embodiment of evil.

313 C.E. Edict of Milan.

4 B.C.E.–29 C.E. Supposed lifetime of Jesus of Nazareth.

27 B.C.E. Founding of the Roman Empire.

200 B.C.E. First clashes between Romans and Teutons.

390 B.C.E. Celts invade and plunder Rome.

500 B.C.E. Celts go to Britain.

1200 B.C.E. Celtic culture in what is now France and West Germany.

1500 B.C.E. Approximate building date of Stonehenge.

2200 B.C.E.–14,000 B.C.E. Minoan period of the Aegean civilization.

2630 B.C.E.–1530 B.C.E. Egyptians start building pyramids.

3500 B.C.E. Start of Egypt's Old Kingdom.

3600 B.C.E. "Civilization" begins in Sumeria.

8000 B.C.E.–1500 B.C.E. Neolithic period (approximate).

13,000 B.C.E.–8000 B.C.E. Mesolithic period (approximate).

2,500,000 B.C.E.–13,000 B.C.E. Paleolithic period (approximate).

The Modern World

England passed the Witchcraft Act of 1735 under the power of King George I. This legislation basically stated that witchcraft was not real and all persecutions should cease. It did allow persecution of those who pretended to possess supernatural powers. Although the general populace still saw witches as evil monsters making deals with the Devil, the notion eventually subsided into the deeper parts of our collective consciousness. In several places, the wise ones and cunning folk quietly began working again as healers.

Although the Age of Reason prevailed in most of society, a resurgence in the esoteric was bubbling beneath the surface. Various spiritualist movements swept over the Western world, particularly in Britain and America, starting around 1850. Such a movement piqued interest and thought on reincarnation, psychic abilities, and healing. Séances became quite popular. For some it was entertainment, a spectacle to partake in, but for many it was the birthing of a new religion, one that was often dogged with accusations of trickery and fraud. In some ways, this was the first breath of the modern New Age movement, which was really bringing older concepts of spirituality to the modern world. Individual stars rose to shine the light of the New Age on the world, and are honored for their contributions, which are still accompanied by the controversy of their day.

H. P. Blavatsky, a Russian émigré to England, brought many concepts of Eastern mysticism to the West, and also revived the knowledge of the ancient Greeks and Egyptians, including Hermetic philosophy. She cofounded the Theosophical Society in 1875, a group dedicated to teaching the ancient mysteries of spiritual wisdom. Blavatsky believed that all religions sprang from the same source of spiritual wisdom, and that she was guided by hidden masters, ascended beings, to found the organization. She is best known for her works *Isis Unveiled* and *The Secret Doctrine*.

In the late nineteenth century, England was a hotbed of occult activity. One of the most influential and well-known groups was the Hermetic Order of the Golden Dawn. The order was founded in 1888 by the occultist Samuel Liddel MacGregor Mathers with Dr. William Westcott and Dr. William Robert Woodman, both master Masons and members of the Rosicrucian Society of England. The material was based on a supposed ancient manuscript found by Rev. A. F. A. Woodruff, a Mason and member of the Hermetic Society who consulted with these men on the nature of the manuscript. The Golden Dawn studied and taught ritual magick, the Kabalah, tarot, psychic abilities, scrying, alchemy, and astrology, most likely drawing from Rosicrucianism and Masonry. The group had many internal conflicts and splinter groups. Famous members include Arthur Edward Waite, William Butler Yeats, and Aleister Crowley, who continued to pioneer magick and exert a strong influence on the newly emerging craft of Wicca.

Of all the modern magicians, Crowley was considered the most infamous, and much of his reputation as "the wickedest man in the world" was well deserved. His life is a story of excess and ego, but also one of a brilliant magician. As a young man, he joined the Order of the Golden Dawn in 1898. Crowley was a student of Mathers, but their constant quarrels ended that relationship. After leaving the Golden Dawn, Crowley was the eventual leader of the OTO, or Ordo Templi Orientis. Through a series of messages from a spirit named Aiwass, Crowley founded the Thelemic Mysteries. This unusual man saw himself as the prophet of the next great age, the Age of Horus, and often referred to himself as the "Beast of the Apocalypse." His most notable works include *The Book of the Law, Magick in Theory and Practice, Magick Without Tears, The Book of Thoth, Moonchild,* and *Diary of a Drug Fiend.*

In 1892, Charles Godfrey Leland, an American author and scholar, published *Etruscan Roman Remains*. The work was based on his study and research of Italian witchcraft, as researched while he lived there, having moved to Italy in 1880. His previous magickal work included research into the Gypsy culture and its magickal systems. In fact, he was the founder of the Gypsy Lore Society. This work set out to prove that not only was there a tradition of witchcraft that could be traced back to Italy, but that the craft was still practiced there presently, worshipping the goddess Diana. Although not stated outright, his work implies study with these Italian witches and possibly initiation into the craft. One witch in particular, identified as Maddalena, gathered folklore, poems, stories, and rituals for his research. The material gathered eventually became another book, *Aradia: Gospel of the Witches*, printed in 1899, and it is for this work that he is best known in the neopagan communities. *Aradia* detailed stories, rituals, and philosophy from a woman living in the Middle Ages, supposedly born in 1313, named Aradia.

Some see her as an avatar of the goddess Diana. Witches liken her to a Jesus Christ or Buddha figure. She came to enlighten the peasants of Italy with teachings of magick and empowerment. Inquisitors' records from this age indicate references to an increase of witchcraft in Italy.

The unusual and often off-putting tone of Aradia's *Gospel* is surprising because previous works by Leland, including *Etruscan Magic & Occult Remedies* and *Legends of Florence*, present a view of witches as misunderstood followers of the Goddess. The *Gospel* shows a tendency toward the Christian stereotype of witches, including material regarding Lucifer and strong anti-Christian sentiment. Although genuine material appears mixed with the *Gospel of Aradia*, since most of it is based on Maddalena's material, scholars wonder why the sudden change. Was this tone from Maddalena playing Leland for a fool, or purposely veiling the information so that it would not be taken seriously? Perhaps the surviving witches adopted ideas from the Inquisition, as the oral traditions broke down. Since Leland died before he completed his next work on the subject, we may never know.

In 1890, Sir James George Frazer published *The Golden Bough: A Study in Magic and Religion*. Frazer was a member of Leland's Gypsy Lore Society and a respected British anthropologist. *The Golden Bough* delved into the mysteries of ancient paganism, particularly in Italy, and strongly emphasized the concept of the Divine King found in many areas of Western magick and religion.

At the turn of the nineteenth century, Edgar Cayce, the now-famous "sleeping prophet," began to give psychic readings. This man had no medical background, but gave very detailed accounts of medical illness and procedures to cure such illnesses. Later readings involved the concepts of karma, spiritual roots of disease, prophecy, and the fabled continents of Atlantis and Lemuria, echoing the work of Blavatsky, though Cayce was a devout Christian. The Christian flavor of his readings might not be tied directly to the witchcraft revival, but he introduced many people to such occult concepts as nontraditional healing and psychic powers. Several organizations sprung up around his groundbreaking work.

Psychiatrist Carl Jung played an important role in the modern mystical revival. Although a contemporary and student of Freud, C. G. Jung's work was inspired by his own psychic experiences. He paved the way for a scientific, analytical look at the mystic's world, investigating the interpretation of dreams, symbols, mythology, I Ching, tarot, the collective consciousness, synchronicity, and archetypes. His interest in ancient alchemy and Gnosticism, from a psychological approach, revived interest in both subjects. His work was first published in the early 1900s, and his material was still being released after his death in 1961. Many current mystics who have difficulty with literal interpretations of ancient wisdom seek the work of Jung to give the modern conscious mind an easily understood reference point.

THE WITCHCRAFT RENAISSANCE

In 1951, England repealed the Witchcraft Act. Believing witchcraft to be a superstition, laws against it seemed to perpetuate the ignorance of believing in such illogical things as magick. The scientific and social revolutions were supposed to have squelched belief in spells and witches. In reality, the repeal had quite the opposite effect, and began what is affectionately referred to as the Witchcraft Renaissance.

At the forefront in the new movement of witchcraft was Gerald B. Gardner, a British civil servant who spent some time in Malaysia exploring Eastern mysticism. He was fascinated by the occult and influenced by the work of Margaret Murray, author of *The Witch Cult in Western Europe*, published in 1921. She claimed that the witches persecuted in Europe were practitioners of an ancient religion of European fertility cults based in goddess worship. Her theories were influenced greatly by her own personal beliefs, since scholars cannot find evidence to this link as an organized religion. Murray was correct in the fact that the wise ones were the *spiritual* descendants of the ancient goddess cults and mystery traditions, if not physically linked.

Gardner claimed he was initiated in 1939 into a long-standing coven of hereditary witches practicing the craft in New Forest. This group taught him the "Old Religion" as a magickal art and a personal religion. Based on their research with Gardner's contemporaries, Janet Farrar and Gavin Bone, co-authors of *The Healing Craft*, with the late Stewart Farrar, believe this New Forest "coven" was actually a group of Theosophists. In Gardner's day, anyone involved in the occult was considered a "witch." Gardner formed his own coven in 1953, borrowing and adapting material from the New Forest group and other occult sources. Gardner drew from his previous experience as a Freemason, his time in Malaysia, and his passing acquaintance with Aleister Crowley. Rumor has it that Aleister Crowley actually wrote Gardner's first Book of Shadows, but that is unlikely. More likely, Gardner was probably inspired by much of Crowley's work. Like the forefathers of the modern mystical movements, Gerald was followed by much controversy. Opinions of his character and work varied greatly. He claimed to be re-introducing an ancient religion, but the general consensus is that much of the material is his own invention. Such facts do not take away from the contemporary practice. All religions change over time and go through many birthing periods. The modern movement of Wicca is no different.

Gardner initiated Doreen Valiente, who reworked many rituals in favor of her own Goddess-oriented approach. Valiente was instrumental in shaping the new movement, and this specific tradition was named Gardnerian Witchcraft, after Gerald Gardner. Their original Book of Shadows has been copied from, added to, and adapted by a long line of modern witches.

Clearly Valiente and Gardner were inspired by the work of Leland and *Aradia: Gospel of the Witches*. The "Charge of the Goddess" is often attributed to Valiente, but the original version of the Charge comes from Aradia. Leland actually writes on many of the same topics as Gardner, in reference to the Italian traditions of the *Strega*, or witch, instead of the Celtic mysteries. The Roman occupation of the British Isles could have spread such concepts to the Celtic people, becoming mingled with their own magick. In fact, Gardner spent some time in Italy prior to his publication, where he studied Roman paganism and remarked how the artwork at Pompeii depicted the mysteries found in witchcraft. The art of the witch can be traced to many cultures, not just one. The world owns the tradition of witchcraft, and all are welcome to it.

In 1954, *Witchcraft Today* by Gerald Gardner was published, soon followed by *The Meaning of Witchcraft* in 1959. His writing drew considerable attention, coming on the heels of Robert Graves' influential yet disputed work *The White Goddess*. These works were fueled by a general desire in some of the population for a personal spiritual path. Regardless of the origins of the material, Gardner is credited as a spiritual forefather.

The Witchcraft Renaissance blossomed in the 1960s and 1970s, inspiring covens in Europe, the United States, and Australia. Gardner is considered the modern founder of Wicca, and his work is one of the reasons why the craft has spread so far and wide.

While Gardner was busy cultivating his brand of the Old Religion, other forms sprang up elsewhere. Since witchcraft was no longer considered a crime in Britain, other hereditary traditions made themselves known, like Gardner's New Forest coven. They, too, claimed descent from more ancient traditions, kept alive in secret during the Burning Times. Though I do believe in the possibility of many such covens scattered about Europe and even America, I think they are far rarer than most would have you believe. Folk magick has been practiced in many families that were not unbroken lines of witches. My family practiced magick with my grandmother's generation, but they were also staunch Catholics. The Goddess survived in the form of Mother Mary, but none of my more recent ancestors would have claimed the title "witch."

Others took Gardner's foundation and built new traditions, reflecting their personal tastes. The most famous is Alex Sanders, the self-proclaimed "King of the Witches." Sanders was already familiar with ritual magick and claimed to be initiated into a family tradition by his grandmother when he was seven, after he stumbled upon her in ritual. His tradition is known as Alexandrian Witchcraft, although it bears a close resemblance to Gardner's.

In other groups, the word *witch* was stripped away, focusing on the pagan elements, founding the neopagan movement. Somewhat divorced from Wicca, these were the foundations of our modern Earth-based religions. Keen interest in Native American mysticism and shamanism developed as part of the New Age movement. Since these shamans were never persecuted by their own people, their traditions survived and were thought to be somewhat similar to the practices of ancient tribal witches. Native people began a period of openness in sharing this material, though some objected. While Native American spirituality seems safe and honorable to the mainstream public, those same people often view witchcraft with the stigma of evil perpetuated during the Burning Times. Witches often point out the fundamental similarities between Native American practices and those of the witch.

Women dissatisfied with the roles of traditional religions flocked to the goddess religions, creating feminist branches of Wicca, including Dianic covens. Archeological discoveries of a goddess culture in Anatolia from the Neolithic period, at Catal Juyuk, Mersin, and Hacilar, were published in 1966. This new evidence of the ancient world coincided with the rising feminist movement in the West during the late sixties. Both contributed to the growing awareness of the Goddess in the Western mind. Feminine roles were changing and awareness grew. The discovery of a matriarchal culture valuing feminine ideals and spirit was a wake-up call to the end of the patriarchal age, dominated by masculine deities and customs. History revealed a forgotten part of the world's past. Those involved in neopaganism and neo-witchcraft sought the divine in both the Goddess and the God, honoring masculine and feminine.

In 1972, witchcraft was granted the status of a legally recognized religion in America when the IRS granted the Church of Wicca tax-exempt status. Witchcraft is now protected by the First and Fourteenth Amendments in the United States. Ordained priests and priestesses enjoy all the same rights as traditional clergy.

The traditions and movements have branched out many times, forming a complex web including almost as many traditions as practitioners, creating an eclectic mix. Witchcraft is very personal, and you can no longer really say there is a "right" way and a "wrong" way to practice it.

The branches of the witchcraft tree continue to grow up and out, forming a deliciously complicated pattern. Everyone has an opinion on where it has been, where it is now, and where it is growing, but such facts seem fluid, never completely defined or documented, as are the mysteries of witchcraft itself. Like the roots of our history, the branches of our future are heading in many directions at once, exploring new territory and reaching to greater heights.

Recommended Reading

When God Was a Woman by Merlin Stone (Harcourt Brace Jovanovich).

Origins of Modern Witchcraft: The Evolution of a World Religion by Ann Moura (Llewellyn Publications).

Flavors of Witchcraft

The witchcraft tree is branching out in different directions. Although many branches cross and interweave with each other, there are differences between the modern traditions. You could fill a book describing these differences. The purpose of this chapter is to give you an idea of the different paths within modern witchcraft. Most teachers teach in a specific tradition. I encourage an eclectic, personal tradition with a solid foundation.

When I first got involved in witchcraft, my mother and I took classes together. We learned witchcraft with a heavy Celtic slant, but neither of us were Celtic by family lineage. My mother is Italian and I am of Italian/Polish/Lithuanian descent. Finding material on Italian witchcraft was a revelation because we were not initially exposed to it. In fact, it was fairly unheard of in the pagan community at the time. We didn't really know it existed. Though I still have a strong Celtic slant regardless of my blood, my mother has taken to her craft as never before, inspired by the practices of her own ancestors and her memories of her parents' and grandparents' acts of Italian folk magick and tea leaf reading. A great number of people who do not feel witchcraft is their personal calling would be surprised by the number of cultures historically involved in the craft.

Common Ground

Before we learn the differences between traditions, let us look at the fundamental similarities. Witchcraft is a personal path, and these beliefs may not be held by every individual, but they are commonly accepted by the mainstream pagan community.

Pagan originally meant "of the land" or "country dweller," referring to rural people and their beliefs. As Christianity grew and took control of Europe, pagan became identified with any of the non-Judeo-Christian religions, and to some it was equated with heretic, an enemy of the Church's truth. Some equate the word *heathen* with *heretic* or *savage*, but it means "one who lives on heaths." Church officials wanted to replace pagan beliefs and practices with Christian ones, so much so that pagan holidays were adopted into the Christian calendar to get converts. As the word *witch* is reclaimed, so is the word *pagan*. Now it refers to a larger group of beliefs with many different traditions and practices. Although I dislike using a Christian analogy to explain paganism, I've found it useful for new students coming from a traditional background. Pagan is to Wiccan as Christian is to Catholic, meaning Pagan and Christian are larger groups with smaller traditions within them. All Wiccans and witches are pagans, but not all pagans are witches. Many identify themselves as pagan, but may not identify with a specific tradition, such as witchcraft. And within the heading of witchcraft are several other smaller divisions. I've spoken to a few witches who feel witches or Wiccans are the clergy of the pagan people, but most strictly pagan folk I know would not agree with that definition. Technically, we are neo-witches and neopagans, meaning "new," but few people use this term outside of academic writing.

Divinity is inherent in all things, material and spiritual. The divine force is apparent in all life and form. Spiritual does not mean divorced from the physical, earthly realm. The Earth is actually one of the most divine forms in all creation. All life, all nature is the divine manifest, and most pagans honor the Earth as a living being, the source of life. In our mythology, the Earth is viewed as Mother, or even Grandmother, the source of all life on Earth. The Earth Goddess can be seen as a symbol of life and interconnection, or a sentient consciousness available for communication in her own right. Science is slowly catching up to the idea of the Earth being alive, and not a lifeless rock. British biologist James Lovelock first proposed the "Gaia Hypothesis" in the

1970s, named after the Greek goddess Gaia, stating that all life, including humanity, is part of a complex biosphere organism. Others have extrapolated that hypothesis into a theory that the Earth is a living being, and all things on Earth are akin to cells within her. To witches, there is no doubt that the Earth is alive.

The divinity, or life force, present in all things expresses itself in several different ways in witchcraft. Most common in this faith is the expression of the divine not only through the Earth, but also through the Goddess, the great mother, and the God, the all father. Through the actions of this polarity, Goddess and God, life is created.

As the Goddess is manifested through the Earth, she is also inherent in the Moon, the changing cycles matching the twenty-eight-day menstruation period. The concept of a Triple Goddess—Maiden, Mother, and Crone—seen in the waxing, full, and waning Moon, is rooted deeply in the pagan consciousness. Her three identities could also be the Moon, Earth, and Underworld Goddess. The Triple Goddess is seen as the giver of life, sustainer and destroyer, all in one. The mythologies of old contain the Triple Goddess image. Different cultures alternately see the Goddess in the Sun, ocean, rivers, sky, and spiraling galaxies.

The God is manifested through various faces, including the Sky Father, encompassing Mother Earth; Solar King; Horned God, the lord of animals; and the Green Man, the lord of the harvest. The God is most aptly seen as dualistic. On the waxing, or warming, half of the year, he is life bringer, the god of light, Sun, and growing things. On the waning and withering half of the year, he is the god of darkness, death, animals, and the hunt.

Each image or archetype in our collective consciousness reveals one aspect of the divine, God and Goddess alike. Neopagans and witches have adopted the gods and goddesses of various pantheons as expressions of the Goddess and God. Usually these expressions function as rulers over a particular aspect of nature or human life, such as a deity of storms, the sea, the Moon, hunting, or magick. Usually they have more than one attribute. Even as expressions of the divine, the gods and goddesses are very real, connecting to our innermost selves.

Although witches are polytheists, meaning they acknowledge and honor more than one deity, they recognize the one spirit running through everything. Perhaps the word monist, one who recognizes the divine in everything, is a more appropriate term, but most pagans identify themselves as polytheistic. The gods and goddesses are expressions of that one spirit, leading to a more personal relationship with the divine.

The one spirit is what I call the Great Spirit. The Goddess and God move in the love of the Great Spirit. They are different aspects of the divine. Infrequently, some Wiccan traditions call this one spirit *Dryghten*, a word said to be Anglo-Saxon and best translated to "lord," but without the gender quality, referring to the creative force that is both male and female, the source of all things. Some see this Great Spirit as the Goddess exclusively, who gave birth to the God through her self-fertilization. Ancient myths, such as the Greek creation story, start with the Goddess who gives birth to her son/husband to continue creation.

Critics say that witches worship nature, and to a certain extent that is true, but in reality we worship the creative force found in nature. In essence, we honor life, everywhere, and see the divine in everything and everyone.

Witches have nothing to do with the Christian Devil. To believe in the Devil, one must already believe in the Christian mythos, and most witches feel their spiritual roots predate Christianity. We are not naive. We do believe that harmful forces exist and precautions must be taken, but we do not subscribe to an ultimate author of evil or the concept of sin. An ultimate evil and an ultimate good is a polarity never found in nature. In Christian myths, God is all-powerful, but the Devil still exists. For this to be a true polarity, they must be equal to each other, but in Christian mythology, they are not. In Wicca, we focus on the polarity of the Goddess and the God, and the love of their union that births life into being. Love is the focus, not conflict. The concept of light versus dark, good versus evil, was actually adopted from Zoroastrian religions.

STEREOTYPES

That being said, let's discuss the typical witch stereotypes. All witches do not wear black. We can wear anything we like. Black is appropriate for ritual because it is a dark goddess color, and it attracts energy. Rituals are celebrated at night for the same reasons, though many take place during the day as well, depending on the tradition.

Witches can feel empowered to wear black outside of the ritual space, but wearing black is not a requirement. Black and late-evening rituals were also practical during the Burning Times. If you were afraid of getting caught, black cloaks would hide you at night in the forest from prospective witch hunters. Black is also the color of clergy, used by priests and rabbis. Perhaps they adopted the practice from witches.

Witches do not perform animal sacrifice, though it may have been a part of our distant history, as it was in Judaism and many other religions. Many Wiccans are animal rights activists and environmentalists, subscribing to a theory of "harm ye none." Witches do not abuse children in or out of ritual as a part of their faith, nor do we perform curses.

Witches and other pagans do believe in and practice magick. Magick is the art of making change, manifesting your dreams, and banishing the things that no longer serve you and hold you back. Though the effects can be quite startling and powerful, magick usually manifests in the form of unusual coincidences and connections. The first time you have success with magick, and even the second or third time, you might dismiss it. After repeated successes, however, you know you are no longer working within the fabled "Law of Averages," and that some other force, namely magick, is at work. *Magick* is usually spelled with a *k* by modern practitioners, to distinguish it from illusion and sleight-of-hand tricks.

Spells, specific acts of magick, can be created through ritual or meditation. To a witch, spells are like prayers. They are simple acts of sending out an intention to the divine, asking it to manifest. The difference between spells and prayers is that witches study the nature of the universe to understand better how to create change. Many people who pray think it is a give-and-take process, where one has to give up something "sinful" to receive the boon of the prayer. Though there is always an exchange of energies, witches know that the universe is ever abundant.

We do not label ourselves white or black witches, as was done in the Burning Times. Though the distinction of white and black magick can still be found in the initial lessons of high ritual magick, most modern witches do not subscribe to it. Magick is ruled by intention.

THE WHEEL OF THE YEAR

The seasonal shifts and holidays are extremely important. The Wheel of the Year is celebrated through ritual holidays falling on the equinoxes, solstices, and points in between called fire festivals (figure 3). The modern Wheel is a collection of rites taken from European lineages, primarily Celtic and Teutonic. The modern Wheel tells the story of the Goddess and the God, through many faces and myths, as they grow and change through the seasons of the year. The changing seasons help Wiccans get into immediate contact with deity, harmonizing them with the world.

The winter solstice, also called Yule, is when the Sun's light starts to grow. Cultures across the Northern Hemisphere saw it as the birth of the young God. Many of the familiar Christmas celebrations were taken from Yule, including mistletoe, Yule logs, and decorating evergreen trees with lights (candles), a symbol of the everlasting Goddess and the return of the God of Light. Although still deep in winter, the light and life are returning to the world.

Imbolc comes on February 2, a fire festival often dedicated to the goddess Brid (pronounced "Breed"), or Bridget. Brid is the triple goddess of light, and a patron of the home, healers, poets, and smiths. Some compare her to the Greek goddess Hestia, the goddess of the home and hearth. Candles are lit and homes are blessed. Advent wreaths are a remnant of Brid's crown of candles. Imbolc is sometimes known as Candlemas.

Ostara, the spring equinox, is the celebration of the Goddess rising and the Earth's resurrection. She returns from her winter slumber and brings with her the first signs of spring. The festival is named after the Teutonic goddess Ostre, the egg or seed goddess. Blessing and planting seeds and painting eggs are part of these traditions. Although named after Ostre, the Greek myth of Persephone rising from the realm of the dead to usher in the growing season with her mother, Demeter, also resonates on the equinox.

Beltane is the fire festival of May 1. Traditionally, herds were driven between two large bale fires of sacred wood to purify them of any lingering winter illness. Modern purification rites, both with fire and water, are performed on Beltane. It is dedicated to the young, fiery god Bel. The God has grown from the winter solstice into a young man, and claims his role as the Goddess' lover. Sexuality and passion are enjoyed on Beltane, and May Pole dances are traditional, representing the union of the God into the Earth Goddess.

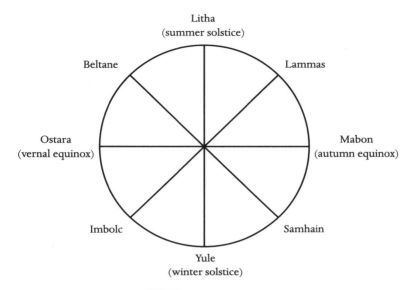

Figure 3: *Wheel of the Year*

The summer solstice, or Feast of Litha, is the divine marriage of Goddess and God. They are at the peak of their power, as the land is in full bloom and the harvest is expected. The day is the longest of the year, giving us an extended period of twilight, when the doors to the faery realm are open wide and we may celebrate with the spirits of the otherworld. Some traditions see this holiday as the battle of the divided light and dark aspects of the God. The dark king is victorious, claiming the throne with the Goddess.

Next is Lammas, the fire festival of August 1. In the Irish traditions it is known as Lughnassadh, after Lugh of the Long Arm, a god of light and grain. His talents are many and unequalled. Games and sports are played on this feast. Though originally named Lugh's Funeral Feast, after his mother's death, it is now associated with Lugh's own death, as the sacrificed king of the grain. Corn-dolly effigies are burned and the first grains of the harvest are cut and given as an offering to the gods in thanks. The sacrifice of the old God ushers in the bounty of the first harvest.

The second harvest is the fruit or wine harvest on the fall equinox. Named after the Celtic god Mabon, who gets lost in the Underworld, this is a time to journey to the dark. Wine is one of the ways to open the magickal passages between realms. Myths of other harvest gods, particular those associated with wine, such as Dionysus, are celebrated.

Samhain (pronounced "Sow-wen") is the traditional meat harvest and the Celtic New Year. Falling on October 31, it has been turned into modern Halloween, but was a very important pagan festival. Samhain is the day of the dead. Since the herd was slaughtered and the meat was salted or smoked for the winter, this was the day when the first of the herd was slaughtered, opening the veils between the worlds. Since the day is one of death, ancestors who have passed on are associated with it, coming back through the veil to give blessings and advice. Soul meals are prepared for the dead, goodbyes are said to lost loved ones, and candles are lit to mark their way back. Eventually this thinning of the veil became a fearful event, and costumes were worn to scare away the walkers between the worlds, though originally it was a normal part of the culture, with no fear or dread.

These eight festivals are called Sabbats, though the individual traditions celebrate them differently. The term harkens back to the Burning Times, to the Hebrew Sabbath, when witches and Jews alike were prosecuted as heretics. Modern witches have adopted the word. An Esbat refers to another type of ritual, usually a Moon ritual. Esbats are typically private circles, for covens, small groups who work magick together. Community and family are usually welcome to the Sabbats, which are more celebratory in nature. With Esbats, the goal is working magick in an intimate setting. Esbats usually coincide with the Full or Dark Moon. Witches celebrate the thirteen Moons of the lunar year. The term *circle* is sometimes used synonymously with Esbat, or with a group of practitioners, but a circle specifically refers to the ritual of the circle, a ceremony of celebration and magick called a witch's circle, moon circle, or magician's circle. Circles are cast in both Esbats and Sabbats or any other magickal event, depending on the tradition.

Life rituals, or rites of passage, are marked along with the holidays. Like tribal people, pagans mark turning points in life with ceremony or ritual. Traditions are individual, but usually birth, coming of age, handfasting (marriage or partnering), elderhood, and death are celebrated.

Personal Freedom

Lastly, witches seek freedom from dogma, the freedom to personally delve into the mysteries of the divine and find our own answers. There may be recommendations and guidelines in each tradition, but there is no official bible. Our bible is the cycle of seasons. Our songs are the songs of the Earth. No one central authority exists. The experience of others can help us find our way, but ultimately we walk individual paths. Others can support, guide, and comfort us, but cannot do it for us. We are our own intermediaries to the Goddess and God. Each individual strives to be his or her own clergy. Magick is used because it works, as is meditation and psychic abilities. We don't need to believe blindly because we are guided by experience. Witches don't simply believe, we do. Such free spirits recognize that no one person or religion has the answer. Being polytheists, we gladly acknowledge other points of view without feeling threatened. Most of us come from other traditions and seek to escape past dogma. Some still feel anger over the persecutions of the past and blame dogma and intolerance, but for the most part, witches do not harbor any biases against other religions. We live and let live.

Traditions of Witchcraft

Each of these paths within the craft contains a different focus. None are completely right or wrong, but are only correct for an individual at a certain time in life. All have their merits and drawbacks. For the most comprehensive study of modern pagan groups, particularly in the United States, I highly recommend *Drawing Down the Moon* by Margot Adler.

Alexandrian

The tradition founded by Alex Sanders is quite similar to the Gardnerian style. Sanders claimed to have his own brand of witchcraft given to him by his grandmother, but in truth it was very similar to Gardner's. His previous background in ceremonial magick added to the evolution of the craft, and, as a natural showman, he attracted quite a number of people to witchcraft. Sanders was called the "King of Witches" within his tradition, but was not recognized as a king in other traditions of witchcraft. It was simply an honorary title given by those in his lineage. Like Gardnerian covens, Alexandrian covens have survived into the present era and one must be initiated into an existing coven to claim this lineage.

Cabot

Long-time public witch Laurie Cabot established two traditions intertwined together. Her first, Witchcraft as a Science, looks at witchcraft from a practical, analytical point of view, while her Cabot tradition focuses on the religion. She views it as a pre-Gardnerian tradition, based on her original training, genetic memory, Celtic heritage, and her own inspiration.

Celtic

Celtic witchcraft is not a specific tradition in the sense of a formal lineage, but denotes one practicing witchcraft with a distinctive, if not exclusive, Celtic flavor. Rituals, myths, and godforms are chosen from Celtic lore, and often based on scant information about the Druidic tradition.

Christian Wicca

Although I was initially hesitant to add this category, the emergence of "Christian witches" is becoming more prevalent. Often, eclectic witches have no reason to leave behind their original Christian faith, and instead incorporate elements of both into their personal traditions. Folk magick survived by veiling itself in Christianity and incorporating the mythology. Unfortunately, Christian witches get curious looks from pagans who have renounced Christianity and see the two as incompatible.

Dianic

The Dianic tradition is considered a branch of feminist Wicca, honoring the goddess of the Moon and hunt, Diana, known as Artemis to the Greeks. Dianic covens are often made up exclusively of women, and some are exclusively lesbian as well. Usually these covens focus their energy on the Goddess as the Great Mother and creator. It is important to note that not all feminist traditions are necessarily Dianic.

Faery (or Feri)

This is a tradition founded by Victor Anderson and Gwydion Pendderwen. Anderson was initiated into a loosely organized coven of witches in Oregon at age nine. They called themselves faeries, and he learned their magick and ritual, prior to the traditions created by Gardner. Inspired by Gardner's work, and later an Alexandrian Book of Shadows, Anderson and Pendderwen, a friend of the family, formed a coven and wrote the rituals of the Faery tradition. Author Starhawk was initiated into the Faery tradition. Some use this term for any traditions honoring the faery folk.

Eclectic

Eclectic witches are those who follow no specific tradition or path, but feel free to borrow from many different traditions and cultures. An eclectic witch understands the fundamental rules of magick, but creates rituals to suit personal needs and tastes. There are suggestions, but not hard rules. One might be equally adept working with Celtic, Greek, Hindu, or Egyptian gods. Such a practitioner can be in a coven, solitary, or both. This freeform style of witchcraft is one of the most popular because it grants such freedom and lacks a hierarchical structure. One can be initiated by another, or perform a self-initiation ritual to the Goddess and God.

Gardnerian

Gardnerian witchcraft is considered the most traditional form of witchcraft, from which most modern paths developed. The material was from Gerald Gardner's own experience, creativity, and inspiration, along with the input of Doreen Valiente. As Gardner's fame spread and he initiated more people into the craft, his tradition moved across Britain and eventually to Europe, the United States, and Australia. To be a member of this tradition, one must be initiated by another member.

Greco-Roman

Most people are introduced to paganism through the classical Greco-Roman mythology taught in many school systems. This encounter starts a love affair in the budding neopagan with these godforms, and, later in life, such individuals choose to work actively with these deities. Greek and Roman myths contain many of our first glimpses of the witch. Some speculate that the true origins of witchcraft and much goddess worship came from territories surrounding Greece, such as Thrace and Thessaly. The mystery cults of Dionysus and Demeter evoke powerful magick in our hearts. Greek and Roman covens are in existence today, but they are not necessarily unbroken lines of a specific witchcraft tradition. They are usually reconstructions based on Greco-Roman material, but if some Celtic family traditions supposedly survived to the present day, then perhaps Mediterranean traditions survived as well.

Green Witchcraft

Green Witchcraft is a fairly broad category, sometimes used synonymously with Celtic witchcraft, kitchen witchcraft, faery traditions, or natural, herbal magick. Herbalists who aren't actually practicing Wicca sometimes refer to themselves as green witches.

Hereditary (or Family Tradition)

Hereditary witches claim a lineage prior to the inception of Gardnerian witchcraft. They state that their own individual traditions were passed on through family members, and that they are hereditary witches through blood lineage. After the witchcraft acts were repealed, some family traditions came out of hiding. Perhaps others remain out of the public eye and have no wish to join the Witchcraft Renaissance.

Radical Faery

This is not a formal tradition, but a loose movement of gay men seeking pagan and witchcraft spirituality, reclaiming the word *faery* as a word of magick and mystery. The gatherings are very primal and playful, not based on a rigid structure, but one of joy.

Seax Wica

Raymond Buckland created the Seax Wica tradition. Originally a Gardnerian and instrumental in bringing that tradition to America, Buckland founded his own tradition in the early 1970s using a Saxon heritage. Seax Wica is more open and democratic in practice that either Gardnerian or Alexandrian Wicca.

Solitary

Solitary witches are those who practice without a coven, and usually do not benefit from the training of a coven. Instead they learn on their own, from books, speaking with other witches, and from nature and the gods. You can become a solitary through self-initiation, or you can come from another tradition and choose to practice alone. Solitary witches are often also eclectic witches.

Stregheria (Italian)

The practice of witchcraft in Italy is called Stregheria, and a witch is a Strega. The words refer to the tradition of Italian witchcraft documented by Charles Leland, claiming a pre-Gardnerian tradition mixing ancient Roman and Etruscan practices. Some are formerly initiated into the traditions, while others of Italian descent claim the word. Raven Grimassi, author of *Italian Witchcraft* (previously called *The Way of the Strega*), is greatly responsible for reviving interest in this little-known path and major root of witchcraft.

Wiccan Shamanism

Wiccan Shamanism is a creation of Selena Fox, High Priestess of Circle Sanctuary. This path combines Wicca with core shamanic techniques, modern psychology, and a multicultural view. Rituals are akin to African or Native American gatherings with drumming and music, ecstatic trance, and personal vision work. Shamanic Witchcraft or Shamanic Wicca is used to refer to other practices that incorporate these ideas, but are not necessarily under the direction of Selena Fox.

OTHER MAGICKAL TRADITIONS

The following practices are not specifically forms of modern witchcraft, but are usually associated with magick, ritual, and neopaganism.

Asatru

Asatru is a form of paganism strongly associated with Wicca. Where many modern Wiccans focus on the Celtic heritage, the Asatru are the modern followers of the Aesir, the ruling race of gods of Norse mythology. The Asatru often focus on runic magick. Sometimes classified as conservative by other neopagans, the Asatru focus on their own cultural heritage and do not incorporate material from other cultures, such as tarot or I Ching, though an individual practitioner might use these tools. While most of the Norse path identify with the Aseir in general, some use the term Vanatru as followers of the Vanir tribe of gods. Followers of Odin might take the name Odinist. Pagans of the Norse tradition often prefer to be called heathens.

Brujería

Brujería is a witchcraft tradition from Central and South America. Women are *brujas* and men are *brujos*. Like their European counterparts, they work natural magick through herbs and charms, and healing through magick and folk remedies. Though the role and function of the bruja is nearly identical to the witch, this tradition bears no direct connection to the evolution of Wicca, other than a growing interest for those exploring the witchcraft traditions around the world.

Celtic Reconstructionist

A few Celtic pagan groups are termed "Celtic Reconstructionist," though "reconstructionist" can be applied to any cultural tradition. The term is used to differentiate them from a Wiccan tradition. Celtic Reconstructionists seek to the follow the ancient Celtic traditions as closely as possible, based on modern, scholarly knowledge. If a practice, such as the formal magick circle, is not documented in the surviving literature and myths, then it is ignored in favor of something more verifiable.

Ceremonial

Ceremonial magick refers to many different traditions, but most are usually based on the Kabalah, Hermetics, Masonry, alchemy, or the work of various factions of the Golden Dawn, which used all of these. Thelema, the tradition of Aleister Crowley, is grouped with ceremonial magick. Ceremonial magick is also called high magick, while witchcraft is called low magick. "High" and "low" refer to levels of technical knowledge, not power. Practitioners refer to themselves as magicians or mages, not witches, but some witches have incorporated elements of high magick into their own practices. Ceremonial magicians are often pagan, but do not have to be.

Chaos Magick

Chaos magick is a term applied to a philosophy, not a tradition. It is credited to Peter J. Caroll as the forefather, though his book *Liber Null* did not use the words *chaos magick*. The philosophy grew out of English occultism in the 1970s and early 1980s. In many ways, it was inspired by Aleister Crowley. Crowley's work was not as important as his life. Though unpleasant to so many, his life was an exercise in experimentation. From that varied experimentation, he created a continually evolving worldview, his own tradition that changed as he changed. Though he set his works as a guide for others, if we follow his example, we would not take his work verbatim but make our own tradition based on our own experiences. Chaos magick embodies an "anything goes" attitude, similar to the popular sneaker commercial slogan "Just do it." Theorizing about magick is fine, but do it, experiment, and use whatever works. Do not be attached to the system. Sources for material can be not only Celtic one day, and Greek the next, but Star Wars and Cinderella. If a pop-culture image works for you, then use it until it doesn't work anymore, and then try something new. Chaos magick grew out of ceremonial magick, and favors the modified use of symbols and sigils, but branches off wildly from that point. I've heard this philosophy described as eclecticism to the extreme.

Druidism

Druidism is a pagan reconstructionist movement based on the teachings of the Druids. Since the original Druidic tradition was oral, little direct ritual and teaching is available. The Druid revival started as early as the 1600s and continues today. While the word *Druid* implies one who is specifically following a Celtic path, using Gaelic in rituals, early reconstructionists applied a much broader definition to the word, incorporating Christianity and Masonry into the practice with little knowledge of the pagan Celtic culture. Many in reality did not consider themselves pagan groups, but philosophical societies, though they are far less common today. Groups organize in "groves" rather than covens, and several large Druid organizations exist. Isaac Bonewits, author of *Real Magic*, has been at the forefront of the neopagan Druid revival.

Egyptian

Egyptian magick is alive and well in the twenty-first century, though it's gone through some changes. Like so many ancient mystic traditions, no one is quite sure about exact

Egyptian practices, but neopagan groups have reconstructed traditions based on the Egyptian myths, texts, symbols, and ancient mysteries. Many contemporary pagans are drawn to the image of Isis and Osiris as the divine Mother and Father, even if they do not practice in an Egyptian tradition.

New Age

New Age spirituality is not necessarily a tradition of magick, but has many things in common with witches, pagans, and magicians, since they often get lumped together, particularly in bookstores. New Age practices include meditation, healing, spirit guides, crystals, herbalism, psychic abilities, chanting, ceremony, and visualization. Blavatsky, Cayce, and even ancient pagan teachings influence the collective view of those involved in the New Age. Most are quite supportive of the craft, but there are some misunderstandings. The biggest misunderstanding is the assumption on behalf of pagans that those in the New Age are "flaky" and only preach "love and light." On the other hand, New Agers see pagans as being "dark" and "depressing." The point of the New Age is the ability for everyone to get along, to live and let live.

Santería

Santería is a religious tradition that was brought to the Americas from Africa though the slave trade, focusing particularly on the Yoruban tribes. The word comes from the Spanish *Santo*, meaning "saint." The faith contains a pantheon of gods called *orishas*. When in the New World, the orishas were disguised as the saints, because the slaves were forced to convert to Catholicism. The religion is the practice of honoring and caring for the orishas, which bring blessings. Priests and priestesses conduct ceremonies, healings, and blessings, making magickal charms and speaking with spirits. The role is congruous with the witch or shaman.

Shamanism

Shamanism is the magickal and healing practice of the Native American cultures. The word *shaman* is Siberian, but it refers to the medicine men and women of the indigenous people in Siberia and North, Central, and South America. Shamans enter a trance state, often through the use of meditation, drumming, dance, or psychotropics, to pierce the spiritual veil and commune with spirits, ancestors, and power beings, to bring wisdom, healing, and energy to the community. Shamans are part religious leader and part lore keeper, doctor, herbalist, and counselor. Anthropologists have noted that these roles were filled by similar people across the world, coining the term "core shamanism" to distinguish between the traditional American shamans and their global counterparts. Since the general belief is that ancient witches were the shamans of Europe, modern witches can look to the practices of the Americas to find missing links in the Wiccan heritage.

Voudoun

Voudoun, or Voodoo, is a polytheistic religion with roots deep in Africa, but was brought to the New World via slave trading in French colonies like Haiti and New Orleans. The practice is similar to Santería, though Santería has a decidedly Spanish flavor. The gods of Voudoun are called *loas*, meaning "laws," and are also linked to the Catholic saints. Though the practices of Voudoun and Santería are not witchcraft per se, they serve the same function as witches in these transplanted African societies. Thanks largely to Hollywood, Voudoun is the only religion with a stigma worse that witchcraft, but the African traditions are quite loving and healing, like the craft.

Quite a number of other pagan traditions draw on different cultures, including Sumerian, Finnish, Slavic, Hindu, Asian, and Polynesian. Some subscribe to the name *witch* or *Wicca*. Most do not. Many other traditions, associations, churches, groves, and covens exist, all practicing their own brand of the mysteries. The neopagan resurgence gives us all the spiritual freedom to devise the magickal tradition we want and to claim the heritage, names, and titles that serve our highest good. Though it is always important to know where your practice comes from, the most important factor is to know where it is going.

RECOMMENDED READING

Drawing Down the Moon by Margot Adler (Beacon Press).

THE WITCH'S PATH

The witch's path is not an easy road to walk. Through the roots of our history, we have seen the persecution of those who practice the art of magick and the mysteries of the Goddess and God. Though death is not the result in this day and age, witches are still discriminated against. If you can handle the difficulties, the life of the witch is very joyous, filled with never-ending study and exploration. Witches learn many disciplines to ply their craft. One must be a dedicated student, but also have the passion, the fire, necessary to live life as a witch. Witchcraft is constantly adapting and evolving, calling creative, daring people to it.

One must be aware of internal feelings and conflicts to be a master of the soul and motives. Witches were traditionally healers and in the past played the part that psychologists and therapists do now. Then, as now, the old adage "Physician heal thyself" is critical. Before you can counsel others, you must be aware of your own issues. Most important of all, a prospective witch must be fully grounded in the "real" world. We dive into the spiritual, but not to the detriment of our daily lives and responsibilities. Because we deal with the magickal realms, we must always know how to return to the physical. Magick is not an escape from reality. Unlike other traditions, the physical is seen as the divine, the Goddess and God, manifest. A strong link to the Earth and all that lives on it is crucial. Seekers are often drawn to witchcraft because of the allure, the mystery and power, expecting life to be easy after proclaiming themselves witches. Magick can make things flow more smoothly in life, and the peace of mind that a spiritual practice brings can make it appear to others that life is perfect; but witches are people, and have the same hopes, dreams, and problems everyone else does. They view them through a witch's magickal eyes.

If the path is new to you, stop and think for a moment. Why do you want to study this material? Do you want to become a pagan, witch, Wiccan, or other magickal practitioner? If so, why? What is appealing about it? Have you looked at other spiritual paths and traditions? I ask these questions not to discourage you, but to make you think about your intentions before you open the door. If you are only reading and experimenting to educate yourself on this possibility, that is wonderful! Education is a great thing. Always look before leaping into something. If you intuitively feel drawn to this path, then follow your intuition. That is one of the most important lessons I've ever learned. Intuition, your inner voice, is key.

If you decide you want to study witchcraft and become a witch, look at the qualities long-practicing witches have: self-awareness, respect, responsibility, and love for life. Possessing these attributes does not automatically make you a witch. They are great qualities for anyone, but they hold a special importance in the heart of the witch. Not all witches agree on all these points, but the general intent is the same.

Most importantly, a witch in the world must be self-aware. This means practicing some form of introspection. It could be meditating, daily ritual, writing in a journal, or hiking out in nature. Anything will do, as long as it stills the mind and allows you to reflect on yourself and your relationship with creation.

Self-awareness stimulates a desire for respect and self-esteem. In fact, it is essential for further study and success in magick. Wiccan rituals are based on a concept of Perfect Love, what others call unconditional love. If you cannot love yourself, you'll never generate a feeling of Perfect Love for a ritual. You will never feel the unconditional love given to you by the Goddess and God, and you'll never be able to return the feeling.

When I got involved in witchcraft, I was a very angry young man. Not violent, but angry at the world for what I thought was its cruelty and unfairness. Raised and schooled in Catholicism, I drifted to agnosticism. I believed in something, but I wasn't sure what it was. At one point I turned to science, but it left so many questions unanswered. I had several unusual experiences growing up that science could not explain by anything other than my imagination, but they were so real to me. I found witchcraft at just the right time. My first serious teacher stressed self-love and self-esteem as the keys to all magick. I knew I lacked these qualities, and began a regular meditation, journaling, and affirmation practice to bring healing and self-love.

If you have respect for yourself, you can have respect for others and their views, even if you do not agree with them. Respect includes all forms of life. A witch realizes through magickal experiences that all things are alive, brimming with magick, from the trees and plants, animals, and oceans, to the big city and even specks of dust.

Part of respect for yourself and your world is responsibility. Thoughts, words, and actions are vehicles for power, but very few people take full responsibility for all three. With the development of magickal ability, your thoughts can manifest as easily as your words and actions, so a witch must be careful about manifesting harmful thoughts. This isn't as easy as it sounds, but it is an essential step to empowerment. As your power grows, you must take full responsibility for it, or do not seek it out in the first place.

Responsibility also manifests in your personal life, as you interact with the world. Witches conduct themselves with integrity if they choose to aid others through divination, healing, spiritual counsel, or a helping spell or ritual. Many see those on the path of the old as caretakers of the world, those who see and hear the Earth's secret life. Such caretaker instincts often manifest in acts of community responsibility, including participation in civil, animal, and environmental rights movements.

The most important quality of the witch is a healthy dose of love for life. You must seek to enjoy the pleasures of life on all levels. A key to such enjoyment is a good sense of humor. Laughter is the best form of magick. A witch who can't laugh at himself or herself is taking things a bit too seriously. The world is a place of wonder and magick. Be focused on your task, but not so focused that you do not enjoy the ride.

With an awareness of these qualities, you can seek to incorporate them into your daily life. But how do you actually become a witch? No easy answer exists. Traditionalists believe that it takes a witch to make a witch, meaning you must find and study with a witch. After a period of training, you are formally initiated. Those harkening back to the older meaning of witch, as wise one, believe you take a pagan faith and practice it, learning your craft and your personal path. After amassing knowledge and wisdom, you can call yourself a witch. People will start to seek you out for advice, readings, teachings, and aid, like they did in the old days. Unfortunately, that can be a difficult road since the old hedge witch is not as widely needed in this world due to conventional medicine and psychology. Not all witches walk the path of the healer or counselor, and the majority keep their practice private and personal.

Eclectic witches often state that only the Goddess and God can make you a witch, and your initiation is a personal matter between you and them. You can train from books and initiate yourself when you feel you are ready. Many witches of the world are self-initiated. Self-initiation has its ups and down. The freedom and personal expression is wonderful, but the lack of a face-to-face mentor can be tough. Eclectics often study with many teachers, classes, and traditions, but forge their own path. There used to be a stigma attached to informal witches, but self-initiation is becoming more widely accepted. If you choose this road, material found in *The Inner Temple of Witchcraft* is an excellent foundation for building your personal power and knowledge. From this foundation, you can continue on the path of the witch, or delve into other areas. The remaining chapters are structured as lessons, with exercises and homework, culminating with a self-initiation ritual.

Magickal Record Keeping

One of the key ingredients to the witch is introspection. Such work is facilitated if you have a record to look back on, to see where you were, where you are, and where you hope to be.

If you don't keep a regular journal, now is the time to start. A journal is a place for you to write about your day, the events in your life, and how you feel and think. No one has to read it but you. You might surprise yourself. To borrow an idea from Julia Cameron's *The Artist's Way: A Spiritual Path to Higher Creativity*, write at least three pages a day, either in the morning or before bed. Make the commitment to yourself to do this everyday. If you can't think of enough things to fill three whole pages, write "I can't think of what to write" or something similar for three pages. Eventually you will get bored and start writing about your life. And you can't write everyday about your life without examining what is in balance and what is out of balance. Such introspection will urge you to bring balance, harmony, and happiness to your life. If you skip a day, don't beat yourself up, but start again and reaffirm your commitment to continue. The act of journaling can be life changing.

You will also need to keep a magickal record. Witches and wizards of old were known for their spell books, grimoires, and dusty tomes of magick. Witches keep a Book of Shadows, the ritual book used by Gardnerians and Alexandrians, hand copied from High Priest/ess to initiate. Over the years, spells, meditations, and other information are added to it, making the information more personal. For eclectic witches, the Book of Shadows is a magickal journal, filled with their own rituals, spells, and experience. You will be recording your experiences from subsequent exercises and meditations. Later, you will write out and record spells, potions, and symbols from your practice.

Each of these can be separate notebooks or journals, or all in one. You can divide one book into sections for easy reference, or let them blend together. I used to separate my magickal journal from my mundane journal. At first I think I was afraid that I would one day think this witchcraft stuff was crazy and stop, and wouldn't want to be reminded about my foolishness. So I kept them separate. As I grew as a witch, the two became intertwined more than I would have ever thought. My everyday life is magickal, so how do I separate them? I eventually got a leather binder and divided it into sections.

The importance of magickal record keeping reminds us of the secrecy of the old craft. Due to the persecutions and conversions of the new religions, the specific traditions of witchcraft were mostly lost. Modern practitioners resurrected the new traditions from the garments of the old, and records are kept now so the traditions will never be lost again.

Secrecy is important for another reason. Acts were kept silent not only because it was safer to do so, but because the magick worked better when you kept silent. Thinking about or sharing your spells with others takes away from the energy as it tries to manifest your will. Visualize an act of magick as sending out a ball of energy. This ball will go out into the universe to do whatever you told it to do. Talking about that ball calls it back. Some of the energy comes back to you, unfulfilled. If you talk back too much, you sap the energy of the ball and sabotage your spell.

THE WITCH'S PYRAMID

The precept of silence comes from the teaching of the witch's pyramid (figure 4). This is not an actual building, but a philosophy of magick based on the image of the pyramid. Many feel that magick and the essence of witchcraft came from the land of the pyramids, Egypt, from the ancient goddess religions of the Nile.

The base of the pyramid consists of four points, one for each of the four elements. The first is earth, and the concept "to know." This is your clear intention. You must know what you want before you can make it happen. Most importantly, you must know yourself and your true will. Is the result in your best interest? Earth is the element of physicality and practicality. All "real world" things fall into the realm of earth, like health, money, and home. The second point is "to will" and the fire element. You have the strength of will to manifest your clear intention. Without proper will, magick cannot work. Self-esteem and self-knowledge are keys to bolstering your will. Fire is your willpower, your passion and drive. Fire guides the way. The third point is "to dare" and the air element. You dare to actually do magick and follow it up with action. You have faith that it will manifest. You have the belief that it is possible. Air is the power of the mind, of logic, communication, and creativity. The fourth point is "to keep silent" and relates to water. Water is the emotions, the mystical and unknown. The top point of the pyramid is the element of spirit and the Wiccan Rede, the only true rule of Wicca: "Do what thou will and let it harm none."

Secrecy is important, though you can share your work with other witches, teachers, and like-minded people, because they will not detract from your energy. If you lack such a community, a Book of Shadows is an excellent way to share your experiences without talking to those who would not understand.

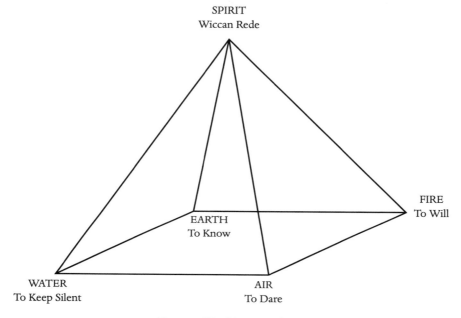

Figure 4: *Witch's Pyramid*

WITCHCRAFT AS A MYSTERY SCHOOL

Ancient cultures provided mystery schools, places where seekers of the unknown were initiated into the mysteries of life and magick. Such training was not for everyone, but for those desiring a deeper experience of spirit, possibly leading to a role in magickal orders of priests and priestesses. The temples in Egypt appear to be an interlocked system of schools and orders. New Age scholars, armed with past-life memories and channeled information, believe that the pyramids were not burial chambers, as commonly believed, but initiation chambers. The shape and position of the pyramid directed vast invisible energies through the supplicant.

Various figures of ancient Greece, some mythical and some factual, including Orpheus and Pythagoras, are credited with heading the Greek mystery schools. The common Western teachings with which we are familiar, such as math, medicine, music, drama, mythology, and athletics, have been incorporated into the foundations of Western civilization, but our recent ancestors conveniently left out the ancient Greek teachings of mystical philosophy, alchemy, sacred geometry, and spirituality. Spiritual training, to a certain extent, was included in such schools as part of basic education. A well-rounded individual must be versed in all aspects.

As the rise of the modern world approached with the rise of Rome, one could argue that these mystery schools died out, as the mystical became less a part of culture and more a force to be feared. The mysteries most likely continued in the fabled secret orders of magicians and mystics. The Eastern adepts, in India and Asia, held their long-standing traditions. The Druids, as an organized order throughout Celtic society, had their own spin on the mystery-school teachings. The wise folk, the shamans and medicine people, always had the mystery teachings, but attained them through a more personal, informal path. The mysteries were revealed from teacher to student, and from the spirit world directly. Through the teachings of the wise folk, the mysteries would live again.

Modern Wicca has, in effect, become a new mystery school, encompassing both the formal and informal, study and personal experience. You can learn the experiences of magick in a solitary tradition, with a group, as a student to a mentor, through a book, or by talking with others and listening to nature. Most of us combine many of these methods to get to our own mysteries. The basic goals of the mystery school are the goals of the modern craft: controlling consciousness, understanding the true nature of the universe, purification, and connecting with higher will.

The first goal is the experience of an altered state of consciousness, which opens the doorway to a new world. Witches voluntarily enter trance states through meditation. These altered states are the peace and tranquility of the adept, or the ecstasy of the shaman.

Once you open the door, the second goal is an understanding of the true nature of the universe. To the Hindus, the true nature of the universe is to see past the *maya*, the name they give to the illusion of separateness that most people see. When you see past the illusion, the maya, you realize that all things are one. Witches look past the veils between worlds, understanding that all is alive, all is divine, and all is eternal, though form changes when passing through the cycles of life. Most importantly, witches learn that one's actions have an effect throughout creation, and what you do comes back to you. Acts of magick are practical and helpful, ultimately empowering the individual, but the true lesson is to understand that all things are connected by seeing tangible proof of this connection in your daily life.

Either prior to learning how to enter altered states of consciousness, or afterward, one usually experiences rites of purification. We purify ourselves with elemental rituals, incense, candle flame, salt, and water. Ritual baths are also appropriate before acts of magick and celebration. These are all minor rites of purification; the true purification comes from events in life. Some ancient sects and traditions, particularly in the Eastern world, have strict dietary requirements, sometimes with fasts during certain times of the year for a physical purification. I know witches who fast for three days of the Dark Moon, purifying their system. In general, when you make a connection to spirit, you start to take better care of yourself because you realize that you are spirit, too. Changes in eating and exercise habits naturally create physical purification.

The greater rites of purification also include nonphysical levels: the mind, emotions, and spirit. Mystery-school training, including some versions of the modern-day Gardnerian initiations, use a bit of fear and shock to heighten your awareness and the connection between your mind, emotions, and body. Shamanic initiations are famous for making you face and conquer the fear of death. Facing your fears, angers, prejudices, and sorrows is part of the introspective process, showing up in meditations and journal entries. Those that do not serve your highest good need to be cleared, released, and healed. Limiting thoughts and behaviors are first identified and then changed. A witch creates through an aware consciousness, not from the dark and unknown thoughts lurking in the subconscious.

The last aspect of the mystery school is contact with higher will. Higher will is not the choice of your ego, but of your spirit, your soul. Higher will guides you to your true purpose in life. It is not *your* will, but that of the Goddess and God. Through magick, we exercise our personal will and magickal selves in conjunction with divine will, the power of the Goddess and God, to manifest in our life. It is a partnership with the divine. Through those acts, we come to know divine will. We learn to trust it, flow with it, and merge ourselves with it. Once we do, no doors are closed, because we are in the right place, at the right time, doing the right thing, always.

THE PATH OF INITIATION

Individuals seeking the path of witchcraft traditionally go on a quest of "a year and a day" before committing to the craft. This time period is from Celtic mythology, signifying a year of preparation and a day to reflect again before dedicating to the path. In that time, one learns the foundations of witchcraft, magickal training, and personal development.

You should not be as concerned with results or magickal power as you are with the lessons the path presents to you. Everyone has psychic or magickal abilities. They are inherent in our human makeup, like having eyes, a nose, or a mouth. Some will find that they are more talented in certain areas than others. With proper training, most people can learn to read and write. A few will go on to write great novels. Others struggle with a grocery list. There are myriad levels of aptitude. Magickal talent, however, does not make a witch. Dedication to the craft and your personal path does.

This book is a course that is divided into thirteen lessons and many exercises. At the end of each lesson is suggested homework. The goal is to work through this material in a year and a day, with enough time to read other sources and reflect on the decision to become a witch. Such a decision entails a lifelong commitment.

If you complete one lesson every three weeks, you will have ample time to review and reflect within the year-and-a-day period. Feel free to adapt this schedule to suit your needs. Your personal pace might be much quicker or slower. It is far better to take longer and truly commit to your study than to take less time and do it haphazardly.

I suggest marking your calendar with the week's expected work and deadlines. If you can arrange a specific "study" night to do this work, then do so. "Tuesday evening" comes more regularly and often than "later" does. Make a commitment to yourself. A few exercises suggest the participation of a partner. If you know someone interested in this path, set up regular meetings to practice and guide each other through the exercises. Having someone to share your experiences with is a great way to build your support through this study and practice. Although I've loved my times as a solitary witch, it can be a hard road. Having a magickal and psychic playmate is a great asset.

The end of this book is marked with a self-initiation ritual. It may be the first of many such initiation rituals. Rituals are important and powerful. They signify beginnings, endings, and intentions. The universe, divinity in action, will support your intentions if they are clear. The biggest obstacle for most people to manifest their dreams is a lack of intentions. If you want to study this material, make a commitment to it and perform the following intention ritual. It is not an initiation into the craft, but a proclamation to the Goddess and God of your sincere desire to understand and experience the path of the witch.

EXERCISE 1

Intention Ritual

1. Get a new white candle, matches, a piece of paper, a black pen, and some black thread. If you like incense or have any other objects that are special to you, like a crystal, stone, bowl, or anything else, you can get them out, but they are not necessary.

2. Find a quiet spot to work, where others will not disturb you.

3. On a small piece of paper, write out your intentions for this work. Do you seek to be a witch, learn witchcraft, or just know more? If you are comfortable calling on the Goddess and God, do so. If not, you can address it to whatever divine force you are comfortable using, such as God, Great Spirit, the Tao, or the Universe. Here is an example:

   "I, (state your name), ask in the name of the Goddess and God for aid in my studies of witchcraft. I intend to complete this work successfully within one year and become a witch if this is correct and for my highest good. I ask to be open to all experiences and understand all lessons given to me. So mote it be."

   ("So mote it be" means "it is so." It is a common affirmation in witchcraft.)

4. Hold the white candle. Think about spirituality. Think about divinity and the Goddess and God. Invite them into your life, or reaffirm your bond with them. Light the candle. If you have incense, light it now.

5. Spend a few moments reflecting on the definition, history, and qualities of the witch. Think about where witchcraft has been, and where you hope to go with it.

6. Read your intention slip out loud. Then roll it up like a scroll and tie it with the black thread, binding it together and sealing your intention.

Keep the paper someplace special, where you will not lose it. You will use this slip as part of your initiation ritual in a year. In a later chapter, you will build a meditation altar. You can then keep the candle and intention slip on the altar.

HOMEWORK

- Get one or two blank books to use as a daily journal and Book of Shadows.
- Daily journal—Write three pages a day.
- Look for any potential study partners.
- Exercise 1: Intention Ritual—Perform and record your feelings and experiences about this ritual in your journal/Book of Shadows.
- Set your study schedule.

Lesson 1
The Magickal Mind

Witches do magick, plain and simple. But defining what magick is can be much more difficult. One of the reasons why the words *witch* and *witchcraft* have such a stigma attached to them is because of people's inability to understand magick. Even practitioners disagree on the definition of magick because it is such a personal art. Some outside of the tradition think magick and spells are a way of claiming power over someone else, of controlling or harming. This misunderstanding leads to defining witchcraft as some form of evil. Although magick has been used with such intents, this is not the true purpose of magick. If anything, magick is learning to flow with the soul of nature.

One of the best definitions of magick I've learned is from the works of Aleister Crowley. Crowley defined magick as "the science and art of causing change in conformity with will." Witches define magick as both an art and a science. Magick has basic rules and structure, like science. They are not moral codes, but conditions that allow magick to occur. As an art, magick also has a creative, individual component. As long as it conforms in some way to the "scientific" laws of magick, you can vary it to your own individual tastes. "Causing change" are the important words here. Magick is not speculation; it is actually making something occur. Lastly, "in conformity with will" means that the change you are creating matches your intention. Magick is learning to work with change, with the forces that create change, and to shape the outcome to match your intention. One definition of Wicca that we already discussed is "to bend and shape." You are bending and shaping natural occurrences to fit your will.

A spell is a specific act of magick to cause a specific change. You can have one magickal ceremony, and in it do several spells for different results. To my friends and family not involved in witchcraft, I describe a spell like a prayer. In many mainstream traditions, one prays to God for help, support, healing, or manifestation; in essence, to create change. A spell is a similar petition to the powers of the universe, but uses a different method to send the petition out into the universe. The principle and basic mechanics are the same, like the science part of our definition of magick, but the execution is different. To further the analogy between prayer and spells, I come from an old European Catholic family. My ancestors prayed to various saints to fulfill an intention. Each saint has a different province or specialty. In witchcraft, different goddesses and gods are petitioned, each having a different realm of rulership in life. The choice of patron and the symbolism used in the ceremony make up the "art" of spell casting.

Once people outside of paganism can relate spells and magick to something they may have done personally, the concept is no longer as scary. Once something as arcane and secretive as a spell is defined as "my tradition's way of saying a prayer," much of the unknown is dispelled, and we can build a dialogue with those who have difficulty accepting nature-based paths as valid religions.

Though you don't have to do magick to follow this spiritual path, such training is part and parcel of becoming a witch. You do not have to actively cast spells to make the concepts behind their working a part of your everyday life. One part of magick that is not usually focused on in many books and classes is that magick is any change caused by your will, including internal changes. We tend to focus on external changes, manifestation in the physical world, as "proof" that magick really works. We all need to see the results of our actions, but some of the most important, profound, and healing magick comes though an internal change, a shift in perspective or consciousness.

In that sense, if you choose this path of the witch, you may not necessarily be doing spells and rituals all the time, but you will undeniably be doing magick. Magick is a part of each breath we take and every action we make.

The Three Minds

Making magick means understanding the parts of yourself involved in the process. We tend to focus on our conscious mind as the director of our will, but in truth, we have at least three minds. Understanding and accessing the three minds is the key to magick.

The first is the conscious mind (figure 5). That is the mind most familiar to us. The conscious mind contains the personality and the ego identity. The part of us that is conscious, awake, and handling the details of day-to-day life is our conscious mind. The tools of the conscious mind are reason and logic, and its qualities are analysis and alertness. It perceives life in a linear, three-dimensional fashion. One event follows another. Events are chained together in a line moving through time. Those behind us are the past, those occurring now are the present, and those to occur are the future. This mind can spend a lot of time reflecting on the past and planning for the future while handling the present. Here is where you formulate your needs and desires for your life and for your magick. The drawback of the conscious mind is its perception. Though a linear perception is necessary for our day-to-day life, it limits our ability to process large amounts of information or energy, the very stuff of magick. The conscious mind is also called the middle self.

Our second mind, the psychic mind, is both the key and doorway to our magickal talents. This part of you has a greater natural ability to process energy and information. Unlike the conscious mind, the psychic mind is not necessarily bound by the limits of linear perception. Great leaps of intuition can be made, skipping over the logical chain of thoughts to reach a conclusion much faster. Intuition is opening up to the information available in the universe by accessing psychic ability. Psychic ability is not necessarily "movie magic," using your mind to bend spoons and move objects across the room, but rather processing information you would not logically have. Knowing who is on the phone before you pick it up is as psychic as acts of mind over matter. We all have an intuitive ability. We are all psychic. Some learn to use their abilities to a greater degree.

The psychic mind is also called the lower self, but not in the sense of lower as bad, evil, or even lesser. Many religions that have demonized personal power and psychic ability might believe so, but the concept of the lower self actually comes from what psychologists call the unconscious and subconscious. By relaxing our conscious mind, we can move through the doorway of our personal subconscious and into the great unconscious, a realm of greater awareness and insight. Unfortunately, we are not often aware of it, hence the term *unconscious*. After hearing this, many desire to erase their conscious, ego self to instead live in this world of intuitive knowing, but each balances the other, serving an important need. If we did not have a linear perception, we would not know to eat and sleep and generally take care of our physical self. For this, the conscious self is necessary. Many desires that fuel magick and spells come from the conscious. The psychic self is also called the lower self because it is seen as more primal and instinctual, acting before reasoning things out. Animal instincts and the lessons the natural world brings to us are often said to be connected with our lower psychic self; accordingly, many nature-based spiritual paths encourage the use of psychic and magickal abilities. Other mystical traditions call the lower self the younger self.

The greatest job of the psychic mind is playing the role of intermediary between the conscious mind and the divine mind, the third mind. The divine mind is the aspect of the creative spirit within us, connecting us to the greater whole. You could call this God. Many witches call this Goddess. I call this the Great Spirit since I come from a tradition that honors both Goddess and God as part of the greater whole. Their love and interaction create all life. Our personal divine mind is the level of the super consciousness or what is called the higher self, or older self. It has a greater view from its position, spiritually speaking, than the ego self. The higher self can see where we've been and where we are headed. Like the lower self, it is not bound by linear time. In fact, it is simultaneously aware of all things and times. Because the conscious mind would have difficulty processing so much information, our divine self gives us information in small bursts of insight, epiphanies, and revelations. Or the higher self can

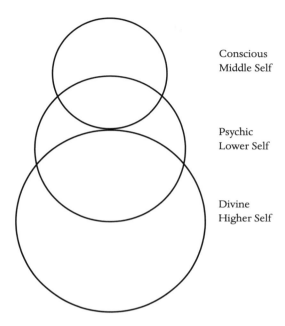

Conscious
Middle Self

Psychic
Lower Self

Divine
Higher Self

Figure 5: The Three Minds

use the lower self, the psychic mind, to relay a message, which takes shape as a dream, symbol, or flash of intuition. However, such messages need to be decoded through our cultural and personal symbol systems in the collective unconscious and personal subconscious.

In Hawaiian shamanic traditions, the lower self is believed to take the raw material it is given from the thoughts, words, and actions of the conscious self. When we sleep, the lower self brings these raw building blocks to the higher self, which then creates our life. We do this continuously throughout our life. Similarly, magick is consciously building a relationship with the lower and higher selves, to form a co-creative partnership. A spell is like giving a very specific request to our higher self, along with all the necessary building blocks to bring the change into our life. The higher self, connected to all higher selves everywhere, to the entire spectrum of life in the universe, can coordinate and help fulfill our spell.

Movie Magic versus Real Magick

Many people get involved in witchcraft because of what I like to call "movie magic," and have difficulty understanding what the essence of magick is all about. They expect special effects: lightning bolts out of the sky and rolling mists over the hills. I am lucky to have been privy to many a magickal night outside where unusual things have occurred, but they are added benefits, not the goal of magick.

Magick is all about manifesting change, in our inner or outer life, in compliance with our will. The channels that bring us this change can seem very mundane, but to line up many seeming "coincidences" is the art of magick. Let's say you want a new job. You know what kind of job you want. You do your magickal spell and the next day you go to a party. You didn't want to go to the party, but felt you should be there. There you meet someone who mentions that his company is hiring. After talking a bit, this person gives you the name and number of who you should call. That person has a job opening that is perfect for you, and by the end of the week you have a new job. Coincidence, or magick? At first you are inclined to think coincidence, but if you live the life of a witch, you find more and more of these coincidences happening in response to the intentions you have voiced to the universe. Intuition is the guide to such fortunate "coincidences."

While I was being interviewed as a subject for a college student's term paper, the subject of magick came up. She was studying the social groups, customs, and beliefs of those in the pagan subculture and wanted to ask me a few questions. After talking through a pleasant dinner, she looked at me a bit like I was crazy and said, "I have good things happen to me, too, but I don't think I'm doing magick." She couldn't quite understand why I did. Over the course of the evening I came to see her as a very powerful person, both working full-time and going to school, making her way in the world. She was very intelligent and organized, yet open and intuitive while she guided the interview. I have no doubt that she practiced her own brand of magick. You don't need candles, robes, spells, and herbs. You don't need to know the definition of magick. She didn't. You do need to access the other facets of yourself, your psychic, intuitive mind, and your divine self, to manifest with your willpower. I believe she did. I think many people who would never call themselves witches still do magick. People are magickal by nature. I tried explaining that to her, but she had difficulty with the concept that she created these coincidences, that they were not just the result of good luck. The difference for witches is to actively and consciously pursue this relationship with the universe and ourselves.

THREE REQUIREMENTS

The goal of the practitioner is to bring the three minds into harmony, into alignment. Once you have a good relationship with them, magick is much easier. Regardless of the form of magick you practice, from pagan rituals to creative visualization, there are some common steps to follow to align the three minds. Along with the three minds, or aspects of self, there are three other requirements.

First, you must have strength of will. Do you desire the outcome? If you don't care what happens, then why should the universe? Your desire, your willpower, sparks the process. Any strong emotion can start it. Usually need and desire, self-love, or better yet, unconditional love can be the fuel. Part of magickal training is to be able to access these feelings, to muster the energy whenever you need it, yet remain calm and centered.

Second, you must have a clear intention. It doesn't matter if you have the willpower to succeed. If you don't know what to apply your willpower toward, nothing will occur. You must have a specific idea of the desired result. You can form the idea through visualization in your mind's eye, through the power of the word, either spoken or written, or through knowing what you want.

It is at this step where we can qualify our intentions. In magick, we tend to focus on the result, and not necessarily on how it manifests. In the intention for the new job, the goal was to get a new job in the field desired, not to meet someone at a party who would give you a lead for new job. The goal of employment was more important than how it happened. This leaves the way in which the spell can manifest open to the universe. If you do a spell for money, it doesn't matter where the money comes from. It could be the lottery, returned taxes, a prize, or a gift. We do not want to limit where the money originates from. But we do want to protect ourselves from channels of manifestation that might not be for our overall benefit. The money could also as easily come from insurance for an accident in which you are injured, but no one wants to get injured. In many witchcraft traditions, all spells and intentions are qualified using the words "for my highest good, harming none." For the example regarding money, think about why you need the money. Is it to pay for something specific? If so, make that your goal, your end result. Always focus on the ultimate goal rather than the means of getting it. You give yourself more opportunities that way. The divine is infinitely wiser and knows far more options than our middle self can perceive.

Lastly, you need a method to direct your energy, your willpower and intention. Usually methods of energy direction involve some form of altered consciousness, resulting from either a meditative practice or ritual. The reason why rituals and tools are so common in the magickal traditions is because they serve the greater purpose of helping us direct our energy and intent. If they didn't work, they would be discarded for something that did.

ENERGY

If we are going to talk about directing energy, you must have some awareness of what energy is. The word *energy* evokes images of power lines and outlets, or more personally your metabolism, but there is invisible energy all around us. This energy is part of us and our environment, as is the energy we direct when we do any magickal work.

Many forms of energy exist. Most that we know of fall into a range, a spectrum of frequencies, that can be detected via scientific means. The most common is the visible light spectrum, the rainbow, but there are many forms of invisible energy above and below physical light, such as radio and television waves and radiation. These energies are all part of the electromagnetic spectrum. We are also aware of a range of energies that are physical vibrations, or sounds. Although scientists have agreed on the characteristics and ranges of these quantifiable energies, metaphysicians have known about a whole other range of energies.

Currently, most of our "evidence" of spiritual energies comes from personal accounts rather than objective, scientific data. Every individual describes the experience in a unique way, so we sometimes have diverging opinions on the spiritual energies.

Different spiritual traditions call these forces by different names, and each name has a specific cultural connotation.

Let's start with personal energy (figure 6). Personal energy is the energy within and emanating from your own being. It is the energy of your body and all its systems, and it includes such things as metabolism, body heat, and nerve impulses. It is also the energy from your nonphysical systems, your energy bodies and chakras. We shall delve deeper into the anatomy of the energy body later, but for now, understand that you have a nonphysical component to your body, your spirit, so to speak. The interaction of your spirit and body creates a field of energy around your body. Modern practitioners call this the aura. The energy flowing into these energy systems, like blood flowing through the physical body, is called ki, or chi, in the Eastern traditions. It can be absorbed from the environment and processed by the body. We replenish our store of vital personal energy through sleep, though some people are naturally more energetic than others. Ki and chi can also refer to other forms of energy we will be discussing. Kundalini, a word from the Hindu traditions, is another form of personal energy, but more specifically refers to the energy found at the base of the spine that can rise through the spine, activating the spiritual centers known as chakras.

To witches, the most important energies to connect to are those below our feet, the Earth energies. This is the energy of the planet and the Goddess, the consciousness of the world that sustains us. It has been called mana or shakti kundalini. Most perceive this energy as feminine. Earth energy is not only the energy inside the planet, but also the energy around the planet, such as the magnetic field, and grids of energy, called ley lines or Earth grid lines. Sacred sites, such as Giza in Egypt and Stonehenge in England, are renowned for being focal points in the grid system of Mother Earth. Think of the grids like acupuncture meridians in our bodies. They let invisible energies flow to promote health and life.

Above the Earth is the energy of the sky. Cosmic energy is also a fitting description for this energy because it encompasses the energy of the Sun and stars, in fact the energy of the entire universe, raining down upon the Earth. As many pagan traditions associate the Earth with mother and Goddess, the sky is usually linked to the masculine deities. Sky gods are prominent in many mythologies as father figures, protectors

Figure 6: The Four Energies

and providers. In the Hindu traditions, the invisible life force riding on the breath, absorbed by us through the food and water we consume and the breath we take in, is called *prana*. It is interesting how this Hindu energy called prana is very similar phonetically to the Hawaiian name of life force, *mana*. Prana, mana, ki, and chi, along with a whole host of other names, such as orgone, od, odic force, pneuma, numen, telesma, and ruach, describe a basic life energy found in all things.

Divine energy is a catchall category for energies not included in the masculine/feminine or above/below polarity. There are many other kinds of spiritual energies and beings, with many different flavors and descriptions. Witches work with divine energy through the ritual of the magick circle, creating what is traditionally called "perfect love and perfect trust." In other words, pure divine energy, what we could call unconditional love, is used to create sacred space for our rituals. This energy is all loving and all knowing, beyond all polarities, yet encompassing them all.

EXERCISE 2

Feeling Energy

The purpose of this exercise is to physically feel some of this spiritual energy that you personally generate. Many students find this easy with a little practice, but others have difficulty because they do not know what to look for. I feel this energy like very weak, very subtle magnetic repulsion. If you were to take two positive ends of a magnet and try to put them together, you would have some difficulty. The fields of energy offer resistance. Take that feeling and expect something a bit less dramatic or concrete, and you can feel the resistance offered between the fields of your hands. They are not exactly opposing charges, so they do not offer the same kind of resistance as two magnets.

Magnets are the way I would describe the feeling. Since this is individual and subjective, others perceive it as a temperature shift. You could also feel a slight tingle or "pins and needles" sensation, as if your hands are "asleep." Others feel a pressure or even texture. Everyone feels it differently.

Once you feel it, you will be able to manipulate this energy through your will and intent. This is a fundamental building block for magick and psychic development.

1. Hold your hands about three feet apart, palms facing each other. Close your eyes if you would like. You are aware of any new information you receive from your hands, but you are not judging the experience or trying to create it. Allow it to happen naturally.

2. Bring you hands closer together, slowly. Be aware of the sensation. Notice any feelings that come in waves or layers. These are the levels of your aura, your energy body. Some layers offer more "resistance" than others. Try it several times, with eyes closed and then open. If you have difficulty, start over, but begin by rubbing your hands together vigorously, as if you were trying to warm them up. This will increase your hands' sensitivity.

3. When you are done, wipe your hands together as if you were wiping excess water off them. This removes any other energies you might have picked up along the way. End all of these energy exercises with such a wiping motion.

EXERCISE 3

Ball of Energy

1. Start as you did with exercise 2, but when your hands are six inches apart, imagine that you are holding a ball of energy. At first this ball is like an empty bowl, a shell, but you are filling it with the energy between your hands.

2. As you breathe out, imagine that you are blowing out energy, exhaling from your mouth, and also "exhaling" from your palms. This energy helps fill the ball. Feel it fill up. Intend to make the ball thicker and more solid. At first this will feel like you are playing pretend and making it up, but such play-acting is the way energy responds to our thoughts. By acting as if the energy is changing, it does.

3. Once you have a "solid" ball of energy floating between your hands, you can literally play with it. You can make it smaller and more dense. You can

stretch it out like taffy. Discover how mutable energy can be, responding to your intent and commands.

4. When done, bring your hands together and imagine you are absorbing the energy. Then wipe off your hands to remove any excess.

Later, as you learn to work more with energy, you can draw more energy from your environment, and not necessarily your own personal energy, to create energy balls. They can then be "charged" with an intention, such as healing, and given to other people, animals, plants, and places to make your magick. You will not be limited to balls of energy, but any shape and size you can imagine. I like to weave energy "webs" of protection around myself and my home.

Now that you have a feel for the power of your own personal energy, if you have a partner in this work, or a willing friend or family member, you can discover how your energy interacts with others.

EXERCISE 4

Feeling the Aura

1. As in exercise 2, sensitize your hands by rubbing them together, but instead of placing the palms facing together, put your arms out with palms facing out, as if you were gesturing to stop.

2. Stand at one end of the room while your partner is at the other. Close your eyes and slowly walk toward your partner, having your partner guide you if you get off course. As you could feel the energy between your palms, you are looking for a similar feeling when you reach the edge of your partner's energy field.

3. Keep your eyes closed, but take note of the various levels of energy you feel. Move back and forth to explore the sensations.

4. Repeat the exercise, this time with your eyes open. Stop where you feel the first layer of resistance. Have your partner raise his or her arms straight out

in front. Usually the perimeter of the aura is a hand's length beyond the reach of a person's arms. I've found that depending on an individual's boundaries and current emotions, it can be larger or smaller, but in general, it is around an arm's length. Where did you feel it? Most feel it near this perimeter, though you can also feel other "layers" closer to the body. Reverse roles and try the experiment again.

EXERCISE 5

Pushing and Pulling Energy

Like your ball of energy was an exercise in control, with this next experience, you will learn how your energy can affect and influence other people in very subtle ways. Again you will need a partner.

1. Stand facing each other, with only a few feet between you. The receptive partner should have his or her eyes closed. Make sure this person is standing up straight, but is not braced against any structure.

2. You then try to use your willpower, breath, and intent to "push" your personal energy out and influence your partner. Use a gathering motion in the space around you to gather your personal energy as you inhale. Use pushing motions as you gently exhale, sending the energy toward your partner.

3. Take notice of your partner. If there is a third person in the room, this person might notice the action more than either of the exercise partners. Usually the receptive partner looks like he or she is slightly swaying back, even if he or she did not consciously feel it.

4. Reverse the process by gathering the energy between you both, and pull the energy forward with your intention. Inhale and sweep your arms toward your body as you bring the energy closer. You may notice your partner pulling forward a bit. Repeat these steps several times until you feel comfortable with them. Then ask your partner, still with eyes closed, what he or she is feeling.

EXERCISE 6

Earth Walking

This exercise expands your experience beyond the realm of personal energy and into the feelings of Earth energy. Our ancestors slept on the Earth and exchanged energy with it every day. Most people barely touch the Earth now, with the ubiquity of shoes and floors. Earth walking, along with other exercises in this book, helps us come back into balance with the energy field of the Earth. Earth walking is a simple meditative walk outside. Start in some natural setting, on grass, in a field or park, on the beach, or in the woods, rather than on concrete or asphalt. If you feel comfortable enough to do this barefoot, so much the better, but with practice, you will feel this experience through your shoes.

Walk slowly and meditatively. Be aware of the Earth below your feet. Be aware of your personal energy, the auric field around you, touching the land, where your energy mingles. As you inhale, imagine that you are not only breathing in through your mouth, but breathing in through your feet. My yoga teacher tells me that a wise man breathes through the soles of his feet. I think that applies to a wise witch, too. Imagine drawing in life force, Earth energy, through your feet as you walk. This energy grounds and centers you. It bolsters your metabolism and energy level, creating health and joy in the moment. For now, don't worry about doing anything special while exhaling. Breathe normally. The excess energy will be released naturally through your daily activity. We release energy all the time. Focus on the connection you make to the Earth.

When on these walks, look for a quiet place that could serve as a meditation spot for later exercises.

When you feel you are done with this experience, walk and breathe normally and resume your day-to-day activities. If you feel too energized, too charged, get on your hands and knees, placing your palms on the ground. Imagine the excess energy flowing out of your palms and even pouring out of your head. You release only the excess energy to the Earth, grounding yourself. As you release this energy, you can place the intent that such energy be used for healing the planet. This is a basic method of grounding yourself if you are not releasing excess energy. There are other ways to ground yourself. If you can't reach down, you can imagine the energy flowing out of your hands and feet into the ground. You can hug a tree. Imagine the tree taking the excess energy for its own healing, and grounding it through the roots. You can even imagine yourself as a tree, and let the energy drain through your own "roots."

When you feel comfortable with the Earth energy, you can include breathing through the crown of your head, to connect with sky energy. Try the sky energy alone to get a feel for that particular vibration. Then try both Earth and sky energies together. Ground yourself as I just described if you need to bring yourself back to normal perception. Sky energy can make you more lightheaded, open, and aware than Earth energy, so be sure to take care. Simple walking meditations can be as powerful and enlightening as any other exercise in this book. Do not underestimate them.

The greatest lesson to learn about working with these energies is that all energies and powers are fundamentally neutral, meaning they are not good or evil. At times we can pick up on the energy of a place or person and feel it is "bad" energy, but it is only energy being used for a less than good intention. Intention rules everything. Electricity is electricity; it can be used to power a light bulb, a life-support machine, or an electric chair. The energy itself does not judge its use, so people who use the energy must take responsibility. Personal, Earth, sky, and divine energies can be used to heal or harm, depending on the intention behind the action.

LEVELS OF CONSCIOUSNESS

While practicing all the previous exercises, you probably noticed that you felt a little different. Your perceptions were different because you were using other senses, other parts of your consciousness. Shifting consciousness is the key to magick. If magick is aligning our three minds, our conscious and psychic minds with the divine, you need an easy method to quickly align these three separate energies. The more self-aware you become, the more the three minds come into alignment, but for now we need techniques to help that process.

By voluntarily changing your state of consciousness, you do not lose consciousness or identity. You can still hold your intent, but such a change brings a greater awareness of your own energy, abilities, and power. The ancient Greeks called this state of greater awareness *gnosis*. Gnosis literally means "knowledge," and it referred to the mystical, divine knowledge available to those who enter this state. Personal revelations and psychic experiences occur during gnosis.

Everyone's brain functions through waves of activity. These patterns of waves, measured in cycles per second, or hertz, each contain very specific characteristics. Individuals may express different abilities at each of these levels, but anyone can physically enter these levels. We do it all the time. The trick is to do so voluntarily.

Normally the brain functions at beta level, our normally waking consciousness. It is the time when we are generally awake and alert, doing our jobs and interacting with people. This electrical rhythm's frequency is normally thirteen to sixteen cycles per second.

The level that most people in the magickal world refer to when talking about meditation, magick, and spells is alpha. Alpha state is right below beta. Alpha is described as being relaxed, yet aware, but I imagine you are most familiar with alpha when you are probably not all that aware. When you daydream or otherwise "zone out" of conscious beta level, you have entered alpha, which is measured at eight to thirteen cycles per second. If you learn to purposely enter this state, you can stay aware. The advantage of alpha is greater contact with your psychic mind. Accelerated learning and increased memory occur at this level. Intuition and psychic abilities are accessed. Think of alpha as a meditative state. You can meditate at this level and go deeper into your inner experience, or you can enter a higher alpha state, or what I call ritual consciousness, remaining calm, relaxed, and aware, yet still being able to walk around, light candles, speak, and so forth. People often worry about getting into alpha because at times it does not feel that much different from beta, particularly when you get used to it. Students often worry if they can reach alpha at all, but everyone passes through it as they go to sleep each night.

Theta brain waves take you into a deeper meditative state. You could call it a trance state. At this level, you can pay more attention to the inner reality and make a stronger connection to the divine. You also enter it during sleep. Theta is measured at four to nine hertz.

The lowest level of brain functioning is the delta wave. Delta is the state of deep sleep, deep trance, and coma. The brain functions on four or less cycles per second. Those who acquire more advanced and conditioned nervous systems through training, like yogis and other mystics, can bring the body to this level while keeping the mind conscious.

There are several states above the normal beta level that prove interesting. First is high beta, clocking in at sixteen to thirty hertz. This is an extreme state of alertness, what is called "battlefield conditions." When you are in a more aware mode of perception due to life-and-death situations, fear, and adrenaline, you are in high beta. Above high beta the brain waves spike into K complex, measured at thirty to thirty-five hertz. This is the experience of divine inspiration, where things become clear for one brief moment. K complex is also called "the eureka experience." Superhigh beta is above them all, falling in the range of thirty-five to 150 hertz. Expansive and somewhat uncontrollable spiritual experiences occur here, raising consciousness. Extreme out-of-body experiences, kundalini risings, and crown-chakra activation occur at this level.

Notice how both lowering and raising the brain waves can lead to mystical experiences. In this practice we will be focusing on techniques to lower your brain-wave level and heighten your awareness, but spirituality can be found in many different places. As you have a spiritual experience, your brain waves could jump up, but you remain peaceful. It is also important to remember that these brain-wave measurements are averages. Different parts of the brain can be associated with different brain waves, so you are not necessarily in any one state with 100 percent of your brain. The brain is a mysterious organ that we still know little about, but it appears that these brain waves hold a key, like a gatekeeper, to our mystical experiences.

SHIFTING CONSCIOUSNESS

Voluntarily changing from one state of mind to another is not as difficult as it seems, but it does take practice and training. The techniques take one of two paths. They can be inhibitory, slowing down the body and gently entering an altered state, or exhibitory, raising energy and the body's awareness through stimulation to bring on an altered state. Neither is better than the other; they take different paths to the same place. As you practice, one approach or specific technique might suit your personality or tradition more, but it is good to be well versed in multiple techniques.

Gerald Gardner taught eight ways to raise power and enter a gnosis state for magick. The use of Eastern practices probably influenced his tradition of witchcraft since he worked in the East for many years as a civil servant. Modern witches use a modified version of this Eightfold Path.

Meditation—(inhibitory)—The main inhibitory technique is meditation. Meditation is clearing your mind and entering a relaxed state. Eastern forms of meditation focus on completely clearing the mind and being one with the moment. Often a chant (mantra), hand gesture (mudra), or posture (asana) is used in various combinations to help the practitioner stay focused. Sometimes a visual focus or a special symbol, called a yantra or mandala, is used. Western forms of meditation tend to be more task oriented and linked with the powers of creative visualization, but practitioners often use variations of the Eastern technique, such as prayers and affirmations for mantras.

Breath Control—(usually inhibitory)—Regulated breathing is called *pranayama* in the East. It relaxes and lowers body systems by focusing on the movement of the breath. The breath is related to the element of air, and air is linked with the mind. By calming the breath, you calm the mind. Some types of breath can excite the body and build energy, while others cool and relax. Breath work is usually used in conjunction with meditation. Some practitioners count their breaths to keep clarity and focus.

Isolation—(inhibitory)—Aboriginal traditions have a rite of passage where one spends time in isolation on a mountaintop, cave, or forest to induce a mystical experience, such as the Native American vision quest. Several religious orders impose isolation and silence on members to facilitate contemplation. Fasting is often incorporated into the process, directly altering the brain chemistry through lack of food. Use this method with caution and guidance.

Intoxication—(depends on substance)—Intoxication is the use of various natural materials to induce an altered state, including wine, hallucinogenics, herbal mixtures, and incense. The difficulty with intoxication is moderation. Just enough can open a doorway, but too much can make you lose control. Although we have a history of using these substances recreationally, spiritual traditions use them with great care and reverence, providing specific training and knowledge to function under these influences. With the possible exception of incense, I humbly suggest saving this path for a time when you have more guidance and training.

Sound—(depends on the music)—Singing, chanting, instruments, drumming, and other percussion can lead you into an altered state as you get swept up with the tone and beat. Some will be more relaxing, such as gentle music. Others will be more exciting, like tribal drums.

Body Movement—(exhibitory)—Movement induces an altered view of reality, and can include exercise, dance, asana (yogic body posture), shaking, shivering, spinning, hand movements, and mudras. Many tribal societies and covens use large circular dances as part of ritual. Yoga and martial arts also induce trance states through body forms. The movements do not necessarily have to be graceful to be effective. The Teutonic shamans, those of the German and Norse people, practiced something called Seith magick, basically using the cold to shiver and shake, entering a magickal state through such movements. In the past, some have used binding to slow the flow of blood and enter an induced altered state. I do not personally recommend binding, though I have experienced wonderful meditation in a ritual that lightly tied strips of fabric around energy centers in the body. No blood was constricted, but the light pressure did help induce a deep meditation.

Sex—(exhibitory)—The most exciting path to gnosis, quite literally, is using sexual energy. Masturbation and intercourse are great ways to raise a lot of energy and enter an altered consciousness. Before sexuality came under the taboos of the dominant religions, sex was a much more integral part of magick, and all acts of love were considered worship to the Goddess. The major drawback to this technique is if you are entering an altered state to perform an act of magick, it is very easy to get lost in your own or your partner's pleasure. Ritual sex between a consenting couple in the context of Wiccan ceremonies is called the Great Rite, re-creating the divine union between the Goddess and the God, but it is more often enacted symbolically, through the use of rituals tools like the blade and chalice, rather than physically.

Pain—(exhibitory)—This method includes scourging (light ritual whipping), piercing, branding, and tattooing. Such practices are a part of initiation rituals and rites of passage all over the world. Pain is my least favorite method of altering consciousness, although it definitely alters your consciousness from the normal waking state. Scourging is a practice in both ancient and modern witchcraft, though most shy away from it. A scourge is a whip made of many cords, akin to the cat-o'-nine tails. Modern witches do not seek to break the skin, but to draw blood to that area to induce a trance state. Though this might seem distasteful, flagellation has been used in mystical traditions for centuries. Another aspect of pain is the practice of ritual piercing, tattooing, and branding. These acts mark rites of passage and possibly even initiation. Many involved in these contemporary industries are a part of, or influenced by, pagan and tribal cultures and see the spiritual connotations of these acts.

The Eightfold Path offers many roads to deeper awareness, and some may be more suitable for you than others. This book focuses on applying the more inhibitory techniques, because in my own experience I have found them easiest to teach and reproduce. You need very little in the way of tools or setting. Once you master the basics safely, you can explore the other techniques.

New Assignments
- Exercises 2 through 6—Complete and record your experiences in your Book of Shadows. Continue with exercise 6: Earth Walking as often as you like.

Continuing Assignments
- Daily journal—Write three pages a day.

Tips

- Be conscious and aware of your psychic mind, as manifested as your own inner voice and sense of intuition. Be open to it. Invite it into your life. Expect it. Realize that you are psychic. Psychic means "listening to the voice of your soul." We all can do that. Ask your intuitive, psychic voice for advice, from important life questions to silly inconsequential ones, such as "Who is on the phone?" when it rings. Listen to it. Follow it. Record your experiences. The more you do this and feel vindicated that your psychic voice was right, the stronger it will get.

Lesson 2
Meditation

Meditation is one of the most wonderful paths to gnosis because it leads to many other skills. So much of the witch's way falls under the umbrella of meditation. Some people take the classes I offer not out of any interest in pagan religion, but to learn to meditate and develop themselves psychically. Modern science is now proving the benefits of meditation for stress control and overall health. Learning to quiet your mind and open up to your intuition is the first step to more major undertakings. Don't let the simplicity fool you. Just because something is basic doesn't mean it is always easy or doesn't need to be practiced. To effectively command the skills learned in this chapter, you must practice them regularly.

The first step to a successful meditation practice is to make a space for it in two ways. The first is the outside space, a place in your home for you to meditate. By designating a physical space in your environment, you make a space within you for this change. One helps create the other.

To make a physical space for meditation, I suggest building an altar. An altar is a basic tool in the practice of witchcraft. An altar is just a workspace for your tools. As you progress on this path, specific ritual tools are placed on the altar, but at this point, you are creating a meditation altar. The tools you need are the ones that remind you of your path. Your altar can be a piece of furniture designated solely for this use, or a spot on your nightstand, desk, or bookcase. Choose a place for your altar that you can see when you are meditating. I started with a shelf across from my couch, where I sat to meditate. If you can use one room for only magickal practices, that's great, but most of us lack the space, so the room usually doubles as a magickal room and something else: office, den, living room, or bedroom. Choose a comfortable room, where you can mark out your own territory, if only a corner.

On the altar, place any items that make you feel good, including any magickal trinkets you have picked up along your path so far, such as candles, incense, statues, crystals, feathers, stones, tarot cards, and tree branches. Use anything that signifies magick for you. Arrange them in any manner that feels intuitively correct for you, and change this arrangement as often as you like. Let this altar be a focus for you. Every time you walk into the room, you see it and are reminded of your meditation practice.

You don't need these tools or an altar to meditate; the meditation itself is an internal practice. These physical tools can help you develop a regular practice and serve as a reminder. By building a practice in a regular space and at a regular time, you develop good meditation habits. If you cannot set up an altar, do not let that stop you from meditating.

Mark your meditation times with a simple ceremony, a "tuning in" process to delineate this time as different from your normal, day-to-day life. Start by lighting a candle on your altar. Use a white candle until you learn the significance of other colors. If you like incense, burn some. Certain substances help create a sacred space for meditation and ritual. They do this by "raising the vibration" or spiritual energy of a room. Most are also known as substances of protection for this reason. Frankincense and myrrh are favored by the witches in my coven. You will soon associate these scents with meditative and magickal work. Then say a simple intention to set the stage for the space. Your intention could be formed like this:

"I ask in the name of the Goddess and God to receive my highest guidance in this meditation."

Or:

"I ask the Goddess and God to protect and guide me in this meditation."

Such statements are programming yourself and your space with the experience you wish to have. Intentions of protection, guidance, healing, or experiences for the highest good are best. Clarifying for your "highest good" requests that the experience be guided by your divine, higher self, rather than your ego.

Now sit down comfortably before your altar space. Posture is important. Don't strain any muscles. Everything should be comfortable and relaxed. Wear loose clothing. Some people wear special meditation clothes. This can help shift your mind from daily life to a meditation practice, but it is not necessary. You can either sit in a cross-legged position, what people used to call "Indian style," or if you are more flexible, a lotus or half-lotus position with your feet up on your thighs. The lotus position does not necessarily make for a better or worse meditation. Use a cushion for comfort and support. If cross-legged is uncomfortable, then sit up in a flat-backed chair with your feet flat on the floor and your palms in your lap or resting on your thighs. This position is sometimes called the Egyptian meditation style because so many Egyptian statues are found in this pose. You do not want to cross your arms, and unless you are sitting Indian or lotus style, you want to avoid crossing your legs, too. It tends to disrupt the flow of energy in the body, and I've noticed that those who do it have more difficulty. Your hands can be in your lap, resting on your thighs, or with one hand cupped in the other with your thumb tips touching. Traditionally, women put the right hand into the left, and men put the left into the right. You can also rest the wrists on the knees, palms up, holding thumb and first finger together. My student Alixaendreia presses the tips of her spread fingers together gently, in the shape of a tent, thumb to thumb, index to index, etc., with a space between the palms for her most powerful meditations. Each finger relates to one of the five elements, and she stimulates those energies with this hand position. She discovered it intuitively, but it is an Eastern mudra. Do what is comfortable for you. You can lie down flat on your back, if that is what is most comfortable, but be sure not to fall asleep. If you do find yourself falling asleep in meditation, switch to an upright position. Upright positions with a straight spine aid the flow and focus of energy.

ENTERING ALTERED STATES

Relaxation is the first step in meditation, and it is often forgotten. By preparing your body to meditate, you ease the transition from focusing on your outer reality to your inner reality. Sometimes all the body needs is permission from the mind to relax. Through relaxation, the magickal worlds open up for you.

Breathing is a big component of relaxation. The basic technique of meditation is to observe the breath. Breath is one of the ways to shift your consciousness. Deep and relaxed breaths lower your brain waves from beta into the lower states of meditation. Control of the breath, particularly through counting exercises, leads to a meditative state quite quickly. Just allow the breath to develop naturally and do not do anything that is uncomfortable to you.

EXERCISE 7

Total Relaxation

1. Get into your meditation position.

2. Relax your body. Be aware of your head, from your crown to the back of your neck. Take a deep breath, exhale, and relax all the muscles in your head and neck. Relax your jaw. Relax your face muscles. Relax your eyes and forehead. Feel all tension drain away.

3. Take a deep breath, exhale, and relax your shoulders and arms, all the way down the arms, past the elbows, to the wrists, hands, and fingertips. Waves of relaxation melt away all tension and stress.

4. Breathe deeply and as you exhale, release all tension in your chest and lungs, your upper back, down your spine to the lower back, abdomen, waist, and hips. Feel them completely relax as all tension drains out of you.

5. Take a deep breath, exhale, and release all tension from your legs, starting in your thighs and moving down to your knees. Relax your shins and calf muscles, down to the ankles, feet, and toes. All the tension drains out of you.

6. Breathe deeply and relax. Enjoy the sensation. Scan your body as you breathe. Do you feel any remaining pockets of tension or pain? If so, imagine as you

breathe in that your breath magickally reaches the tension anywhere in your body and takes the tension away as you exhale.

7. Relax your mind. Any thoughts, worries, or concerns from the day melt away and leave with your breath as you exhale. Don't let them concern you any longer. Relax your mental body completely.

8. Relax your heart. Release any unwanted feelings, emotions, and memories as you exhale. Open your heart to the love of the Goddess and God.

9. Relax your soul. As you breathe, feel the pulse and rhythm of life that moves through you and know it moves through all things. Follow your inner light for guidance and protection.

Now add a visual focus to your meditative practice. Like focusing on the breath, turning your attention to an object is a focus for entering an altered state. The very process helps relax the body and deepen the breath. It builds your powers of concentration and clears out a lot of extraneous background noise in your mind. One of the first meditations I learned was to focus on the flame of a white candle on the altar. It is a simple exercise, but something I still go back to when I need to get in touch with my roots. You will probably find yourself coming back to this exercise even after you advance to other skills.

EXERCISE 8

Candle Meditation

1. Start by lighting a white candle on your altar if this is not part of your regular practice. Dim the lights. Sit in your meditative state. Do exercise 7: Total Relaxation.

2. Direct your gaze to the burning candle. Do not stare intently, but face the candle with your eyes open. Let your focus soften.

3. Let the image of the candle fill your thoughts. Focus solely on the candle and stay in the moment.

4. Do not strain your eyes. If they are tired, close them, but visualize the candle in your mind. If visualization is difficult, alternate between opening your eyes

and studying the candle, and then closing your eyes and re-creating the picture in your mind. This will help build your visualization skills. Do not worry if you have difficulty holding the image. Hold the idea of the candle in your mind. Relaxation with focus is more important than visual skill at this point.

5. Do this meditation for a few minutes at first and build to longer intervals. When done, close your eyes, rest, and relax.

You can substitute any object for the candle, re-creating it on the screen of your mind.

Inner visualization is another path into the meditative state, and many people claim it is the most powerful because the talent lends itself to many other magickal practices. You've learned how to feel and experience your own personal energy and the energy of a partner in previous exercises. You have some understanding of this invisible force. But our conscious mind has difficulty processing energy, or even understanding it. That is why we connect with the psychic and divine minds. The psychic mind can process psychic energy, but has difficulty translating the experience so the conscious mind can comprehend it. Our psychic self has to use a code that the conscious self can understand. This code is symbolism. Symbols can stand in for concepts and energy. Personal symbols are private messages from your own unconscious, your own psychic self, to your conscious self, as when we have dreams. General or universal symbols, falling into the realm of archetypes, is how the collective unconscious speaks to humanity.

Visualization is the process of using these symbols. Most people see in their dreams. Other senses may be involved, but dreams mainly have a visual component. Likewise, the easiest method to get a direction or command to the psychic mind is through the use of a visual symbol. Practitioners of magick have always studied symbols, from petroglyphs and ancient alphabets to dream interpretation and vision quests. The symbols of our collective and personal mythology are the ways to direct power. Those who understand the symbols and can project them, through intention, will, ritual, and, yes, visualization, tap into a power we all possess, but few use.

Visualization is a very effective and quick method of altering your consciousness. The advantage of this method is that your "psychic muscles" are activated and "warmed up" from the process, and will function more effectively in deeper meditations.

EXERCISE 9

Counting Down to a Meditative State

1. Get into your meditative position. You can do exercise 7: Total Relaxation and exercise 8: Candle Meditation if you would like. Relaxation and focus before any exercise is great, but this countdown can also be used alone to get into a meditative state quickly.

2. Visualize a giant screen before you, like a blackboard or movie screen. This is the screen of your mind, or what is called your mind's eye. Whenever you visualize or recall anything, or remember a person's face or anything else, you project it on to this screen. You have always had it, but now we are going to give it some attention. Anything you desire will appear on the screen.

3. On the screen of your mind, visualize a series of numbers, counting down from twelve to one. With each number, you get into a deeper meditative state. The numbers can be any color you desire, drawn as if writing them, or appearing whole.

   Now visualize 12, see the number 12 on your screen, 12,

   11, see the number 11 on your screen, 11,

   10, see the number 10 on your screen, 10,

   9, see the number 9 on your screen, 9,

   8, see the number 8 on your screen, 8,

   7, see the number 7 on your screen, 7,

   6, see the number 6 on your screen, 6,

   5, see the number 5 on your screen, 5,

   4, see the number 4 on your screen, 4,

   3, see the number 3 on your screen, 3,

   2, see the number 2 on your screen, 2,

   1, see the number 1 on your screen, 1.

4. You are at your meditative state. Everything done in your meditative state is for your highest good, harming none. You are now counting down to a deeper, more focused meditative state. Count backward from thirteen to one, but do not visualize the numbers this time. Let the numbers gently take you down: 13, 12, 11, 10, 9, 8, 7, 6, 5, 4, 3, 2, and 1. You are now at your deepest meditative state, your magickal mindset, in complete control of your magickal abilities.

5. From this point, you can continue on to other exercises and experiences, or meditate at this level for a while and bring yourself up, counting from one to thirteen and then from one to twelve. Gently start to wiggle your fingers and toes and slowly move to bring your awareness back to the physical.

6. Take both hands and raise them up over your head, palms facing your crown. Slowly bring them down over your forehead, face, throat, chest, abdomen, and then groin, and "push out" with your palms facing away from you. This gives you clearance and balance, releasing any harmful or unwanted energies you might pick up during your magickal experiences. Tell yourself:

   "I give myself clearance and balance. I am in balance with myself. I am in balance with the universe. I release all that does not serve."

7. Ground yourself as needed.

This exercise effectively takes you into a meditative state. Even if you have difficulty visualizing the numbers, hold the concept of them, if not the visualization, in your mind until it grows stronger.

In the first part of the meditation, we count using the numbers twelve and thirteen. Witches follow the natural cycles, particularly those of the Sun and Moon. The solar calendar is based on twelve divisions, like the twelve zodiac signs, and the lunar year is based on thirteen Moons. The Sun is associated with more masculine, linear, and logical thought, so during the active, solar twelve count, you are actively visualizing and controlling what you see on the screen of your mind. The Moon is linked with the intuitive, feminine energies, emotion, and mystery. During the lunar thirteen count, you do not try to visualize or control anything. Simply go with the flow of numbers and allow it to happen. Psychics and witches often rely on feelings and intuition rather than concrete visualization and direct messages. Doing both counts brings us into balance with the masculine and feminine energies within. Both are needed to make magick.

At the end of this countdown, you wave your hands down over your crown and over the front, vertical axis of your body, the chakra line. Chakras are spiritual energy centers in the body. We are primarily working with the third eye, or brow chakra, on the forehead between and above your two physical eyes. This point controls your sense of psychic "seeing," visualization, and what many call the mind's eye. During visualization, this chakra is more active. In fact, during many magickal practices, your energy centers activate, like taking a running car from out of neutral and into gear. They are always on, but in different states of activity, depending on what you are doing. Clearance and balance return these centers to a normal energy level to prepare you to focus your energy again in the physical world. It also helps detach any harmful, unwanted energies you may have come across in your magickal practices, returning you to a state of clarity and balance.

As we continue with further exercises and meditations, refer to exercise 9: Counting Down to a Meditative State to get into your magickal mindset. If you are not comfortable with a visual countdown, you can use the techniques of exercises 7 and 8 to begin meditation. Some people modify the countdown to suit their own needs. You can imagine a set of twelve steps that you are walking down, perhaps in a spiral staircase. This engages not only the sense of sight, but also the feeling of movement. Whenever you complete your meditations and exercises, always end with the last few steps of exercise 9, including counting up, clearance and balance, and grounding if necessary. These help prepare your senses to return to physical reality. The count up is a very important part of the process. Do not skip it just because you become aware of the physical world before you count up.

There are many meditations and exercises designed to help you access these psychic abilities and improve your skill at creating and holding visual images. The next exercise starts with a series of basic shapes (figure 7).

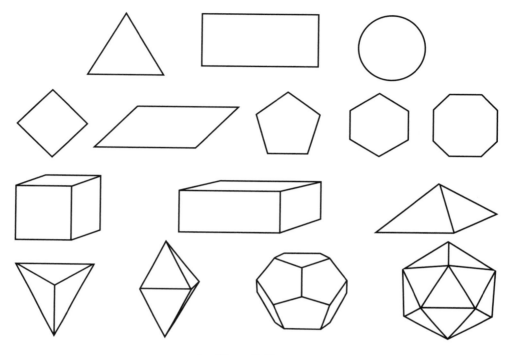

Figure 7: Shapes

EXERCISE 10

Basic Visualization

1. Start exercise 9: Counting Down to a Meditative State to get into your magickal mindset.

2. Again, call up the screen of your mind. Imagine that it is like a board where you can control all the drawings. You can use any color to draw this set of shapes. You might find it helpful to physically raise your hand and "draw" the shapes in the air in front of you with your finger.

3. Draw a triangle on the screen of your mind. Hold the image for a few moments. Then wipe it away, like wiping away chalk dust. Again, you can physically move your hand with a wiping motion.

4. Draw a rectangle on the screen of your mind. Hold the image for a few moments. Then wipe it away.

5. Draw a circle on the screen of your mind. Hold the image for a few moments. Then wipe it away.

6. Draw variations of the triangle, rectangle, and circle. If you are comfortable with these three shapes, then move on to other, more complex shapes, like a diamond, parallelogram, pentagon, hexagon, and octagon.

7. If you feel confident with these two-dimensional shapes, try working with three-dimensional shapes, starting with the cube, box, and pyramid. Later, try more complex three-dimensional shapes, like the Platonic solids, such as a tetrahedron, octahedron, dodecahedron, or icosohedron. Do not be intimidated by them. Allow them to appear on the screen of your mind and hold the images as best you can.

8. Wipe all the shapes off the screen of your mind and clear it. Then ask for the energy and image of an orange to appear on the screen of your mind. See the orange before you, as if a real piece of fruit is hanging on an invisible tree. Take note of the color, and variations of color. Is it completely ripe?

9. Notice the texture of the orange's skin, the curves and bumps. Reach out with your physical hands and pretend to grab it. The orange is now in your hands. How does it feel? Can you smell it? Peel back the skin. Can you feel the wetness of the juice on your hands? Can you taste it? Use all your senses.

10. Experience the orange fully. Then magickally visualize yourself putting it all back together, perfect and unbroken. Hang it back on the tree on the screen of your mind.

11. Thank the orange, and wipe the image away, erasing it.

12. Return yourself to normal consciousness, counting up, giving yourself clearance and balance, and do any necessary grounding.

If you practice this meditation often, you can skip the shapes, if you'd like, and start with the orange. Replace it. Use any fruit you like, or substitute other objects, like an egg, leaf, or crystal. Although you think you are visualizing an object, you are doing more than that. It's like playing pretend, but you are not playing, you are actually connecting to the energy of an orange from somewhere in space and time. The orange was not physical, but it was real. You were reaching out to it and your mind made a little simulation of it before you, so you could observe it. If you try this exercise twenty times, you will probably get twenty different oranges, unless you have the intention to get the same one each time. Little blemishes and details you might not think to include if you were completely making it up will be there.

Affirmations

Affirmations are beneficial statements we make to ourselves, out loud or silently, to reprogram our deep levels of consciousness. You know that magick requires an alignment of the conscious mind with the psychic and divine minds. One of the methods of achieving this alignment is through meditation, quieting the inner chatter to bring this harmony. From this alignment, magick flows. When people start meditating, many are filled with a sense of accomplishment, while others are unsure if it is really working. This uncertainty can accompany disbelief, doubt, and fear. The root of these frustrations and fears is found in the subconscious, a connecting link to your psychic mind.

Humans are like vast, unlimited computers, capable of quite literally anything we set out to do. We are only limited by our programming, the directions, instructions, and images we contain. As individuals, we program ourselves, but use templates and programs from our family, friends, and society. Unfortunately, at the moment we do not live in the most life-affirming and optimistic world, and our self-programming can reflect that. Every thought and idea becomes a part of our overall programming. If we think we are unworthy, unwanted, or unloved, our self-esteem falls. Feeling confident and good about ourselves is paramount when using our magickal abilities. If our programming prevents us from feeling connected to spirit, our abilities are greatly diminished. When we try to connect to them, the blocks surface. When difficult feelings arise in meditations, at any level, we are attempting to clear through the blocks.

Clearing away the blocks through experience is important, but there is another way to tackle this problem: through direct, conscious reprogramming. Because every thought you have becomes a part of your new programming, consciously think new, helpful thoughts to replace the old programming with the new. Affirmations are the new programming. The idea of inner programming does not replace free will or conscious choice. We choose and create our own programming. Most of us have accepted a log of programming that is not of our own making. Now is the time to take back control and responsibility.

Daily affirmations are a great way to instantly reprogram the subconscious and gain greater access to our personal power. They can be done in meditation, to deeply implant them in your consciousness. They can also be done in a regular beta state with great effect. Here are some sample affirmations that have helped me and my students. This set is great to start out with to build self-esteem and a sense of connection to your own spirit.

> *I love myself. I love all others. I am infinitely loved.*
>
> *I forgive myself. I forgive all others.*
>
> *I am walking in the love of the Goddess, God, and Great Spirit.*
>
> *Everything I do is for the good of all involved, harming none.*
>
> *I am open to my highest guidance.*

For those who have programmed blocks to their own prosperity, using these affirmations can help clear the way to great blessings.

> *I am successful and talented.*
>
> *I am prosperous.*
>
> *I have all the money and resources I need.*
>
> *I am always in the right place, at the right time, doing the right thing.*
>
> *I am joyful in all that I do.*

This third set of affirmations is to open and awaken psychic abilities.

> *All of my senses are growing stronger every day.*
>
> *I am safely opening and increasing all of my psychic abilities.*

I am seeing psychically.

I am hearing psychically.

I am knowing psychically.

I am traveling psychically.

I am psychic.

This last set creates personal health and prepares you to take an active role as a healer. Healing is one of the highest skills learned in witchcraft.

I am completely healthy on all levels.

I am in balance and harmony.

I release all that does not serve my highest good.

I am safely opening my healing abilities.

Many of these affirmations are in the form of "I am" statements. The phrase "I am" is very powerful because it connects the affirmation to the highest quality of your being, your higher or divine self. The phrase goes back to an Old Testament phrase when the Divine, taking the form of a burning bush, says, "I am that I am." You don't have to be Jewish or Christian to use the power of these two simple words. In the kundalini-yoga tradition, a popular mantra is "Healthy am I. Happy am I. Holy am I." In the Silva Mind Control Method, they use "Everyday, in every way, I am getting better and better and better."

The "I am" statements are also in the form of what you want to create, rather than what you don't want. An affirmation of health is "I am healthy" rather than "I am not sick." In the latter, you are focusing on the word *sick*, and may be creating more sickness, even though that is not the intent of the statement.

Affirmations are often said a certain number of times. Sets of three are popular, for not only the pagan Triple Goddess, but for the conscious, psychic, and divine minds. Saying affirmations in sets of three, nine, thirty-three, ninety-nine, and 108 are extremely effective. Others prefer sets of four, for the four elements. The elements correspond to our physical, emotional, mental, and spiritual bodies. Use what resonates most strongly with you.

In a way, affirmations are a form of magick. Once, when too sick to meditate or perform a ritual, I said the affirmation "I am completely healthy on all levels" thirty-three times in the shower, preparing to go to the doctor. I had a nasty case of the flu. By the time I dried off, I felt completely fine. I was not congested or lightheaded anymore. I went to the doctor anyway, and he said I should have come sooner to him, because it looked like my body had already fought it off. He assumed that I had been suffering for a week or two by my progress, and not just two days. That was my most immediate success with affirmations. Now, if it is possible to do this and heal the physical, think how powerfully affirmations work on your subtle mental programming.

Don't feel uncomfortable doing affirmations. When you start them, there is a tendency to feel awkward or foolish. Let yourself feel that way—it will soon fade. Then get back to the affirmations, no matter how silly it seems. That is part of your programming. You are trying to dissolve feelings of self-consciousness so that you can be free to do whatever you want, whenever you want, without embarrassment. Once you start to see how powerful they are, you quickly overcome the embarrassment. The power of affirmations has made me rethink many song lyrics I sing over and over again, as well as using expressions such as "He's a pain in the neck." Your words literally create your reality.

EXERCISE 11

Affirmations

1. Choose at least five affirmations from the previous lists, or create your own. Focus on which qualities you would like to bring to you. Memorize them as best you can, so you will be able to recite them in a meditation.

2. Start exercise 9: Counting Down to a Meditative State to get into your magickal mindset.

3. Once you are at your meditative level, recite each affirmation at least three times.

4. Take note of how you feel when you recite each affirmation. You may not feel anything at first, but you are subtly changing your inner programming.

You may see things, or think of people or places from your past. Let the ideas flow in and out. Do not hold onto them, but remain aware of them. They can give you clues as to what issues need attention.

5. Return yourself to normal consciousness, counting up, giving yourself clearance and balance, and do any necessary grounding.

Instant Magick

Instant magick is the practice of putting your will into motion very quickly, using the power of visualization and attaining a light meditative state through the use of a trigger. There are many names for it: the power of creative visualization, projecting (because you are projecting your will into the future to manifest), or causal magick. It is a form of magick without deep meditation, ritual, or tools, and many discount it because of that, thinking "anyone" can do it so it is not "real" magick, but I disagree. Yes, anyone can do magick if they decide to, and the rewards of instant magick are by no means little. These seemingly insignificant acts help us reevaluate the way we create our own reality from moment to moment.

Such instant spells never cease to amaze me. When you start out in the practice of magick, it is easy to chalk success up to coincidence, even as you learn metaphysically that there are no real coincidences. Still, it's a hard fact to swallow when most of us are told otherwise throughout life. If you are able to integrate this talent into your daily life, your results venture out of the realm of coincidence and into the truly amazing. You then learn to expect the amazing and live a magickal life.

Instant magick is projecting your will forward through visualization and specific intention to create an opportunity, lining up what seem to be coincidences. You do this by entering a light state of alpha, a meditative level where you can still talk, walk, drive, and carry on with everyday life. The sensation is similar to letting your mind wander for a moment, but it is not wandering. In fact, it is truly focusing, but only for a few moments. In those few moments, you state silently or out loud what you want to happen, or visualize it. You do not even need to close your eyes. Imagine it for a moment.

You reach your light magickal mindset through intention. By programming a trigger, you can reach this state no matter how stressful a situation is. There are many times in life when we need access to our magick and meditation skills, but circumstances do not give us the time, space, and quiet we are accustomed to having. The trigger helps us. It is like a post self-hypnotic command that says, "When I do some specific motion, I will enter a light trance state." Triggers can be hand motions, gestures, words, or images that, when performed, help us reach our magickal mind.

Although you can choose any trigger you like, I suggest a simple hand position. I originally learned from Laurie Cabot to cross my first and second fingers to activate my trigger. She taught it as the basis of our expression "I'll cross my fingers," when we want something to happen. Children's games associate crossed fingers with lying, and that root also probably comes from witchcraft, when the craft was associated with harm. I was surprised to find out that this position is actually a mudra in Hindu mysticism. Author Gurunam (Joseph Michael Levry) says, "If you need a favor, or have a wish, such as wanting a raise, all you have to do while asking for it is cross the middle and index fingers. . . This procedure balances your energy, thereby momentarily increasing your magnetic field for your desire to be fulfilled."[1]

Other mudras that are potential hand positions for your trigger include putting the thumb and index finger together, putting the thumb and middle finger together, or even putting the thumb with both the index and middle fingers together.

Experiment in meditation and see what feels comfortable to you. The reason why I suggest simple hand movements is because grand and sweeping gestures attract attention, and you want to be able to do this when you drive and have a conversation with someone and not necessarily explain what you are doing. In Celtic myth, thumb sucking is a trigger for inspiration and wisdom, though I don't suggest using it in public. Some use a specific word as their trigger into the trance state and a word to end the trance state. Use what feels comfortable to you. You do not necessarily have to vocalize the word to make it effective.

Once you program your trigger, you can use it for many different effects in your everyday life. Here are some of the more traditional ideas used by witches. I combine

---

1. Gurunam (Joseph Michael Levry), *Lifting the Veil* (New York: Rootlight, Inc.) 42.

visualization with intent. Sometimes I ask the Goddess and God for my intent, silently in my mind, and ask that it be "correct and for the good of all involved."

Accelerated Learning

Hold your trigger when reading a book, studying for a test, or listening to a lecture. The teaching will penetrate deeper and be more fully understood. When you need to recall the information, use your trigger again. Some people can re-create the pages memorized on the screen of their mind, and "look up" the answers.

Affirmations

Use your trigger when you do affirmations and you don't have time to get into a meditative state.

Animal Communication

You can project your thoughts to animals, and receive impressions from them as well. Try "speaking" to a pet or other animals, and see if it responds. This communication is not limited to animals, but also extends to the consciousness of plants and even minerals.

Bending Time

Believe it or not, time, or our perception and movement in it, is not as immutable as you think. Next time you are running late and do not have enough time to get to your destination, use your trigger and imagine yourself getting there exactly on time. I've used this many times to get to jobs on time when running impossibly late. There is a joke that there is "real" time and pagan standard time, running about a half hour late. It does not have to be so, if you use instant magick.

Body Control

We have far greater ability to control our bodily systems than we currently use. Medicine is exploring this frontier through something called biofeedback control, but witches and shamans have known about it for a while. You can control your response to extremes in temperature and pain. The next time you are out in the cold, use your trigger and either imagine yourself warm or unbothered by the cold. I've tested it out on cold New England mornings waiting for the bus, and I'm very glad I learned this skill.

Cosmic Telephone Message

Cosmic telephone message is a quirky way to say you are leaving a psychic message for someone to call you. It is particularly useful when the person is out of reach. Use your trigger and think of the person you wish to reach. Leave a message, like you would on an answering machine, asking him or her to call you. Usually you will hear from the person in three days, saying, "I don't know why, but I was thinking about you."

Early Warning System

Holding your trigger with the intention of awareness in times of danger can keep you alert and prepared for anything. Although I am not advocating any speeding laws to be broken, I use my instant magick to warn me of police speed traps.

Guidance

As you continue with this training and explore the world of spirit guides, you can use your trigger to instantly make a connection to higher guidance and ask questions.

Healing

People have a remarkable ability to heal themselves and others. You can use your trigger and visualize yourself or the other person getting better, more healthy and vibrant. Other techniques will be explored later, and your trigger can help you access them instantly.

Internal Alarm Clock

We all have a biological clock. Our bodies know what time it is by the cycles of the day, and if we are in tune with them, we can know, too. My student Heather does not wear a watch. She does her trigger and asks Spirit what time it is, and gets an accurate time. I use my trigger before bed and visualize a clock with the time I need to wake up. I tell myself and my body that I will wake up refreshed at that time. Although I love to sleep in, I get up when I do this, feeling fine. It can also be used as part of a morning meditation, for those suffering from insomnia. When you wake up, set your internal alarm clock for the time you plan on going to bed, and sleep will come much easier.

Memory

Use of your trigger improves memory. Use your trigger when meeting new people, to remember their names. When you introduce yourself, think your name as you say it, so your new friends will hear and remember it on a deeper level.

Parking Spaces

My favorite trick of instant magick by far is visualizing a parking space near the door of my destination about fifteen minutes before arrival. Almost always, there is one. Don't pick an exact space, but an approximate location. When I was going to a city college and working in a major urban area, parking was always scarce, but this little bit of magick proved very valuable. My friend Rich uses his trigger when driving on congested highways, to visualize a space safely opening up when he changes lanes. You can even use your instant magick to get unstuck from the mud or snow.

Protection

Enter your light meditative state when feeling unsafe and ask the Goddess and God to protect you from all harm. This activates your personal shield of protection. Call on your protective spirits. You need not know them to ask them to intervene for your highest good. You will learn more specific techniques of protection and how to meet spirits as we progress through the lessons.

Reduce Anxiety

If you have a tendency to get anxious under pressure, or stress easily, use your trigger and tell your body and mind to calm down. Use it for any performance situation, public talks, meeting new people, visiting family, and job interviews. Use your trigger if you feel road rage or need to cool down after a long day and can't fully meditate.

Repairs

As our intention can heal the body, strangely enough it can also repair inorganic systems. I've used my trigger to visualize ailing cars, computers, and office equipment working. I even use it when signing on to the Internet. I know a crystal healer who successfully uses crystals on her car, so visualization on machines is not far-fetched.

Usually this magick is a stopgap measure, but it can be more permanent. At one job, I was a computer-systems administrator, not because of my knowledge and skill with computers, but because of my ability to experiment and do magick. I think I kept the system running through sheer willpower, and after I left, I heard from my office friends that the system crashed and took quite a while to repair.

Traffic Lights

Another popular use of the trigger is to get traffic lights to turn green, but this can be dangerous. What if you switch a circuit that makes your light green without turning the other lights red? It is far better to start your journey and visualize all lights being green, getting you to your destination on time, than to try to "force" each set of lights to turn green as you approach.

Victory

Some feel this is cheating, while others think of it as using all the resources at their disposal, so I'll let you make the call. Your instant magick can manifest your success at contests, sports, and games of chance. It is quite effective for dice games. I don't necessarily consider it cheating, because everyone is projecting their will at the game. I know lots of people who are not witches who unknowingly practice instant magick. Since they don't believe in magick, they call it good luck.

Weather Magick

When in difficult or dangerous weather, particularly while driving, use your trigger to project a clear and safe path for yourself.

You need not be limited by these examples. Just as I found special tricks to fit my lifestyle and needs, you will expand your instant magick into new areas. The most important thing to notice about all these acts is how mundane they are. I am not putting simple magick down; I am just emphasizing that the simple acts of life can be infused with magick. Your everyday reality is a vehicle for living a magickal life. Many people who follow a spiritual path resign it to a particular time when they are "being" spiritual, usually once a week at a service. Don't think magick is relegated to a few special times a week when you sit down and prepare to do it. Witches weave the threads of magick, family, home, and world together because they are all parts of the web of life. Integrating your magick, and more importantly your magickal viewpoint, into your daily life is a very important step.

Although technically these simple spells should work for you regardless of your path or tradition, if you do see yourself on a spiritual path, I would suggest thanking the divine powers, the Goddess, God, and Great Spirit, for every gift, even those that did not occur. If an act of instant magick does not happen as you intended, there is probably a reason for it. Perhaps being late for work even though you tried to bend time might have prevented you from being in an accident. Giving thanks is a great lesson for any path, because gratitude opens up a whole new world of blessings.

Now that you have an idea of what instant magick can do, try this meditation to program your own trigger. This exercise should be repeated several times to ingrain the program into all levels of consciousness.

EXERCISE 12

Programming Your Trigger

1. First decide on what trigger position feels comfortable to you. I suggest your first two fingers and thumb together or crossing your middle and index fingers.

2. Start exercise 9: Counting Down to a Meditative State to get into your magickal mindset.

3. Once you are at your meditative level, physically perform your trigger on one or both hands. I like to program both hands so I have a choice as to which one I use, depending on the circumstances. If I trigger both hands, I feel I go a bit deeper.

4. State to yourself, "I program this as my instant magick trigger. With this trigger I can instantly access a light meditative state and all my magickal abilities, for the good of all, harming none." Say this statement three times.

5. When done, return yourself to normal consciousness, counting up, giving yourself clearance and balance. Ground yourself as needed.

When you hold this trigger position, you enter a light magickal mindset. When you need to get out of this state, release the trigger. The process is that simple.

Finding a Place of Power

One of the most important tenets in the traditions of witchcraft is the sacredness and power of the natural world. Making space for meditation in your inner reality by building an altar or shrine and then maintaining a practice is an important step. Another foundation stone in the process is to find a place in nature that is special and sacred to you, if possible. It does not have to be deep in the woods, but someplace accessible to you, to serve as another meditation spot where you can commune with the forces of nature as a pathway to yourself.

Some of your magick will seem easier or harder outside of the safety of your home because you are communing with all manner of new energies. This can be in a park, a trail in the woods, a beach, a stream, a lake, or someplace off the beaten path where you feel safe, comfortable, and relaxed. You may find such a spot as you continue your earth walking from exercise 6. Use common sense in selecting your area. If you are not an experienced camper or hiker, do not pick a place deep in the forest, far from help, in case you get lost. If you live in an urban environment and can't find a suitable place in a park, then don't worry, but the next time you are out of the city and in the country, try practicing your meditations there.

Make or find a shrine at this spot, even if it is temporary. You do not need to put candles or incense in your shrine unless you want to do so, but try sitting by a special rock or tree that helps you make this connection. Spontaneous psychic experiences have been known to happen when you venture forth into nature, in search of a place of power.

NEW ASSIGNMENTS

• Exercises 7 through 12—Complete and record your experiences in your Book of Shadows. Incorporate them into a regular routine at least three times a week, if not daily. Early-morning or late-evening meditation times are usually best, but do not meditate lying down in bed, or you will always associate meditation with sleeping. Sit up. Do exercise 12: Programming Your Trigger at least three times. Practice the orange meditation often, using all your senses. Use instant magick in your daily life.

CONTINUING ASSIGNMENTS

• Daily journal—Write three pages a day.

• Honor and recognize your intuition. Continue to ask it questions.

TIPS

• Prepare your space and set the mood for meditation. If you would like, use some soft, repetitive music or perhaps a water fountain.

• Develop your inner narrator. Take the voice within you that may act critical and skeptical, and give it a job to do. Train it to be your coach rather than distract you. Silently tell yourself to relax your body and mind. Silently instruct yourself through each step of the meditations, as if someone were there to help you. If you get internal criticism, thank the voice for sharing, but kindly ask it to sit down and focus on the task at hand. This inner guide will help you become your own best teacher.

• Always make sure to count yourself down and count yourself back up. Always give yourself clearance and balance at the end. Always check in to see if you need to ground more after the meditation.

• Don't rush. Relax and take your time. You can spend quite a while with relaxation and breathing before getting to specific exercises. Let your body and mind tell you when you are ready, and then count down.

• There is no real "getting there." Some sessions seem deeper than others, but many students expect to feel "under," as if they were at a stage-hypnotist show. There are many levels of meditation, and all of them are valuable. You can still be in a meditative state and have your mind wander. The alpha state is much like daydreaming, and when we daydream, our minds wander. When you recognize this, bring your thoughts back to the experience at hand. Don't feel you are failing because your mind is wandering. Sometimes you are distracted by outside noises. That happens to everybody. You are learning to bring more focus and direction to your meditation time, but that takes a lot of practice. Witches are walkers between worlds, and must be conscious of both, but as you practice, you will begin to withdraw your senses into the inner world for greater lengths of time. Do not berate yourself when meditation does not fulfill your expectations. Bring your focus back and do your best.

- You shouldn't fall asleep when meditating. If you do, reevaluate your sleeping and eating patterns, as well as your work habits. Take care of your physical body.

- Some people meditate better in the early morning hours. Others, like myself, meditate better at the end of the day, before bedtime. Experiment and find out which time, if any, is best for you.

Lesson 3
The Magick of Science

At one time, science and spirit were a single discipline, but the two broke apart in Western culture, and did not mix again until the twentieth century. The twentieth century is looked at as a time of dispelling the occult and paranormal, but science, strangely enough, has led us back to the mystical through some interesting theories and the advent of a new paradigm that borders on the spiritual, and not the mechanical. The threads of many different disciplines lead to the view of the universe as a holistic system. One of the first was the somewhat controversial theory of quantum physics.

The basis of quantum physics began in several stages in the early 1900s, and is attributed to the contributions of six men: Niels Bohr, Paul Dirac, Albert Einstein, Werner Heisenberg, Max Planck, and Erwin Schrödinger. Originally the theories were not an attempt to create a new discipline or scientific paradigm, but to account for odd experimental results that did not conform to the generally accepted classical rules of physics.

Though a *quanta* refers to a bundle of energy, the smallest discrete amount of energy that can be measured, quantum theory does not deal exclusively with the microworld, but the entire universe. The previous scientific paradigm described the universe in terms of distinct divisions, and in particular two separate groups, particles and waves. Particles held a position and waves had momentum. The building blocks of all matter and energy were either in particle or wave form. Everything was believed to be separate and distinct; every part is in its own space and time, linked only through observable forces. Classical physics is very rigid and predictable. Events happen due to an observable cause and effect. Conditions can be maintained and controlled in experiments to repeat the process with the same results.

However, results of many new experiments with subatomic particles did not fit this classical model. Some results were "nonlocal," occurring without an observable cause. The further one dove into the microworld, and divided the particles of matter into smaller and smaller units, the less they behaved like individual units. The distinction between particles and waves grew fuzzy. At times, a unit such as an electron behaved as a particle. We think of an electron as a ball of energy with a negative charge, circling the nucleus of an atom, like a planet orbiting the Sun. In other experiments, an electron exhibited the characteristics of a wave. It depended on the experiment. In fact, it is speculated that such energies only have a particle form when we are looking at them. It is like saying that the universe changes when we turn our back on it, but then conforms to our expectations when we observe it. We can never know both the position (particle) and the momentum (wave) of a quanta at the same time. Observing one changes the other. In fact, they may not possess both attributes at the same time. This is the core of Heisenberg's Uncertainty Principle. Suddenly the particles of matter, which we thought were solid and dependable, became fuzzy and nondescript. Certain energies, such as x-rays, were always believed to be in wave form, but under certain conditions, they exhibited particle properties. Suddenly everything we knew about physics was called into question.

Scientists discovered the power of the observer. Somehow the interaction of the observer, once considered independent of the experiment, had become crucial to the way experiments were conducted, and the results were subtly influenced. The behavior of the phenomenon would change, depending on who was observing it and what thoughts, feelings, and expectations the observer had. Controlled conditions were no longer "controlled." Gradually scientists started coming to the conclusion that the "pieces" of an experiment were not separate unto themselves, but part of a larger whole, extending beyond the experiment and including the observer and quite possibly the whole universe.

Leading us in a similar direction, but from a completely different route, was the neurosurgeon Karl Pribram and his work with the brain, memories, and vision, starting in the 1940s. Until then, scientists believed that specific memories were located in specific regions of the brain. Through research with animals and people with specific portions of their brain removed, he discovered, along with his mentor Karl Lashley, that the individuals did not suffer specific memory loss, coming to the conclusion that memories were not held in specific areas, but nonlocally, throughout the brain. The mechanism allowing the brain to accomplish such a feat was unknown to him until he discovered the model of the hologram.

THE HOLOGRAM

The hologram plays an important role in understanding these new scientific advances, so let's discuss it in detail. A hologram is a three-dimensional sculpture of light. It is a recorded image, like a photograph, but a photograph is flat, with only two dimensions. The hologram is three-dimensional. You can look at it from any angle, and it looks real, with depth and texture. If you try to touch it, you realize it is not solid, but a construct of light.

The hologram is created through the use of a special form of light, a beam of coherent light called a laser. A laser beam is split through the use of a device called a beam splitter. One beam is bounced off the object to be recorded. The second is directed with mirrors until it collides with the reflected light of the first. These two beams create an interference pattern, two patterns overlapping (figure 8A).

Any two waves can create an interference pattern, but those of the laser beam are special. To understand an interference pattern, think of a pond. When you drop a pebble into the pond, it creates rings moving outward. When you drop two or more pebbles, the rings cross each other, creating an interference pattern.

The resulting interference pattern from the lasers is recorded on a special film, called a holographic plate. The pattern itself looks nothing like the object. Upon close inspection, it looks somewhat similar to the waves in the pond. But when you shine a laser through the holographic film, it creates a three-dimensional image of light, a hologram, of the object (figure 8B).

The most interesting property of the hologram is the pattern. Each piece of the film contains all the information of the pattern. If you rip the holographic film into two pieces, and shine a light into one, you get the whole image, only smaller. You can divide the film again and again, until you reach the limits of the technology, but theoretically, the pattern can continue to be reduced and still contain the image. The film will deteriorate the image at a certain point.

The main points to remember about holograms are that the pattern created from two beams of energy can store three-dimensional information, and that the storage is nonlocal, meaning each piece of the pattern contains all the information necessary to recreate the image.

The holographic model of the brain, in which each part contains the whole, provides an interesting answer to the way the brain receives information, retrieves memory, and creates our point of view. Since our memories are recorded holographically, brain damage does not necessarily remove specific memories or even functions. The brain can "trick" us into thinking that our internal processes are external. We cut our hand and feel the pain in our hand, but the pain is actually caused through a chemical reaction in their brain. The sensation of "phantom limbs" to people missing them could simply be a holographic memory of those limbs, as recorded in the interference pattern of our brain. The memory accidentally gets played back, feeling very real, but has no basis in physical reality.

Taken further to its logical conclusion, Pribram opened a door to a whole new world, where our perceived outer reality is actually occurring internally. The world may not be as solid as we think, but perceived by the brain in holographic terms. The world only becomes familiar as it enters our senses, but in actuality, the world is an interference pattern.

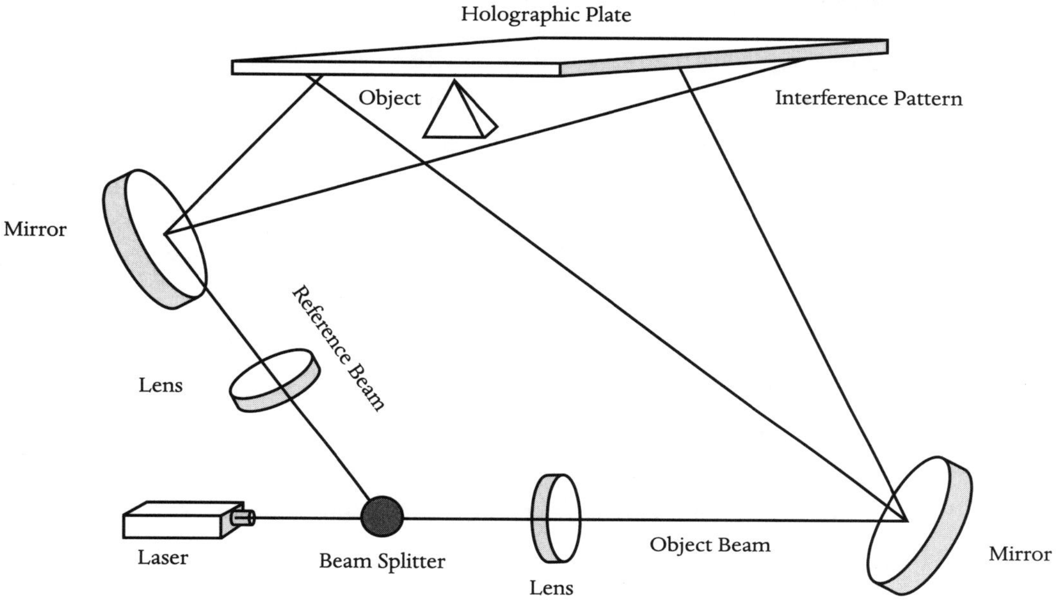

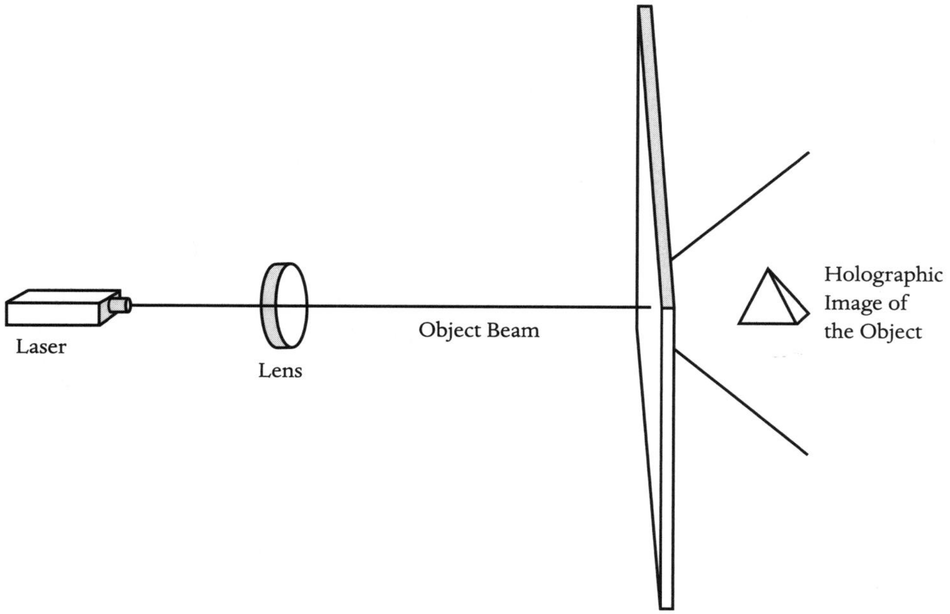

Figure 8A: *Recording a Holographic Image*

Figure 8B: *Projecting a Holographic Image*

Fields of Consciousness

In 1952 on the isolated Island of Koshima, scientists were observing the behavior of Japanese monkeys *(Macaca fuscata)* by giving them sweet potatoes dropped in the sand. They liked the potatoes, but disliked the sand clinging to them. One female monkey solved this dilemma by washing the potato, and subsequently taught her mother and friends. Soon potato washing became a cultural trend and many learned to wash. From 1952 to 1958, all the new young monkeys practiced washing, while some of the older ones held to the older practice of eating them dirty. That fall, the scientists noted something very strange. Once a certain critical mass was reached on Koshima, and all monkeys of the *Macaca fuscata* species on that island started washing their potatoes, monkeys on other islands, separated by water, also began to wash their potatoes. These monkeys were not taught this skill, but somehow knew. No information was transferred on any recordable level. The practice came into the general consciousness of the monkeys.

Though not a controlled experiment, this lead to the postulation that a species is connected by some invisible field of consciousness. When a small number of the species, in comparison to the entire population, learn new information or a way of life, it remains their individual knowledge. When a critical mass of those with the knowledge is reached—in this case it was speculated to be one hundred—the information becomes part of the race's consciousness, available to all. The story of the Japanese monkeys is told by Lyall Watson in the book *Lifetide,* but other experiments have been conducted since, with animals and even people.

The hundredth monkey theory supports the concept of morphogenetic fields, whose main proponent is Rupert Sheldrake. Sheldrake, a pioneer in the biological sciences, built on the work of Hans Spemann, Alexander Gurwitsch, and Paul Weiss, who in the 1920s each independently proposed that morphogenesis, the coming into being of form, is organized by fields of energy. Sheldrake developed his morphic field theories, influenced by Hindu spirituality, Sufism, and Goethe. This theory proposes that each species creates a field with low energy, but with vast amounts of information, acting as a cumulative collective memory for that type of organism. The morphic fields include information on the genetic, behavioral, social, cultural, and mental levels. This would certainly include the information transferred through the hundredth monkey theory and go far beyond it. Such fields cannot be seen or measured, and move across space and time, but directly influence the development of a species, built up from the life of all beings in said species. These fields, too, are nonlocal. Physically, they act as a geometric influence, a template or blueprint for development. DNA acts as a resonator, or antenna, to pick up the influence of the field. Each species' DNA "tunes in" to the appropriate species field.

We can tune in to the information of the morphic fields, not only for physical development, but for any information in our species. Our brains and memories retrieve information from the field when needed. Although we contain individual identity, characteristics, and knowledge, we also share in the wealth of identity, characteristics, and knowledge of our species.

On the spiritual front, morphic fields could be pointing the way to consciousness beyond the physical, and we can speculate about the existence of nonphysical beings, ghosts, angels, goddesses, and places such as heaven or the Underworld as part of these nonphysical information fields. C. G. Jung's collective consciousness could be one aspect of these energy fields being explored by science.

The Holographic Universe

The last piece of the puzzle was delivered by a quantum physicist named David Bohm. Our brain researcher, Pribram, actually discovered Bohm's work on the advice of his own physicist son. Bohm started studying quantum physics in the 1930s and was fascinated by the interconnected aspect between subatomic particles, though most other scientists gave it little recognition. Through his experiences teaching, writing, and researching, he became dissatisfied with the theories of quantum mechanics and searched for greater understanding. Through various experiences, including exchanges with Albert Einstein, who was also unhappy with the direction of quantum physics, he came to the conclusion that the universe behaved as a vast and complex hologram. Through his study of the degrees of order, he became focused on the fact that beneath our physical reality, what he called the explicate (unfolded) order, was the hidden world of the truer reality, the implicate (enfolded) order. The implicate order is like the holographic film, an interference pattern. When the correct light is shined through it, the implicate order creates the explicate order that we are familiar with. Our perception of objects, and the entire world, is caused by countless unfoldings and enfoldings between the two orders. Bohm published these theories in the early 1970s and then most comprehensively in 1980 in the book *Wholeness and the Implicate Order*. Although many in the scientific world agree with his findings, the holographic universe theory remains controversial.

The philosophical implications of the holographic universe are vast. Our comfortable reality is an illusion created by patterns of energy interacting with our senses, our consciousness. Mystics from the East always called the world the maya, meaning "illusion." Our separateness is an illusion, our oneness the truth. The hologram, where all fragments contain the whole, seems to be the ideal model for this—the witches'— view of the universe. Nonlocal energy fields, extending across time and space, influence us all the time. Our brains, or more importantly, our minds, behave like miniature universes, if a sense of size can even be applied. Nothing is completely individual or isolated, existing in a vacuum. All things are connected. The observer is the observed. We, and the entire world, are all constructs of light, holograms, believing we are solid because we are in the hologram of the universe. We are really energy. Matter, time, and space are all forms of energy.

To the witch, to the mystic, this is no surprise at all, though the words and symbols are new. The underlying principle of spirituality is the connection between all things. Even as we create new models and paradigms to replace quantum physics, holograms, and morphic fields, they continue the general trend of wholeness. Modern research into fractals, infinitely complex patterns that exhibit repeated patterns under greater magnification, and superstring theory, the theory expanding the universe beyond three dimensions of space, follow in the footsteps of describing a vast and complex, yet whole, universe. Ancient myths often speak of a weaver goddess, weaving the universe into form. Perhaps she weaves with "superstrings." These stories, including scientific theory, explain what we know in our spirits.

The most primitive model of the hologram, two systems creating a third, an interference pattern, is the image of the Vesica Pisces (figure 9). The Vesica Pisces is two circles overlapping to create an "eye" or "fish" shape, often drawn alone as a popular Christian symbol. In sacred geometry, the spiritual study of shape and its role in creation, the Vesica Pisces is called the Eye of God, and through it all things are created. The two forces, or polarities as we will later learn, can be viewed as anything: black/white, light/dark, creation/destruction, or chaos/order. Many would say good/evil, but witches see the Goddess and the God as the two patterns of creation. Their love brings about the third pattern, our reality. Our reality is the "eye" of the Vesica Pisces.

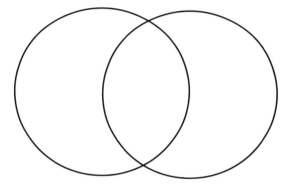

Figure 9: Vesica Pisces

Perhaps the ancients understood the hologram far better than we give them credit for, and we are just rediscovering the spiritual wisdom that we had cast aside because we did not understand.

CONTINUING ASSIGNMENTS

- Daily journal—Write three pages a day.
- Honor and recognize your intuition. Continue to ask it questions.
- Practice the orange meditation.
- Use instant magick in your daily life.

Recommended Reading

The Holographic Universe by Michael Talbot (HarperCollins).

Stalking the Wild Pendulum: On the Mechanics of Consciousness by Itzhak Bentov (Destiny Books).

The Tao of Physics by Fritja Capra (Bantam Books).

LESSON 4
THE SCIENCE OF MAGICK

You don't need to understand how a car works to drive one, and you don't need to study magick theory to do a spell, but magick theory is a science that can be studied. I know many people who have opened a book, done a spell, and had great success with it, but they had no idea how it worked. Magick theory allows serious students of the craft to find an intelligent, sophisticated model of the universe that deals with the use of abilities usually dismissed by mainstream society. Doing a ritual or reciting a spell can seem silly the first time around, but understanding the reasons behind the ritual or chant can lend it credibility. Without this, a portion of our mind is always doubting our magickal actions. Many old superstitions have a basis in metaphysics, but if you do not understand that basis, they continue to be superstitions. Despite popular opinion, witchcraft is not superstitious. The practitioners of this craft have very specific reasons for doing things. An educated witch understands how real magick works in the modern world and can discuss it intelligently even with someone who may not necessarily believe in it.

Since the dawn of civilization, there have been philosophers asking the tough questions, seeking to understand. As cultures developed, these philosophers took up specific disciplines and now ask questions in relationship to science, philosophy, psychology, art, and religion. Until fairly recently, the boundaries between idea, science, and mysticism were not as clear-cut.

The Greek scholar Pythagoras was well versed in many areas, including the occult, geometry, medicine, and poetry. We tend to know Pythagoras for his contributions to geometry and math, but his knowledge and teaching encompassed far more than just math. Even some notable scientists, like Newton, famous for codifying the laws of gravity, were esoterics, studying the mystical as they studied the physical. Many sciences grew out of what are now considered occult traditions. For instance, alchemy birthed the science of chemistry, and astrology is the father of astronomy. But since we live in a culture that tends to elevate the rational, logical, and scientific over the mystical, we have discarded segments of many scholars' work, keeping only the portions relevant to us at this time. Well, if these individuals were so intelligent and gave so many contributions to our modern culture, why do we assume that the material we do not understand or agree with is foolish? Couldn't there possibly be merit in their esoteric studies as well?

These scholars sought to understand the nature of the universe and how humanity interacts with it. In ancient cultures, the use of magick, charms, and psychic abilities was not only well documented, but accepted as fact. Scholars, who often were practitioners of such arts, desired to understand intellectually the evidence right before their eyes, to know intimately how will and intent interacted with certain forces, through symbol, charm, chant, or ingredient, to effect a change. As a result of this quest, occurring in many places in the world, over many eras, various theories and laws were established. These are not laws in the sense of morals of a society, but are similar to the laws of the physical sciences. As an example, gravity worked before anyone used the term "Law of Gravity." Magickal laws are the same. They are statements based on observations that work whether we pay attention to them or not. These laws are some of the best explanations we have for the phenomena of magick, spells, and psychic powers. Since the modern magickal community is not as united as the modern scientific community, there is no general agreement on what exactly these "laws" are, although those who choose to study magick theory come across various texts with the same basic ideas described in a multitude of ways. Because the Christian Church saw many of these texts as heretical, they were often written clouded in symbolism, and were difficult to decipher unless you understood the symbol system. Depending on what tradition and culture of magick you study, you may prefer one form over another. Modern magickal scholars have coined many of their own terms, building on the foundations of the past, to better explain the process of magick. Magick is not a musty old discipline, but a strong growing tree, weaving together branches from the ancient and modern worlds.

The Hermetic Principles

I've read many different variations on Hermetic philosophy, but the version that I most consistently refer to is the one first introduced to me, a book called *The Kybalion*. *The Kybalion* was written anonymously by "three initiates" and published in 1912, but the work within is ascribed to Hermes Trismegistus, or Hermes "thrice great." Who Hermes is, or was, is not generally agreed on. Most recognize him as a great master and teacher of spiritual wisdom, dating back to ancient Greece or Egypt. Some believe he was a god who came down to humanity to teach the arcane arts of alchemy, magick, and philosophy.

His name, Hermes Trismegistus, refers to the Greek god Hermes, known as Mercury to the Romans. Hermes was the messenger of the gods, traveling freely between worlds, in many ways like the shaman traveling to the upper and lower realms. He is well-known for his quick and inventive mind, and credited with giving humankind writing, musical instruments, and commerce.

The Egyptian god Thoth is associated with Hermes. Thoth is known as the scribe of the gods and is one of the oldest and most powerful Egyptian deities. While Hermes kept a youthful image, Thoth was more the archetypical magician, and sometimes appeared as a man with the head of the ibis bird or an ape. In some ways, he acted to the Egyptian pharaoh gods, like Ra, Osiris, and Horus, as Merlin did to King Arthur, as the monarch's advisor and mentor. Perhaps the Greeks were referring to two different gods, using Hermes to refer to the Greek messenger god and using Hermes Trismegistus to refer to the imported Egyptian sage god, hoping to avoid confusion.

No one knows if Hermes Trismegistus was literally a human, or simply a myth that developed around these teachings. Legend tells us that his wisdom was originally written on emerald tablets. In any case, the exact origin does not matter as much as the teachings themselves. The Hermetic texts have gone through many translations, and like the Bible, some argue about how much of the "true" writings remain and what was seeded with the thoughts, ideas, culture, and interpretations of the translators. Much of Western ritual magick, particularly those ritual-magick traditions tracing back to the Golden Dawn, are considered Hermetic traditions, based in part on the writings of Hermes Trismegistus. The word *hermetic* literally means "sealed," as in the medical world. In this case, it can mean "sealed," or "secret knowledge." Since such ritual magicians influenced the development of modern Wicca, the study of these writings and concepts is an important part of the education of a witch.

The seven principles I learned from my teachers and *The Kybalion* were keys to my understanding of magick. Much Hermetic text is shrouded in symbolism and is hard to understand, therefore *The Kybalion* is not easy for the modern reader, but is easier than some other works attributed to Hermes. Once I understood the ideas behind each Hermetic principle, I found that they each had a practical application to my craft. In this chapter, I have included an exercise or meditation to help you better understand each Hermetic principle.

Hermetic magick can more accurately be called Hermetic alchemy, and Hermes Trismegistus was considered a master alchemist. This sort of alchemy does not deal with the transformation of base metals into gold, but the transformation of the practitioner from baser materialistic consciousness to golden enlightenment. These principles give us a structure to understand how we create our own changes, or the transformation of the self. This is the highest art of magick, in any tradition. By coming into our own power, and responsibility to that power, we understand that we are spiritual beings living in a material world, all interdependent on each other.

As you grow to understand each principle separately, you will begin to form a larger picture of the universe, which is not significantly different from the larger picture of quantum physics and holographic theory discussed in the last lesson. Amazingly enough, modern science and ancient philosophy are basically saying the same thing.

THE PRINCIPLE OF MENTALISM

The Principle of Mentalism states that everything in the universe is a "creation of THE ALL." THE ALL is a nongender, nonpantheistic way of referring to the divine, whether you call it God, Goddess, the Source, Tao, Prime Vibration, First Cause, Mother/Father/God, or the Great Spirit. This force is also known as the divine mind.

The Principle of Mentalism tells us that we are all thoughts of the divine mind, existing within the divine mind. The borders of creation are encompassed by the divine mind, and all of creation is permeated with the divine mind. Everything is composed of the same thing—the divine mind. We appear to be separate, but in truth, we are one. In the Hindu tradition, this separation is called the maya, or illusion of the world. Spiritual practices are used to see past the illusion to the truth. In *The Living Gita*, Sri Swami Satchidananda uses this beautiful example: "Water appears to be a wave. But the wave after all is nothing but water. If we see the wave only as a wave, and not as water also, then it's an illusion. We should discriminate: 'Yes, I see it as a wave. Because it rises up, I give the name, wave; but it's the same water rising up.' That's discrimination—seeing the same essence behind all the names and forms."[1]

Imagine your own mind, for a moment, as not only a consciousness within your head, as Westerners tend to visualize it, but as a place. If this place is your mind, you have a lot of control over what is there. You can choose to create a beautiful scene, populate it with characters, change it, or even destroy it. All these things can have detail, depth, and character to them. They are individual, yet part of your greater whole, your mind. Although ultimately you are in charge, these images have a measure of free will. As you dream and daydream, your creations often do the unexpected. The thoughts, feelings, and intentions you have control this mindscape, though the "characters" can take interesting turns.

Now take that model and expand it to the entire universe, all of creation. Remember that both the brain (or mind) and the universe are described as a hologram. They have much in common. Our universe, on every level, *is* the mind of the divine creative being. Everything in it is a thought that the divine has created, just as you do with your

---

1. Sri Swami Satchidananda, *The Living Gita* (Yogaville, VA: Integral Yogi Publications, 1988) 153.

daydreams and visualizations. Just as you create, the divine mind creates, showing us that the nature of the universe is very mental. Therefore, the universe, and everything in it, responds to thoughts because it is composed of the thoughts of the divine. If the divine created us and everything else as a thought, and we are capable of creating our own thoughts, then they, too, are divine and filled with power. The universe and everything in it will respond to our thoughts. Thoughts invested with energy become reality. This is magick.

Creation is an ability and power we share because we are part of the divine. We are all creators on different scales. When we choose to create together, in partnership, there is true magick and power. One of the necessary ingredients of magick is a clear intention, and what is a clear intention if not a clear thought? Learning to project your thoughts out into the world is a primary step to making magick.

Here are some exercises to show you how powerful your thoughts can be and how other objects and people, which are only thoughts in the divine mind, like you, easily respond to your thought energy.

Exercise 13

Mental Projection

Choose an inanimate object to "receive" your mind as you project it. Common items include jewelry, coins, or crystals. I've found natural objects to be easier to work with than plastics and synthetics. Objects made of one material are usually best to start with, rather than combinations of substances. The object does not have to have any special significance to it.

1. Hold the object in your hand and start exercise 9: Counting Down to a Meditative State to get into your magickal mindset.

2. Hold the object in both hands and feel it. Does it feel heavy? Light? Be aware of the object in your hands.

3. Even with your eyes closed, be aware of your thoughts and perceptions. We tend to confuse our mind with our brain, and "think" we are up in our head, even though our mind is throughout our body. But take your perception of

being up in your head, behind your eyes, and feel your sense of awareness slowly move down to the back of your head and your neck. Focus your attention on these places and let the sensation descend to your shoulders. All your awareness is on your shoulders and moving down your arms, as if your mind is traveling down your arms.

4. Continue the movement down your arms and then to your hands and fingers. Your mind keeps moving, from your body and now into the object you are holding in your hands. Feel your mind enter the object and merge with it. Your mind is now part of the object. Your thoughts are now part of the object.

5. Notice your new perceptions. What are you experiencing? What do you see? What do you feel? What do you hear? What do you smell? What do you taste? Can you feel the energy of this object? Can you pick up any information from it? Intend to merge with it.

6. When the experience is complete, feel your mind traveling in the opposite direction, back out of the object and into your hands. Feel yourself travel up your arms and shoulders, back into your head and behind your eyes.

7. Return yourself to normal consciousness, counting up, and giving yourself clearance and balance. Do any necessary grounding.

After doing this exercise, many of my students who have no scientific background accurately describe molecular shapes. Others have a very surreal experience, and when they enter the object, they receive storybook images with symbolic, dreamlike information—the internal structure of the object is a castle, forest, or mountain. Many do not have a visual experience, but feel vibrations, hear noises, and experience gut-level, intuitive flashes.

Once you feel comfortable with this exercise, expand on it. Try many different substances and materials. If you continue on this path and gather ritual tools, you will consecrate them with your intention. Learning to connect with an object mentally is a great asset when consecrating your items. If you have any items on your meditation altar, connect with them.

Next, on the screen of your mind, call up objects that you do not physically have in your possession, but desire to connect with mentally. In exercise 10, you called up onto the screen of your mind an orange. You thought it was a simple visualization exercise, but in truth, it is much easier to connect to the energy of an orange somewhere out in the universe than to create your own. You were actually connecting to the energy of the orange, somewhere across space and time. If you've tried that exercise more than once, you'll notice how it changes. Hold the fruit on the screen of your mind, but instead of observing it visually, project your mind into it as you did in the previous exercise. Try this variation several times, each time calling up a different object. Try fruits, vegetables, crystals, and metals. Touch a wall in your home, and project yourself into the wall, into the building material and the insulated space in between.

The last variation of this exercise is to try using living, cellular material. You've already moved on to fruits and vegetables, which you can do physically or nonphysically. Now try a plant, a living, growing plant. Notice how different living tissue can feel compared to the other material you've used. Lastly, try it on a pet. If you do not have a pet physically with you, or one that will stay near you long enough to try this exercise, call an animal up onto your screen through your intention. Notice how animal tissue feels different from plant tissue. Ultimately though, they are all forms of thought, responding to your thoughts. We are all thoughts in the divine mind.

I have one last exercise to demonstrate the power of thoughts: cloud busting. Cloud busting has gotten a bad rap as New Age nonsense or the power of self-delusion, but for many people, this simple, powerful exercise opens the door to a whole world of psychic and spiritual development. When my student Tom first introduced it to me, I looked at him a little strangely since I had never heard of it before, but he told me how it lead to his spiritual path. Once I tried it, I could understand why. If you don't think your thoughts affect the world, think again.

Cloud busting is exactly what it sounds like, busting or breaking apart clouds with the power of your mind. In modern times the phenomenon is associated with Dr. William Reich and his study of orgone energy. Orgone is the good doctor's take on what mystics have called prana or chi, the subtle energy that flows in and around all things, moving from personal energy to sky or Earth energy and back again. Cloud busting is actually a technique taught in many Eastern and native traditions.

Get a clear view of the sky on a moderately cloudy day. Do your instant magick trigger. State the intention that this be "correct and for the good of all, harming none." Pick a moderate-size, individual cloud. Focus your attention on the center of the cloud. Concentrate all your attention on the intention of making the cloud break apart. Imagine projecting your thoughts out to the cloud to break it apart. Visualize it breaking apart. In your mind, ask it to break apart. Be patient. Within a few minutes, the cloud should break apart. You may not make it disappear completely, but "break off" a piece. This talent improves the more you practice, but it does not always work. Sometimes it is best for a cloud to stay together for the higher good of the local weather patterns.

Cloud busting actually clears the mind. The element of air is the energy of the mind and mental body. By clearing clouds with your thoughts, you are clearing out the feelings, thoughts, and programs that "cloud" your own mind.

The Principle of Correspondence

The Principle of Correspondence states, "As above, so below; as below, so above." This seemingly simple statement contains some of the most important tenets of witchcraft and magick. The whole contains the part, and the part contains the whole. By studying the patterns of the known world, one can apply this knowledge and wisdom to the unknown worlds. The principles of geometry used on small objects in a classroom can be used to measure the vast, almost unknowable distances between planets and across the cosmos. The simple truths and patterns found in the physical world can also be found in the spiritual realms.

Cycles and patterns repeat infinitely, from the largest scale to the smallest scale. Think about the structure of the solar system. You have one large body, the Sun, at the center. Orbiting around this center are several smaller particles, the planets, arranged at regular intervals. Now think on a smaller scale, to the atom. The atom has a nucleus at the center of it. Circling around the nucleus are smaller particles, electrons, spaced at regular intervals. The atom and the solar system are almost maps of each other (figure 10).

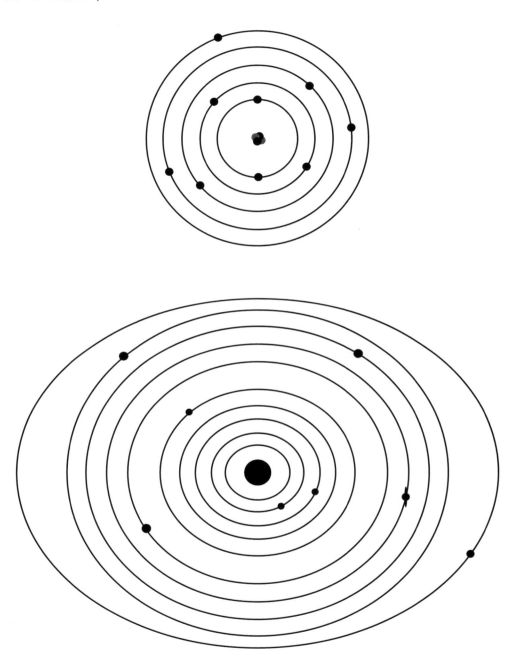

Figure 10: *Atom and Solar System*

Everything contains a map of the cosmos, reflecting the patterns of creation in the smallest scale, what is called the microcosm, and in the largest scale, the macrocosm. Our holographic model of the universe is basically saying the same thing. One part of the hologram contains all of the information and can be used to re-create the whole. A human cell, a small part of a human being, contains all the DNA needed to re-create the entire body. Every speck of dust contains a world. Every galaxy is like an atom, a building block to a bigger structure that we cannot see at the moment.

The analogy between the brain and the universe, both working holographically, is the most remarkable example of patterns repeating from the small to the large. The study of fractals, the repetition of patterns created from mathematical equations, is another example of correspondence. Fractal shapes are not only seen in computer-generated graphics, but throughout nature in the shape of snowflakes and shorelines.

The Principle of Correspondence is also important to witches because it allows us to compile lists of correspondences to use in magick. Although the hologram tells us that everything contains everything else, the entire model in a single part, magick tells us that certain specific relationships have different kinds of power. Witches use their understanding of these correspondences to create rituals, spells, and potions. The hologram is made of light, and that light can be broken down, divided into the spectrum of colors through the use of a prism. The energies of the holographic universe can be divided as well. The energy within individual substances, colors, planets, elements, days of the week, and ritual tools corresponds with specific energies of the universe. When you want to emphasize a particular energy for your magick, you utilize items that correspond with that energy.

Many different systems exist to divide and subdivide the energies of the universe. As usual, no one system is correct; they are all different views of the same thing, and most work together on some level. Have you ever noticed how some colors evoke certain feelings? Red may make you angry. Green is more alive and vital, yet happy. Blue calms you down. There is a psychology of color because each color corresponds to certain feelings, intentions, and energies.

The same holds true with musical notes, but we do not pay as much attention to individual tones in this society as we do to individual colors. In fact, music may be one of the best examples of the Principle of Correspondence in action. Music is divided into repeating sets of notes. Each set of notes is a scale. The most familiar scale is made of seven notes and sung in children's songs as Do, Re, Me, Fa, So, La, Ti, and then Do repeats. The notes themselves are called C, D, E, F, G, A, B, and C. This series of seven notes repeats over and over again. One person may sing the low C and another the higher C. It is the same note, repeated in a different range. This is called an octave. The Principle of Correspondence is like these octaves, repeating patterns in different ranges. Because energy that can be heard has a lower vibration than the energy of visible light, the scale of seven notes is like a lower octave to the spectrum of seven colors. Perhaps other unseen energies, such as those of the electromagnetic spectrum, are "octaves" to the ones we can see and hear.

Color and sound are one way of building a correspondence system. Some people build correspondence systems based on the four elements: earth, air, fire, and water. The properties of fire are energy, passion, lust, and protection. If you wanted to do a protection ritual involving fire, you might use the colors red and orange, a sword, red roses, or a ruby. They all correspond to fire. Others build a system from astrology. The same spell would probably be based on the planet Mars, a fire planet, named after the god of war. Mars energy is good for protection and aggression. Its color is also red. Many of the correspondences of fire fit Mars. Each system works.

A system of correspondence used in herbalism is called the Doctrine of Signatures. Though credited to Paracelsus, and alluded to in the second century c.e. in the writings of Galen, the basic idea is found all over the world. Since witchcraft is based in a tradition of healers and herbalists, the doctrine is quite appropriate here. The herbalist looks for correspondences of shape, color, texture, and growing season to both the human body and to the elements. The energies of the plant world, formerly unknown, can be applied to the human world for healing. Lungwort has lung-shaped leaves and is used for respiratory ailments. The roots of Solomon's seal look like tendons and are used to either tighten or loosen tendons and ligaments. Hawthorn berries are red, which is the color associated with the heart and blood, and hawthorn is used for the heart. Yellow color (jaundice) is a sign of liver dysfunction. Dandelion has yellow flowers, and it is used to heal the liver. By listening to the language of correspondence, you can uncover many secrets in the unknown worlds.

EXERCISE 14

Correspondences

1. Start exercise 9: Counting Down to a Meditative State to get into your magickal mindset.

2. Imagine in your mind's eye an egg. It can be any kind of animal egg. As in the orange exercise, examine the egg. Pull it down and visualize yourself holding the egg, feeling its texture, temperature, and any other details that come to mind. Do not break it open.

3. As in exercise 13: Mental Projection, project your mind into the egg. Feel yourself enter the egg. First you go through the hard outer shell and penetrate the egg. Notice the egg white, the layer between the center and the shell. Feel it. Move through it. Move toward the center. Enter the third section, the egg yolk. Feel the egg yolk, the center, the core of the egg.

4. If this egg is carrying life, there would be at least one living cell in the center. Project yourself to this cell. See the cell before you as you travel toward it. Penetrate the cell membrane, the cell wall, and enter the cell. Feel the liquid of the cell as you move toward the nucleus. Enter the nucleus and take note of the double helix, the spiraling DNA of the cell.

5. Know that the molecules of DNA are made up of smaller blocks called atoms. Project your consciousness down to this level and feel the atom there before you. On the edge of this single atom is the electron cloud, the energetic, mistlike zone of electrons circling the center. Move through the different orbits, layers of electrons, to enter the nucleus. Observe the atom from the inside out. Look at all the different parts and levels to it.

6. Know that this atom is like all the atoms in everyone. It is similar to every atom on the planet, even the atoms in the core of the Earth. Imagine that you are looking at an atom in the core of the Earth, and expand your consciousness outward. Project yourself outward. Notice the molten core of the planet, and as you exit the core, you enter what is called the mantle, a

thick layer of molten rock flowing around the core. Expand your consciousness through the mantle. Enter the curst of the Earth, a thinner layer of rock and soil. On top of the crust, there are rivers, oceans, winds, people, and even waves of energy, all moving about on the planet.

7. Expand your view beyond the Earth. Take note of the Moon orbiting the Earth. See the Earth orbiting the Sun. Notice the Sun's movement in the spiraling arm of the galaxy. Recognize the similarities, all the correspondences, on all levels of creation, and understand that there is a pattern to this creation. Know that you are connected to something greater, a larger whole, the pattern of life.

8. When the experience is complete, feel your consciousness slowly move back to your physical body, back on the Earth.

9. Return yourself to normal consciousness, counting up, and giving yourself clearance and balance. Do any necessary grounding.

The Principle of Vibration

The Principle of Vibration states, "Nothing rests; everything moves; everything vibrates." Everything is always moving, vibrating, all the time. Even when something looks like it is staying still, it is not. The Hermetic philosophers knew this thousands of years ago, but science has only recently caught up. Prior to the discovery of atoms, physical matter appeared to be stationary, unmoving. Except for living beings with cellular movement, inanimate matter looked to be still. Once the atom was discovered, we understood solid matter to be tiny packets of empty space, where small particles constantly rotate around a center particle. These tiny particles, electrons, are always moving, always rotating, always vibrating. Even when something was "perfectly still," these little particles were moving. How did the philosophers know this without knowing about that atom?

The power of the Principle of Vibration comes from not only understanding that physical matter is always vibrating, but that everything is vibrating, even the nonphysical. In fact, the differences between matter, energy, and spirit are different vibrations.

Matter is a denser, more solid vibration than energy. Energy that can be physically recorded by machines is considered to be a denser vibration than spirit. The physical sciences tend to acknowledge only the physical vibrations, but as we are learning with quantum physics, we are more than our physical vibration. We also contain energy and spiritual vibrations. Understanding how they work and how to control them is an important part of witchcraft.

Have you ever met someone you just did not like, or gone to a place that made you uncomfortable? We tend to say it was "bad vibes," thinking that these words are a figure of speech, but they are true. You are literally picking up on the energy, the vibration, broadcast by a person or place. By knowing this, you can consciously put out "good vibes" to change the energy of a situation. Your thoughts, emotions, and intentions all carry a vibration, and by consciously changing that vibration, you can have a profound effect on your reality. Similar vibrations tend to resonate and gather together. That is why you may be drawn to particular people or places in your life. Likewise, you draw the things that resonate with the vibrations you send out. If you put out vibrations connected with happiness, health, and prosperity, you draw more of the same. If you vibrate anger, illness, or unhappiness, you attract events and people with those vibrations.

Mystics from many traditions talk about vibration, and increasing your vibration to a more spiritual level as a part of the mystic's path. Cleansing incenses are burned to raise the vibration of a ritual or temple. The realm of vibrational healing—using intent, energy, and the vibrations of natural substance such as flower essences and crystals—is fast becoming a part of alternative medicine.

This next exercise helps you consciously control your vibration. You do not need to be scientific about it. You do not need to know anything technical like the frequency or wavelength of your vibration. There are no visuals to this meditation. You only need to know your intent. With what do you intend to vibrate? Think of a quality you wish to possess or think of your affirmations. Affirmations are ways of changing your vibration. You have already done this work without focusing on the vibrational aspect. Think of an energy you wish to contact. Some examples include total health, prosperity, unconditional love, inspiration, or Mother Earth, the Goddess, the God, a place, planet, color, or any of the four elements. Choose one that speaks to you. That will be your mantra for your vibrational statement.

EXERCISE 15

Vibrational Statements

1. Start exercise 9: Counting Down to a Meditative State to get into your magickal mindset.

2. Tell yourself, "I wish to vibrate in harmony with . . ." and fill in your energy or quality. Repeat this mantra nine times, and then relax and feel. Notice the change occurring in your energy, your vibration.

3. If you do not feel anything, repeat the statement again nine times, and feel. Continue with this process and notice the shifts that occur. If you don't feel much after several attempts, you may already have the vibrational quality in you. Try another statement connected to an issue or area you are struggling with.

4. Return yourself to normal consciousness, counting up, and giving yourself clearance and balance. Do any necessary grounding.

You may notice during this exercise, or any time you are exercising your magickal abilities through meditation or ritual, that there is a slight noise or hum. It is not a constant sound, and I don't hear it every time I do magick, but I do hear it often, especially when I am in a group setting. I have heard it all my life at different points. I used to think that I was going deaf, because I listened to loud music and played in a rock band, but not many of my musician friends heard it. Once I started going to pagan gatherings, I realized that others heard it. My friends and I surmised that it was some sort of Earth energy we were hearing. It wasn't until I taught classes that I noticed that it was the most noticeable in groups, and we only heard it when we were doing magickal exercises. I truly believe now that we are "hearing" those spiritual vibrations, like glimpsing something out of the corner of your eye. In the Hindu traditions, this is the sound of Om, the sound of creation. Hearing it can be a sound of spiritual awakening. The pitch deepens over time and with spiritual development. To me it is the Principle of Vibration in action. Don't try to hear it if you don't already. That is not the point of the exercises. But if you do hear something, don't be alarmed. You are listening to vibration.

THE PRINCIPLE OF POLARITY

From *The Kybalion,* the Hermetic student is told, "Everything is dual; everything has poles; everything has its pair of opposites." The understanding of polarity, or pairs of opposites, is very important in magick, and in witchcraft, in particular, because witches desire to find harmony between the extremes.

Everything can be divided into two poles, but the trick to the Principle of Polarity is to understand that poles are not everything, but a range of responses falls between the poles. Any description of two opposites is never absolute. It is a relative description that must be compared to something else. What is hard? It is difficult to describe unless you use an example, or compare it to something soft. Using the pair of opposites, hard and soft, how would you describe a feather? Most would say soft. Then describe a piece of chalk. Compared to the feather, it is hard. Compared to steel, chalk is soft. Hard and soft are not absolutes, but relative degrees on a larger scale. We can change all our perceptions of polarities by using the same mental gymnastics. As the intent in our mind changes, the actual energy changes in our life. Each polarity contains the essence of the opposite, like the Yin-Yang figure (figure 11).

Figure 11: *Yin-Yang*

One unfortunate view in the Law of Polarity is to lump together all the ends of several different spectrums. For example, we tend to equate the words *light, day, positive, good,* and *male.* On the other hand, we equate the words *dark, night, negative, evil,* and *feminine* (figure 12). Although some of these words have obvious associations, such as *dark* and *night,* they are not synonymous. I'm convinced that such a shift in consciousness occurred in our culture in an effort to simplify the complex nuances of the natural world, particularly as the organized religions dominated Europe. I am all for simplicity, but not when it equates dark with evil. I love the dark. Many dark goddesses are loving and sacred to me, and by no means evil. It is easier to give a group of people you seek to control only two choices, all black or all white, with us or against us, rather than give them a range of possibilities to find what is correct and good for the individual. We must realize that there are many spokes to the wheel of polarity, and lumping them together does not serve our greatest good as witches. The eyes of the witch do not recognize only black and white, nor only the shades of gray in between, but the whole spectrum of color found amid the dark and light.

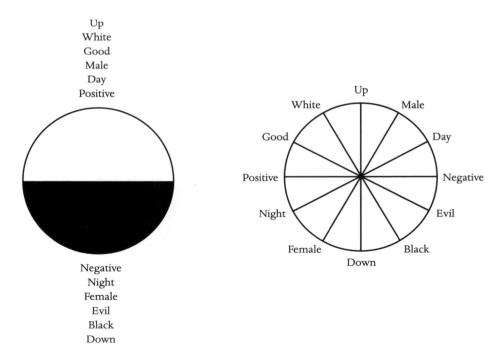

Figure 12: Polarity Wheels

Precision in word and thought is essential in magick. Notice how *negative* is used to mean a "bad" attribute, while *positive* is used to mean something "good" or "desired." We all generally accept these definitions, but they are not accurate in a scientific sense. If you are studying the spirituality, art, and science of witchcraft, you must pay attention to all definitions. *Positive* refers to a positive electrical charge, while *negative* refers to a negative electrical charge. Someone in the scientific world decided that a certain type of charge was negative and named it so. Using *positive* and *negative* to mean "good" and "bad," respectively, causes problems later on down the road, even though it is so common.

Ions are electrically charged particles found in the environment. When you go to a place with churning water—an ocean, a waterfall, or even a bath or indoor fountain— you are taking in ions that make you feel good. Electrically, they are negatively charged ions, yet they promote health and relaxation. You may feel sluggish or sick when you spend a lot of time around electrical equipment, particularly computer monitors, televisions, and microwave ovens. That is because you are absorbing another type of ion that promotes these feelings, positive ions. When you intend to banish all "negative energy," are you banishing negative ions? When you call all "positive energy" into your life, are you calling positive ions, too? Even though you don't mean it that way, your words betray you. If you are banishing all harm, say you are banishing all harm, not just the negative. Your thoughts and words are powerful, and must be precise.

From our discussion of polarity and positive/negative attributes, we come to the concept of balance. This balance is a key point in the Cabot tradition of witchcraft that I learned. Something is only "good" for you, what others call "positive," because it helps you maintain a healthy balance. If the same substance takes you out of balance, it is no longer "positive." If you take a medicine once a day to treat a particular condition, you may call that a "positive" effect. If you decide such "positive" things are only good for you, and decide to take a whole bottle of medicine at once, you have changed a "positive" substance into a "negative" one, making yourself sick. Again, there are no absolutes. Almost any given substance or energy can be helpful or hurtful depending on the situation and your specific needs.

In the book *Initiation,* by Elizabeth B. Jenkins, the Andean priest-teacher Juan Nunez del Prado reveals that "within the world of living energies no positive or negative energies exist. There are only graduations of more subtle and refined living energies and energies that are more dense or heavy . . ."[2] "Remember that 'heavy' is not 'bad.' Besides, what is heavy energy to you could be refined energy to someone else."[3] Energy exists in graduated scales, not absolutes.

One of the most important polarities in witchcraft is the polarity of the Earth and sky. Earth is grounding, material, physical, and emotional, and is associated with the Goddess energy. Sky energy is considered more intellectual, logical yet creative, mental, expressive, and electric, and is associated with the energy of the God. Finding a balance between the two energies is important. This next exercise helps balance all the polarities in you, helping you realize that pairs of opposites within you are different degrees on a scale. By acknowledging this scale, you have the ability to gently move traits and energies you don't like to another part of the scale, transmuting yourself. This is the true art of Hermetic magick, of Western alchemy: to transform the mind, emotions, and spirit.

Exercise 16
Polarity of the Earth and Sky

1. Start exercise 9: Counting Down to a Meditative State to get into your magickal mindset. If you have a particular personal attribute you wish to transmute, think of it now and hold that intention for a few moments.

2. Visualize a beam of light extending down from your spine, grounding you down to the Earth like the roots of a tree, or a balloon tied down. The beam of light is hollow like a straw, and you can draw energy up and down it. The beam connects you to the center of the Earth. As you inhale, hold the intention of drawing up the Earth energy, like sucking up a straw. In your mind, ask Mother Earth to send her energy up to you. With each inhalation, the energy moves further and further up the beam of light.

---

2. Elizabeth B. Jenkins, *Initiation* (New York: Berkeley Press, 1997) 131.

3. Ibid., 137.

3. Feel the energy rise up through the beam of light. Some visualize it as green, brown, black, or blue. It may move quickly or slowly. Feel it reach the base of your spine and flow upward, through your body. Feel the Earth energy move through your belly and up into your chest. Feel it energize your body. Feel it flow through your neck and into your head, and out the crown. Feel the beam of light extend upward, connecting you to the sky.

4. While the Earth energy still flows upward, feel the energy of the sky flow down as you inhale, like water. At first it may be a trickle, or flow like a flood. Let it descend down the beam of light and into your crown. The sky energy flows much faster than the Earth energy, down through your head and neck, through your chest and heart space into your belly, to the base of your spine and down into the Earth.

5. Feel yourself in balance with these two energies. They are not static poles, but free-flowing, living energies. Release your own rigid polarities, the things you wish to transmute, and allow them to flow with you.

6. Slow down the flow with your intent, and allow the remaining Earth energy to flow upward and out, and the remaining sky energy to flow down and out into the Earth, helping ground you.

7. Return yourself to normal consciousness, counting up, and giving yourself clearance and balance. Do any necessary grounding.

Another polarity-balancing exercise I find useful is the scales meditation. You can experiment with it and try it on your own. First think about the different polarities in your life, aspects needing balance. Then count yourself down to a magickal mindset and visualize a hanging scale, like the scales of justice. They are unbalanced because you are in need of balancing. Visualize yourself moving the weights of the scale from side to side until you balance the scales (figure 13). Some of the weights will be objects from your life, symbols of things you need to balance, get more of, or discard. Usually the left side is emotional and personal aspects, while the right is more logical and public issues. Be creative in your scale balancing.

Figure 13: Scales

THE PRINCIPLE OF RHYTHM

With our discussion of polarity, we know that energy has a range and it can move from one extreme to the other, flowing freely. The Principle of Rhythm tells us how it flows: "Everything flows, out and in; everything has its tides . . ." All patterns move in a cycle. As energy moves from one pole to the next, it is actually tracing a circular movement, with its own schedule and pattern, or tide.

Learning to recognize the tides of natural energy is an important part of witchcraft. The seasons are natural cycles honored by most tribal, Earth-loving people. Certain times of the year express a different kind of power than other seasons. Feelings, moods, and even health are altered by the seasons, because of the energy embodied by each turn of the year.

Everything and everyone has their own turn of seasons, or cycles. The ocean tides have a cycle that coincides with the movements of the Moon. The Earth's cycle around the Sun creates a natural rhythm of the seasons. Such movements cause cyclical weather patterns. We forget that the Sun is also moving and creates its own rhythm. The Hindu people call the Sun's, or solar system's, great epochs *yugas*, and each yuga has a different flavor and different correspondences for those living on Earth. The Sun also goes through a sunspot cycle that affects the Earth. Scientists only recently understood it, but the Mayan calendar predicts such activity with accuracy. The ancient Mayans knew the rhythms of the world around them.

The most important rhythms to be aware of are the cycles within yourself. People have their own seasons, too. Women go through a profound cyclical shift every twenty-eight days, and go through the larger cycles of entering womanhood at the onset of menstruation and then entering a season of elderhood at menopause. Although the hormonal cycle of men is not as physically dramatic, they, too, experience internal, chemical rhythms as well.

Have you ever noticed how certain seasons empower you while others debilitate you? Each season is different for different people. Spring is a time of revitalization for most, a time of rebirth, but if you suffer from allergies, an oversensitivity to these energies, you might not feel too empowered by the spring. Likewise, most people dislike the cold of winter, but others thrive when participating in winter sports and outdoor activities. Many people suffer from actual diagnosed seasonal dysfunction, particularly due to the lack of light during the winter months. But everyone has a point in the year when they feel empowered, stronger, more balanced, and in tune. For many it is the month of their birth. They feel excitement for their birthday, which puts them in a good mood. Metaphysically, the effect comes from the Sun being in your personal Sun sign, the sign it was in when you were born.

Not only is this awareness of your own personal cycles an important aspect of "Know thyself," and introspection, but it is far easier to work your magick within your own cycles than to change a cycle that is outside of you. As a sovereign being, you have greater control over your own rhythms. Why swim upstream when the water is flowing at its peak? You know you can wait a bit and find only a trickle.

Being in tune with the rhythms of a particular season, month, Moon, and your own self can make your magick easier or harder. Psychic abilities are easier to access at the Full Moon. The Full Moon amplifies our psychic and astral selves, but it also heightens emotions. The word *lunacy* comes from *lunar*, meaning people get a little crazy around the Full Moon. Anyone who works with the public, with children, or in the medical profession can attest to the power of the Moon. I used to work in customer service, and would mark my calendar and try to plan my days off at the Full Moon.

The following exercise is to help you understand that you have a measure of control over your own rhythms and cycles. You have already controlled the rhythms of your brain waves, breath, and pulse. Through intention, you are going to control your heart rate. The goal here is not the dramatic results many Eastern mystics achieve, lowering the heart rate to a deathlike state. You are just going to gently slow down and speed up your heart rate, and then return it to normal. The range will be well within the normal, healthy heartbeat range, slowing down to only the level of sleep. If this prospect makes you nervous, then please follow your intuition and do not do anything that makes you uncomfortable. Use your own discretion, particularly if you have any heart-related medical conditions.

EXERCISE 17

Heartbeat Control

1. Start exercise 9: Counting Down to a Meditative State to get into your magickal mindset. Ask that this be for your highest good, harming none.

2. Feel your heartbeat, nice and relaxed, slow and steady. Feel the pulse of it move through your body. Feel and know your natural rhythm. You can physically put your hand on your chest or neck to feel your pulse better.

3. With just your simple intention, imagine your heartbeat getting faster, more excited, but keeping within a normal, safe range. Imagine yourself receiving good, exciting news. Feel your heart rate rise slowly. Feel the shift.

4. Then though intention, imagine your heartbeat getting slower, more relaxed. It stays within normal range, but at the level it goes to during peaceful, restful sleep. Feel the slow, steady, yet relaxed heartbeat. Feel the shift from excited to peaceful.

5. Intend that your heart rate return to the level that is correct and good for you at this time. Take notice of the shift. Does it get faster or slower? Relax and allow.

6. Return yourself to normal consciousness, counting up, and giving yourself clearance and balance. Do any necessary grounding.

THE PRINCIPLE OF GENDER

The Principle of Polarity gave us many different pairs of opposites, but the Principle of Gender focuses on one important pair, masculine and feminine. In *The Kybalion*, this principle is introduced with the words "Gender is in everything; everything has its Masculine and Feminine Principles." Masculine and feminine energies, traits, and characteristics are found in everything. Witches recognize the divine as a feminine goddess energy interplaying with a masculine god energy, to create all life, like the overlapping patterns of the hologram.

Part of a healthy, well-balanced life is recognizing the masculine and feminine within yourself, and honoring both. No man is 100 percent masculine energy, or he would be beyond the worst male stereotypes. Likewise, no woman is wholly feminine energy. We each have a unique balance between the two, making us who we are. In general, masculine energy is attributed to the more logical, rational, aggressive, and physical traits. Feminine energy is ascribed to the intuitive, creative, healing, and emotional traits, although there is much debate in our society as to what is really a feminine or masculine trait. Depending on the historical time period, those labels could be different, even reversed. The label does not matter, but the concept does. Everyone has these two forces, creative, expressive energies, and for your own well-being, you must be able to use both. In ancient times, those who had an unusual mix of such energies, particularly lesbians and gays, were honored as healers and shamans in various tribal cultures.

The Principle of Gender tells us that gender is in everything. Gender is easy to see physically in living beings, but could it be in everything? I questioned the existence of gender in my chair, my computer, or the architecture of a building. "Where is the gender in inanimate objects?" I asked. Then someone pointed out that shape and contour, texture and color, give us a sense of gender. Objects and buildings made with many straight, unbending lines and sharp edges give us a masculine sense, because the energy is very linear. Those with curved lines and rounded shapes evoke a more feminine sense, much like the curves of a woman. Soft textures again evoke feminine, motherly images, while harder textures are seen as more masculine. Gender really is in everything. If witches believe that the patterns of the hologram are the energy of the Goddess and God, then why shouldn't everything express their love and union?

In witchcraft, many mystical symbols are ascribed to the masculine or feminine. Traditionally, the Moon is associated with the Goddess. The Moon moves through phases as the Triple Goddess, moving from Maiden to Mother to Crone as the Moon moves from New to Full to Dark. The Sun is considered part of the God; as a light and life giver, his rays help Mother Earth bloom with life. The following meditation helps you connect to the masculine and feminine energies of the Sun and Moon.

EXERCISE 18

Sun and Moon

1. Start exercise 9: Counting Down to a Meditative State to get into your magickal mindset.

2. In your mind's eye, on your magickal screen, invite the image of a beautiful green field at dawn to appear. The grass is lush and moist with dew. The birds are waking up with song.

3. Step through the screen as if you were stepping through a door or window, and stand in the field. You are facing east, and the Sun's beams are rising over the horizon. You can feel and see the light as the Sun rises.

4. As if on fast-forward, the Sun quickly rises in the sky and continues on its arc. You feel the warmth, heat, and light. You feel energies, absorbing the power through your skin. You feel the power of the God, rising in the light, protective yet inviting.

5. When the Sun reaches its apex above you, the noon point, a beam of solar light like liquid sunshine descends down, entering your crown and descending through your body into the Earth. The energy fills your body, each and every cell. You feel completely energized. Your mind is sharp and clear, creative and in balance. Your physical body feels strong and healthy.

6. The Sun continues on its arc and begins to set. In the east, you see the Full Moon rise in the dimming light. The darkness falls as the Sun sets, and the night sky is illuminated with stars. They shine like jewels. The glowing orb of the Moon lights up the field with silver white light, illuminating your skin. Feel the power of the Goddess, powerful yet soft, gentle, and loving.

7. When the Moon reaches its apex above you, at the midnight position, the orb slowly descends down around you, enveloping you in a sphere of silver light. Feel the power of the Goddess enter every fiber of your being. Feel it heal you and soothe your emotions. Feel your own natural psychic abilities awaken even further. Soak up these powerful energies.

8. When the experience is complete, the Moon rises back up and continues its ride across the sky, heading west, toward the horizon. Feel the energies of the Sun and Moon, God and Goddess, balance you and your inner masculine and feminine energies. Feel yourself in harmony with all. When the Moon sets and it is the twilight between night and day, imagine yourself stepping back through the screen of your mind and returning to your physical body.

9. Return yourself to normal consciousness, counting up, and giving yourself clearance and balance. Do any necessary grounding.

THE PRINCIPLE OF CAUSE AND EFFECT

The last of the seven Hermetic principles seems the most scientific. The Principle of Cause and Effect states, "Every cause has its effect; every effect has its cause . . ." When I first heard this, it sounded to me like something from physics class: "Every action has an equal and opposite reaction." As I studied both science and metaphysics, I eventually found the Hermetic definition more useful in my life.

This axiom reminds us that nothing happens by sheer chance. Many things that seem like coincidences have a cause somewhere. The cause may not be physical in nature, but mental or magickal, but it is nonetheless a cause. Often the effect of one action becomes the cause of another, creating a chain of events. Everything that happens not only in your life, but in everyone's life, happens for a reason, has a root somewhere. Every action you take, every thought and feeling you have, causes an effect, to you or to someone/something else. If your every action has a result, you must be careful, and accept responsibility for everything you do.

I originally thought our traditional physics "equal and opposite" law to be more accurate, because it was more specific. I later found out that many metaphysical schools of thought believe that the energy of our thoughts, intentions, and actions are amplified in the universe, and when they return, they return with more strength. All energy eventually returns to its source, but the journey adds inertia to it, making its effects much more widespread. That is why a simple spell with little effort can have great results. Modern witches call this the Law of Three, meaning whatever energy you send out into the universe, it will return to you threefold, or three times as strong. I've found the three to be a bit arbitrary. When you have joy return to you, how do you measure threefold? When you have pain return to you, it may feel like it is tenfold. The important thing to know is that the energy is always amplified.

There is no judgment to this process of cause and effect. There is no punishment or reward any more than there is a moral code to science. Whatever you put out comes back amplified. Many witches will attest to this, particularly when something unwanted comes back threefold. Once you make that mistake, you learn not to do it again. Some think of this as karma. We will explore thoughts on karma when we delve into the lesson on past lives in chapter 16.

In the culmination of the Hermetic principles we have the basic philosophies of Wicca. There is no moral judgment of right and wrong, or good and evil. Witchcraft is based on the concepts of balance, harmony, and cyclical change. There is no moral code of "thou shall" and "thou shall not." There is only one simple code of behavior called the Wiccan Rede. The Rede comes in many forms and names throughout magickal traditions, but the way I was taught is simply, "Do what thou will, and let it harm none." Some take it to mean that you can do anything you like, with no consequences, because it's now "part of your religion." That is not what the Wiccan Rede says. You can do whatever you want, but you must accept the consequences of your actions. The best guide you can use is to harm none. If you harm none, no harm will be returned to you. My Christian friends and students are always so surprised to find how close the Wiccan Rede is to the Golden Rule: "Do onto others as you would have them do unto you." In essence, both are saying the same thing. An extended version of the Wiccan Rede is taught by some covens:

Bide the Wiccan Law ye must
In perfect love and perfect trust.
Eight words the Wiccan Rede fulfill:
An' ye harm none, do what ye will.

What ye send forth comes back to thee
So ever mind the Law of Three.
Follow this with mind and heart,
Merry ye meet and merry ye part.

Any action you take is an exercise in the Principle of Cause and Effect, but for this specific meditation, we are going to work with the cycles of a tree: the effect the seasons have on the tree, and the tree's effect on the environment around it.

EXERCISE 19

Tree Meditation

1. Start exercise 9: Counting Down to a Meditative State to get into your magickal mindset.

2. In your mind's eye, invite the image of a deciduous tree to appear, such as an oak or maple. You are seeking a tree that sheds its leaves in the winter. Just like the orange, feel it take form on your screen.

3. Project your consciousness into the tree, as you did with various objects, physical and nonphysical, in exercise 13. Become one with the tree.

4. The season is spring. Feel the warm Sun shine down upon you. The energy of the Sun awakens you to the world. Feel your sap move through the main trunk. Feel the rain of the early spring showers. Feel the water collect around your roots as you drink it in. Absorb the nutrients and minerals in the soil beneath you. The soil is fresh from all the decaying leaves of winter. Feel the spark of life rejuvenate within you. Feel the buds form at the end of your branches and grow into small leaves.

5. Spring moves into summer as the Sun's light grows brighter and warmer. The light of the Sun activates your cells, transforming light and carbon dioxide into your food. Feel your leaves grow bigger and greener. Feel yourself release oxygen, providing for all the living animals around you. Feel the birds within your branches and the insects crawling around your bark. None cause you any harm. This is exactly as it should be.

6. Summer changes to fall as the Sun's light cools down. The days are still warm, but your energy has peaked. Your sap is running a bit slower. Your leaves are starting to wilt and change color. Feel the rainbow of colors in your leaves. Notice that there are not as many birds around, but the squirrels are diligently busy collecting acorns. You may be making your seeds, acorns perhaps, and preparing to release them. Your leaves and seeds fall to the ground, and your branches are becoming bare once more.

7. Fall shifts into winter as the Sun seems to hide behind the clouds. Everything slows down. You move slower. The world seems to move slower. The air grows colder and you find yourself slipping into a deeper and deeper sleep, a hibernation. You await the spring.

8. Project your consciousness out of the tree, back through the magickal screen and into your body. As the Sun, water, and Earth all have an effect on

the tree, aiding in its changes and growth, realize that your own changes and growth are the effects from many different sources in your life.

9. Return yourself to normal consciousness, counting up, and giving yourself clearance and balance. Do any necessary grounding.

NEUTRALIZATION

Telling ourselves that we must take responsibility for our actions is one thing, but doing it on a daily basis is quite another, particularly if we were not raised in an environment that encouraged such behavior. We all carry around little programs that influence us, the instructions based on our learned behaviors. One way of combating these programs is through our use of affirmation. Another way is to actively deprogram and reprogram ourselves through neutralization.

We can never take back anything we say. If you are ever in a heated argument, you know this. Once it is out of your mouth, it is into the universe for all to hear and react to, as in the Principle of Cause and Effect. The only way we can stop the damage of our words, in a metaphysical sense at least, is to neutralize all harmful words, intentions, and energy. Neutralization is a mental process whereby we consciously send a thought out to ground and cleanse our previous actions. It is as easy as saying "I neutralize that," or imagining an X over any image you hold in your mind. I used to think that neutralization was exclusive to witchcraft, but I have found that reiki masters, shamans, and tarot readers often use this technique as well.

Before I got involved in witchcraft, in college, I used to say "Drop dead" to the people who were annoying me. I meant no harm by it, but through my studies I soon realized that I was responsible for those thoughts, and if something harmful did happen, I would have a part in it. But using the phrase was a habit. I said it without thinking. The lack of thought did not relieve me of my responsibility; in fact, it made it even more important to cleanse myself of these habitual thought patterns.

We all say things unintentionally that do harm, ranging from insults to gossip to malice. It is hard not to get angry when someone wrongs you, but the trick is to express that anger in a healthy way. Tell the person you are angry and get it out, but do not wish harm on anyone. That only brings more harm to you, physically or spiritually.

The next time you say something you regret, follow it, either out loud or silently, with "I neutralize that." I know a wonderful woman named Linda who told me that she says "Cancel, clear." Her intent is to cancel the last thought, and reset herself. If you imagine something unwanted, visualize a white X across the image, or a stamp that says "Cancel." If you do this every time, you will reprogram yourself to release and heal those patterns. I never say "Drop dead" anymore. I can't even imagine it, but I get a laugh out of telling that story. I never thought witchcraft would bring such a fundamental change in my speech, but it did.

A student of mine, Ann, told me a wonderful quotation from an Islamic proverb found in *The Mantram Handbook* by Eknath Easwaran. At first I thought, Islam and Wicca have nothing in common, but with this proverb, I see a common thread. According to an Islamic proverb, each word we utter should have to pass through three gates before we say it. At the first gate, the gatekeeper asks, "Is it true?" At the second gate, he asks, "Is it necessary?" and at the third gate, "Is it kind?" Mythology and shamanic initiations are filled with images of gateways to the Underworld. If we watch the three gates, we never have to worry about neutralizing harmful thoughts.

It should be clear by now that you should never use magick to harm another person intentionally, although there are times when it is tempting to do so. As you learn instant magick, spells, charms, and rituals, you will often want to use these tools when feeling powerless against someone. You are not restricted to neutralizing your own harmful thoughts, but can neutralize the thoughts of others directed toward you. If you feel that someone, magickal or otherwise, intends you harm or speaks badly of you, neutralize it. Never try to send back "bad" energy directed toward you. Neutralize it. That is the responsible way to handle it.

For those who get flashes of harm in their mind right before it happens, it is difficult to distinguish a precognitive flash from subconsciously causing harm. I suggest neutralization in either case. If the events and accidents still occur, I would ask, while in meditation, to know the reason that I am seeing such images, and for more "advanced warning" if I am to use this information to prevent the harm.

OTHER MAGICKAL LAWS

The Hermetic principles are by no means the only system of magickal theory available to a prospective magickal student. They were the first I learned, and I find them to be a most helpful and complete system, but I've taken a shine to a few additional laws that have also helped me. In essence, I think that they are all different ways of saying the same things, but one version might work better for you than another. Magickal laws and paradigms are designed to explain the unexplainable to our rational, linear mind. The more we think we have a conscious understanding of everything, the less likely our conscious mind will hinder our magickal progress. A balance between intuitive knowing and logical thinking must be reached. Metaphysics with no basis or understanding becomes stereotypical New Age babble, but relying too heavily on theory makes magick the province of the laboratory. As with most things, I prefer the middle road.

Here are some additional magickal axioms that I have found useful.

THE LAW OF SYNCHRONICITY

Synchronicity describes two meaningful coincidences that are not *apparently* linked through the Principle of Cause and Effect. The link between the two is through the meaning of such events. Pulling tarot cards that accurately describe the events in your current life would be a synchronous event. In no way does the act of pulling the cards seem to influence your life, or vice versa, but how they coincide can lead to greater meaning and insight when joined together.

Synchronicity is a word coined by Carl Jung to describe such coincidences. His law is called the Principle of Acausal Synchronicity. Later, Isaac Bonewits called it the Law of Synchronicity for modern magickal practitioners. Although grounded in modern psychology, the idea is found in many magickal cultures. The main lesson I learned from this law is to allow my intuition to bring me synchronous events. Such events lead me to a greater spiritual awareness, lesson, or mission in my life. By following the trail of synchronicity, we often find our path.

THE LAW OF ASSOCIATION

This law basically says that if two things have something in common, each can influence the other. The more similarities they share, the more influence they can provide. Such an idea is taken out of the Principle of Correspondence, particularly magickal correspondences. You might use a dollar bill in a ritual to bring more money to you. The dollar is associated with the concept of money. It also has the vibration of money, and can be used to draw that vibration to you. Similar vibrations gather together. Some call this particular application of association the Principle of Abundance.

The two subdivisions of this law are what I find to be useful. The first, the Law of Similarity, says that if two events are similar, the smaller event can be the cause of the larger event. A "small" ritual action can create a larger corresponding change. If you desire to make the Sun shine, you might light a candle as part of your ritual. If you desire rain, you might drip water. This is also known as sympathetic magick. Witches of old would dance around the fire, riding their broomsticks and jumping in the air, mimicking the direction the plants should grow and rise. Later it was misinterpreted as witches "flying" on their brooms. The other sublaw, the Law of Contagion, states that if two objects have touched, they continue to interact and influence each other. That is why magicians often ask for a lock of hair, a fingernail, or a piece of clothing for the intended target of a spell. Magick is sent via these connections to the intended recipient. The stereotypical voodoo doll, usually called a poppet in witchcraft, combines both sympathetic magick and the Law of Contagion.

THE PRINCIPLE OF TRIPLICITY

You may be familiar with the old wives' tale "Things always happen in threes." My grandmother was famous for saying it, be it "good luck" or "bad luck." As with many of these superstitions, there is a truth to it. The universe seems to resonate with the number three. We discussed the Law of Three, where things get amplified three times, or could occur in three parts according to some. Three is important to many witches because of the Triple Goddess. Another example of the use of three occurs in the Principle of Triplicity. Whatever you do magickally, do it three times, once each for the middle, psychic, and divine selves.

THE LAW OF SYMBOLISM

As discussed in chapter 6, symbols are the language of the psychic mind. Our conscious mind does not necessarily understand raw, pure energy. We need an interface, a translator between us and the magickal word. Symbols and words of power are often that interface.

Magickal words and symbols change our inner and outer realities, and we do not necessarily have to consciously understand them to use them. Some people believe that they accumulate power from being used over centuries. The energy of all the previous uses grows into a collective "psychic memory," or energy bank, in the divine mind, allowing anyone who knows the symbol to draw from this collective pool. Others feel symbols and sounds are so primal in resonance with universal forces that they contain power within them. Both views are valid and probably have a measure of truth to them.

Witches use many symbols. The pentacle, or five-pointed star in a circle, is the most common (figure 14). Most movies and books associate it with Satanism, but it existed long before the Christian concepts of evil. The pentacle can be traced back to Pythagoras of Greece, in his work with geometry. The proportions of the pentacle and pentagon can be found at many sacred sites, including the pyramids of Egypt. The star in the circle can also be found in Chinese mysticism, relating to the elemental cycles of feng shui.

In modern witchcraft, the pentacle represents many things. It is a symbol of witchcraft and the mysteries of life. The five points are for the five physical senses, and the circle is the sixth, psychic sense. The circle is the cycle of the seasons, as well as the cycles of life: birth, initiation, love, repose, and death. The points of the star represent the four traditional elements of earth, air, fire, and water, and the fifth element of spirit, or ether. The Triple Goddess and Dual God are found in the five points. The star represents humanity, the image of a person, with two arms and legs outstretched and the head at the top point. The pentacle in this form is a symbol of incarnation, a gateway bringing life force into the world, or sending it out. The star is a symbol used in invocation, to open gateways to the spirits and elements or close and banish them. Because of this, the pentacle is a symbol of protection, much like the cross or Star of David.

Figure 14: Pentacle

I've heard detractors say that the upside-down pentacle is the image of the devil, goat faced, with two ears and two horns. I learned, however, that the reverse pentacle is simply directing energy downward, or into the Earth. If anything, the animal symbolism fits with the original image of the horned god, Pan, Cernunnos, or others, and has nothing to do with Satanism. Satanists use the upside-down cross, too, but most people do not associate all crosses with Satanism. It is an unfortunate misunderstanding, leaving many in fear. Witches never associate the pentacle with evil, regardless of the direction in which it points.

The interlocking *A* shapes symbolizes Alpha, both in the meditative state of alpha brain waves and Alpha as in Alpha and Omega, the beginning and the end. Pythagoras called the five-pointed star the pentalpha. The rich and complex symbolism of the pentacle is what makes it such a perfect symbol of witchcraft.

There is a lot of confusion over the name. Some call it a pentacle, others a pentagram. Technically, a pentagram refers to the five-pointed star. A pentacle has the circle around it, and is often in some three-dimensional form, like a piece of jewelry or ritual tool. In tarot, the pentacle is the symbol of the coin or shield, and is used to represent Earth.

Another powerful symbol used in witchcraft is the triskelion (figure 15). It is now considered a Celtic triple symbol by most pagans, honoring the Triple Goddess or as a symbol of Earth, Moon, and Sun. The origin of the triskelion can also be traced to the Norse, Italians, and Greeks, meaning "three-legged" in Greek. Those on the Isle of Man, between England and Ireland, consider it a special symbol and have a version of it on their flag. The spiral version is the one that is most often used by pagans, though the triple-knot images are sometimes referred to as triskelions. The triskelion can be used as a gateway to opening and increasing psychic powers as well as for protection and honor. Many use it in place of the pentacle. Hang it up in your meditative space or keep it on your altar if you are drawn to it.

To increase your proficiency with visualization, count yourself down to a meditative state and visualize the pentacle or triskelion by drawing it on the screen of your mind. Choose the version you like best. Use it as a meditative focus, and notice the effect that each symbol has on you.

As you can see, these paradigms—quantum physics, Hermetic laws, and other magickal laws—are all saying the same things, in different ways. Understanding them is a great asset, but do not let the process hinder you. The ideas and concepts will become more familiar as you gain more practical experience. These exercises are simple, practical applications of some basic ideas. You will build on them further as you build your magickal foundation.

New Assignments

- Exercises 13 through 19—Complete and record your experiences in your Book of Shadows. Try to incorporate the Hermetic wisdom and worldview into your daily life.

- Do the symbol meditation with the pentacle and/or triskelion.

- Neutralization—Be aware of your thoughts and feelings. Be vigilant and neutralize thoughts that cause any harm.

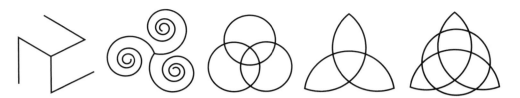

Figure 15: Triskelion and Triple Knot Images

CONTINUING ASSIGNMENTS

• Daily journal—Write three pages a day.

• Focus on a regular meditation practice, at least three times a week if not daily.

• Honor and recognize your intuition. Continue to ask it questions.

• Use instant magick in your daily life.

TIPS

• At times, magick and meditation may feel inauthentic, like you are "making it up" or "using your imagination." Magick is imagination. The power to visualize is imagination. Magick is imagination mingled with your intention. Think of how magickal children are. They haven't lost the ability to imagine and enter the magickal state of awareness. You are working with the magickal forces of the universe, but you must partner with them. Your interface with unseen forces *is* imagination. As you continue, you might have vague impressions or imaginary experiences that turn out to be very meaningful. Record them and remember them. Honor your intuition and experience.

RECOMMENDED READING

Power of the Witch by Laurie Cabot, with Tom Cowan (Dell Publishing).

The Kybalion by Three Initiates (Yogi Publication Society).

Real Magic by Isaac Bonewits (Samuel Weiser, Inc.).

The Hermetica by Timothy Freke and Peter Gandy (Tarcher/Putnam).

Lesson 5
The Art of Defense

One of the most frequently asked questions I get about witchcraft is "Can't something bad happen to you when you do this stuff?" That's the popular Hollywood image. I usually respond with, "No more than when you walk across the street or drive in a car. You could get mugged or into an accident, but you probably won't. In either case, you have to be careful." Likewise, if you are not careful in magick, there are things that could "go wrong" and give you difficulties, but if you know the basics, you can handle most experiences. Precaution is a part of your magickal education, and is not meant to scare you away. You should definitely look before leaping. Everything comes with responsibilities.

Because of monster movies and stereotypical witch stories, many people who do not condemn witchcraft to the realm of nonsense think that there is a monster or demon hiding behind every corner waiting to get them. Magick tends to amplify the intentions given to it. If you learn centeredness, confidence, and compassion, magick will amplify those qualities, rather than your fears. Protection magick and psychic self-defense skills alleviate your fears and bring balance.

Mystics from many traditions are often portrayed as spiritual warriors, battling for the well-being of the community. Mystics are not necessarily aggressors or conquerors, but they know how to defend and protect themselves. Like martial arts, the emphasis is not on provoking a battle, but safely diffusing a threat, often using your enemy's strengths and weaknesses against him. Magickal defenses work much the same way. Witches want to be centered and confident in their own power. Usually that is enough to prevent any unpleasantness from occurring.

If you practice defense, then you should know the potential dangers you are facing. Many people talk about psychic attacks, and they can be real, but genuine attacks are much rarer than most believe. Usually they are unintentional, but that doesn't always help the person on the receiving end. Most people cannot even define a psychic attack in anything more than vague terms. You have to understand the problem before you can solve it. A psychic or magickal attack is the perception of an energy or entity that intends you harm on a physical or spiritual level. People perceive it many different ways, but harmful intent is the common factor.

This type of energy has many sources. The most usual is what people call "negative energy," although I don't use the term, as I mentioned in chapter 8. I prefer the words *harmful, unbalanced, dense, heavy,* or *discordant energy*. Many people put out harmful thoughts and words all the time. Sometimes such energy builds up subtly. Psychically sensitive people have difficulty with this energy, and usually do not understand it. It can figuratively trap people, often in a cage of their own making. Certain environments, such as unhappy homes and offices, promote this energy and you get used to it being part of the "background" noise of the environment.

Usually such energy is unintentional, but there are some people with malicious intent, particularly when they are upset. Anger, fear, and frustration can charge words and thoughts with power. It is a form of harmful instant magick, but since most people do not believe in magick, or even the power of thought and word, they do not believe that they are really doing anything wrong. When you criticize someone else's accomplishments out of jealousy, or wish harm on someone in the future, even jokingly, you are making an attack of sorts. If that person is not centered and stable in his or her power, he or she can be influenced by such actions.

Next there is a malicious intent with people who actually know and understand that magick is real, but do not care. Somewhere along the line they discovered this, through traditional magickal training, books, or just discovering their own power. Unfortunately, they did not discover the Law of Three. If you meet such people, you will probably see the return of their harm much more apparently than they do, though some are aware and do not care.

Harmful energy can manifest as bad dreams or visions, sudden pain, losing many important objects when you are not prone to losing things, or having accidents when you are not accident prone. Some curses manifest as sudden, random sickness when you were perfectly healthy without other factors such as stress, depression, or exposure to the illness. Any kind of "bad luck" is often attributed to a curse. The most important thing is to check your own consciousness to make sure that you are not the root of the problem and are not seeking to blame someone or something else. Self-awareness and introspection are key to this knowledge, hence the journaling and meditation. Ask yourself why you are drawing this experience to you in the first place, regardless of who instigated it.

The source of such intentional attacks range from the Old World curse of the "evil eye" to spells from an accomplished practitioner. My mother's godmother, in an old Italian community, was well-known for removing the *malocchio*, or evil eye, through folk magick. She would break the curse with virgin olive oil, a boiling pot of water, and a needle. Though it was a form of magick, they attributed it to the Virgin Mary. Ethnic communities often bring their folk magick when they emigrate.

Many people unwittingly cause "attacks" because of their nature and behavior. Known in magickal circles as "energy vampires," these people are very low on energy and drain others of their vitality and emotion. I dislike this phrase because it is another Hollywood dramatization and shows no compassion, but it gets the general point across. Most energy vampires are not aware of their behavior. They are people who have been depressed and realize that when they are near certain energetic people, they feel more up and energized. They think that they are being cheered up and do not notice that those around them feel drained. They do not find their energy from an internal source, but from others. As their lives change, many people snap out of this pattern.

Some learn to understand it and either relish it or find themselves addicted to it, even though they want to change. While in college, an acquaintance of mine acted like an energy vampire, being very depressed and draining on my circle of friends. Things just seemed gloomier around her, and eventually we tried to avoid her because she did not seek help for her depression. Some people need to experience such things for their own soul development. We can have compassion for them, perfect love and perfect trust, and yet still draw healthy boundaries for ourselves. As I learned magickal protection skills, she no longer drained me. It is our individual responsibility to prevent such behavior from affecting us. I ran into her years later and she was bright, vibrant, and alive. Change is very possible. She made the changes in her life that she needed to be happy, and her unconscious, energetic behavior changed. One is not fated to always act like an energy vampire.

I was blessed to have a wonderful woman in one of my classes who worked in the mental health field. She described herself as a former energy vampire. She did not realize what she was doing until she got involved in Wicca. She heard about energy vampires and recognized her behavior, then valiantly worked to change it with her new awareness. Hearing her story was a wonderful way to see this phenomenon from the other side. So often the word *vampire* paints a portrait of evil, much like the word *witch*. Remember, people are people, all with their own individual challenges.

Certain unwanted energies are not connected to a physical being. They are perceived as a spiritual entity. In *Modern Magick*, author Donald Michael Kraig calls the most common of these entities the "little nasties."[1] The name aptly describes the experience. You feel an unsettling presence or sometimes "see" strange images when doing magickal work. The entities you perceive are like spiritual scavengers. As the physical planes have some unpleasant life forms that scour refuse, like rats and roaches, the nonphysical realities, the astral planes, have similar creatures. This is an example of the Law of Correspondence in action. Scavengers are a part of nature. They are not necessarily evil, but I wouldn't want one, physical or nonphysical, to run across my foot. They are a part of creation, to be honored, but you must also honor your boundaries of comfort and remove them as needed. I like mice, but I don't like

---

1. Donald Michael Kraig, *Modern Magick: Eleven Lessons in the High Magickal Arts* (St. Paul, MN: Llewellyn Publications, 1988) 76.

them in my home. Remember that these entities can't harm you in any way. They can only unsettle you if you let them.

When you first do magickal work, most of these entities will probably not take much notice. As you build your power, it's like turning on a light switch for the first time. Entities come to check out the new change, but usually leave. Once you raise your energy in a more permanent way though a spiritual practice, you flow so smoothly with the universe that you do not attract attention unless that is what you desire. If these beings make you uncomfortable, use a single banishing pentagram in white or blue light in the direction you feel them, or draw such pentagrams all around you, in the four directions, above and below. A banishing pentagram is a five-pointed star that is drawn by staring in the lower-left point and moving clockwise (figure 16). The energy of this movement banishes all dense harmful energy and seals the space, protecting you like a shield. This is sufficient to send them scurrying, like a magickal "shoo."

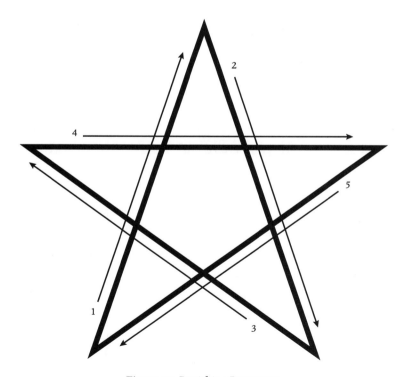

Figure 16: Banishing Pentagram

Other entities are not as benign as the little nasties. Mystics can encounter entities that are trapped in more harmful emotions like anger and fear. They may be the spirits of those who were physical once and died, creating a ghost. Some feel that ghosts make links to people and places that meant something to them, anchoring them to the world. Most of my personal "ghost busting" experiences have not been discarnate beings, but a build-up of a harmful energy. Some entities may never have been physical. They can manifest as scary visions and abusive voices. Others are more mischievous and playful. They could be under the direction of a magician who is adept at controlling spirits, but usually they are acting on their own.

Ultimately, these discarnate beings are seeking attention and have discovered that fear gets them the most attention. Your attention feeds them power, and one of the best ways to get rid of them is to no longer fear them. Use banishing pentagrams. Use the shielding technique described at the end of this chapter. But most importantly, do not be afraid, which is easier said than done, I know. Laughter is a great way to combat fear and harmful spirits. If you laugh, you are no longer taking them seriously. It's a good test to see if a spirit is friendly. Any entity worth knowing should be able to take a joke. Laughter only angers unwanted spirits because you are no longer in fear or awe and no longer giving them the energy they need from you.

The last source of an attack is you. If you think that you are cursed or under attack, the universe will respond in that way. As you study witchcraft, you gather your personal power and learn to direct the energy around you. If you set these talents subconsciously against yourself, you will find that you are the most formidable enemy there is. Awareness is the best protection.

I used to say that the majority of psychic attacks were self-created illusions, but if you feel an attack is real, then it is real, regardless of the source. The key to defeating such acts is to first check in with your own consciousness. Ask yourself if you are the source of your own problems. Often we are, no matter how much we don't like to admit it. Even if there is an external source, think about why you are drawing such an experience to you at this time. There are no accidents. Why is the attack affecting you? If you are centered in your power, then most "attacks" should wash off you like water from a duck. Where is the weakness or root you need to work on for your personal growth? What is the experience teaching you? The answer to these questions will solve your problem and encourage your own spiritual growth.

PROTECTION CHARMS

As you learned with the Law of Symbolism, many magickal symbols have a power beyond our conscious knowledge and have been used throughout the ages for protection. In this day, the Christian cross is a symbol of God's protection. Before it, the equal-armed cross, a symbol of sacredness and balance, was a protective symbol. Other ancient traditions have symbols that are now used for protection (figure 17).

The pentacle is an obvious sign of protection, and many witches do not leave the house without one in the form of a necklace or ring. The ankh, or Egyptian cross with a loop at the top, symbolizes the union of the Goddess and God, in this case, the god Osiris and the goddess Isis, to create a symbol of life. Another Egyptian symbol, the eye of Horus, is used for protection. Horus was the avenging son of Isis and Osiris. His eye is like a lens of power, only allowing in energies that are correct and good for you. The hexagram, or six-pointed Star of David, is most often associated with Hebrew traditions, but it, too, is a symbol of faith and protection.

Other natural substances have the power of protection in them. Certain minerals and stones are well-known for their protective properties. Most are related to the element of earth and grounding. Salt absorbs discordant energy. Sea salt is used in many charms and potions. Iron is the metal of Mars, the planet of war, but also the protector. Iron grounds harmful energy like a lightning rod. Dark crystals, such as obsidian, smoky quartz, and onyx, are protective. Fluorite, usually a green, pink, or purple stone, helps amplify your energy field to create a protective boundary or border. It also cleanses your energy field of harmful energy, like an energy purifier.

Before you carry a talisman or stone, you should cleanse it and consecrate it for your intent. By investing a little of your personal energy in it, you will increase the effectiveness of your magick. You can cleanse an object by leaving it out in the sunlight for a day or two, smudging it in incense or through intent. To cleanse with intent, imagine the object filled with white light, purifying all harmful energy. When it can take no more, hold the object up to your mouth, ask the Goddess and God to cleanse it, and blow on it three times. This act will clear all unwanted energies. Then connect with the object, holding it in your hand. As you projected your mind in exercise 13, do so again, but not necessarily as intensely. You want to make a connection and place your intention, in this case protection, into the object. This is called charging, conse-crating, hallowing, empowering, or blessing a charm. You can use any intention you like, charging things for healing, happiness, tranquility, psychic power, or any other quality. Then carry your charm for daily protection. You can do this for your friends and family, too.

Figure 17: Protection Symbols: Pentacle, Cross, Ankh, Eye, Hexagram, Triple Knot

PREPARATION

Just as you prepare your car before you drive by checking the gas and making sure the oil is changed regularly, preparation work is done before magick or meditation to as-sure a more pleasant spiritual journey.

When you started your meditations, I mentioned using a meditation altar with a candle. From now own, every time you light the candle, charge it, as just described, with the intentions of protection and guidance, or "to have the experience correct and good for me." This establishes an intention and vibration to your session, to receive higher guidance and protection. The intent doesn't have to be with a candle. You can use any object.

Before sitting down, light some incense on your meditation altar. A traditional use of incense is to raise the vibration of an area. If all energy vibrates, you are intending for harmful, unwanted vibrations to be removed, or cleansed, from an area. As some crystals and minerals are known for their protection, other natural materials, particu-larly when burned, are known to raise the vibration of an area to create a sanctuary and sacred space. In this space, you are more protected and peaceful. The vibration aids meditation and protection at the same time.

I use incense of frankincense and myrrh. Frankincense resonates with the energy of the God, while myrrh resonates with the energy of the Goddess. Together they create a unified vibration. The Catholic Church uses it for the same reason. Native Americans use combinations of sage, sweet grass, and cedar. Copal, a resin similar in form to frankincense, is the favored incense of Central and South America. Lavender, cinnamon, cloves, and pine resins also create sacred space.

Look to use natural incense products in your work, because they carry a higher energy. Synthetics might smell as nice, but they do not hold the same magick. Charge the incense for protection before using it. If you dislike smoke, essential oils of the same type can be used. Anoint your candle or wrists with them. Find what works for you.

The last step of preparation is to use banishing pentagrams in the direction of all four walls, above in the ceiling and below in the floor. If you feel uncomfortable at any time during your meditation, you can revisualize your pentagrams and banish any harmful energy, even if it is your own fear. Some people imagine the space filling with white, cobalt-blue, or violet light for protection. You can use any color that you feel is protective, as long as it feels comfortable to you. I shy away from white light because it is too opaque and does not allow the energies in that I desire. When I visualize white light, I make it a "crystal white," like an opal, quartz, or prism refracting all the colors of the spectrum.

SPIRITUAL GUARDIANS

Many spiritual traditions believe in some form of guardian or protector spirit. For some, it is the popular guardian angel. Tribal traditions take the form of an animal. You may feel it is an ancestor or a deity. The duty of this nonphysical being is to aid in your protection, psychically, magickally, and even physically.

When you start your meditations, invite your guardian spirits to be with you, to guide and guard you during these experiences. The very invitation will bring their presence, even when you do not know who or what they are. Ask that they work for the highest good. When in danger, physically or during a meditation that does not feel comfortable, ask their presence to be with you.

SHIELDING

The most powerful magickal protection is to create a shield around you. A shield is energy programmed with the intention of defense. Everyone has energy around their physical body, like a bubble. This energy field is called the aura. The boundary of the aura can be programmed to be your protection shield, preventing all physical and magickal harm from reaching you. Try this next meditation to program your protection shield.

EXERCISE 20

Protection Shield

1. Start exercise 9: Counting Down to a Meditative State to get into your magickal mindset.

2. Be aware of your energy field, the space around your body at about an arm's length. Feel your energy field like an egg or sphere around your whole body.

3. Visualize the edge of the energy field becoming like a faceted crystal. It is clear like quartz or diamond, and hard, strong, and protective. Let the light of your mind reflect in the dazzling facets of the gem. The crystal surrounds you, above and below.

4. Hold the intention of protection from all harm in your mind. The shield will protect you from all harm. It blocks harmful energy and allows in the energy you need for your highest good. I use these words: "I charge my protection shield to protect me from all harm on any level, and reflect love back on the source of the harm." (I repeat it three times and end with a "So mote it be.")

5. Repeat the process as many times as you would like and hold the image. When done, let the image fade from your mind when it starts to wander. You can continue on to other meditations, or end your session.

6. Return yourself to normal consciousness, counting up, and giving yourself clearance and balance. Do any necessary grounding.

The key to the shield is to allow in what you desire and block out only the harmful energy. You do not want to wall yourself off from all helpful energies. A popular defense is to visualize mirrors all around you, returning harm back to the sender, but I cannot recommend this technique at all. Witches vow to never do harm, but mirrors purposely send back harm to someone. The argument for the mirror technique is that the original sender is "karmically" getting what was sent out, but I believe that it is not our job to make sure others "get what they deserve." The universe takes care of that. Willing harm back to another instead of grounding it and neutralizing it is irresponsible. If someone should "walk into the magickal crossfire" and get "hit" by the harmful energy, we would be as responsible. We did not start the conflict, but we perpetuated it when we could have ended it.

You will have to repeat this process to reinforce the program and strengthen the shield. The more you repeat it, the stronger it gets. I suggest doing it every time you meditate for a few weeks. For physical harm, the shield can act as an early warning defense system, keying your intuition in to avoiding disaster.

Do not limit this shield to yourself. You can program the energy around anything to act as a defense. Everything has an energy field, even if it is not a living being. I have one around my car, and whenever I get into someone else's car, I create one. I created a protection charm for a friend and cast a shield around her car. She was accident prone in a serious way. She later got into an accident and said half-jokingly, "It didn't work." True, she had been in an accident, but, for once, had no major injuries. She walked out with minor whiplash when usually she was rushed to the hospital.

More complicated protection shields around a place, often visualized as domes, pyramids, or defensive castles of energy, are called wards. You can create a ward around your home through ritual and visualization. Circle the land with a ring of salt. Bury protective herbs and crystals in key places. Invite guardian spirits to your home, often visualized as angels, dragons, or wolves. Then create the shield with all this energy that you have accumulated.

Other forms of protection include casting a magick circle or doing specific binding spells when someone means you harm. Both topics go beyond the scope of this work as a foundation course, but will be dealt with in the sequel to this book.

The best strategy I learned regarding protection came not from a book on witchcraft, but from an audiotape set on Afro-Caribbean magick called *Jumbalaya*, based on the book of the same name. The author, Luisa Teish, suggests "blessing your enemies away." You invite into their lives all sorts of wonderful blessings and success, so they will be so happy and occupied with their life that they will not bother you. If we do receive what we send out, I would happily accept blessings from my enemies. The best protection is having a defensive strategy where everyone wins.

NEW ASSIGNMENTS

• Exercise 20—Complete and record your experiences in your Book of Shadows. Repeat at least three times in one week. Repeat often to reinforce the protection.

CONTINUING ASSIGNMENTS

• Daily journal—Write three pages a day.

• Focus on a regular meditation practice, at least three times a week if not daily.

• Honor and recognize your intuition. Continue to ask it questions.

• Use instant magick in your daily life.

• Neutralize unwanted thoughts and intentions.

TIPS

• From now on, prepare and protect yourself and your space before doing any meditation. State an intention for protection and guidance. Call on your protection spirits. Burn protective incense. Draw banishing pentagrams in all directions.

• Obtain a charm or symbol of protection, such as a pentacle, and consecrate it. Wear it during meditation, and in your daily life, if you desire.

• Create protection shields as needed, including ones for your home, office, and vehicle. If you have difficulty visualizing shields around other objects, imagine drawing three interlocking rings around your target, one horizontal with the ground and two vertical (figure 18). Then imagine the space in between filling with crystal, creating a transparent shield.

- Use your shield if you ever feel overwhelmed by the emotions and thoughts of others around you. The shield provides protection on the empathic and mental levels, as well as the psychic and physical levels.

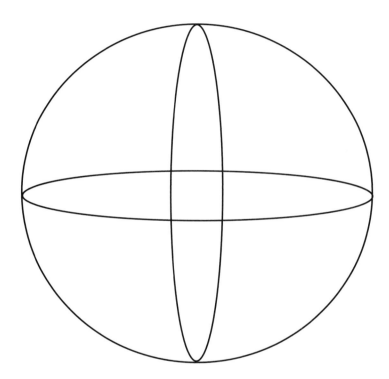

Figure 18: *Protective Rings*

Lesson 6
The Power of Light

In Greek myth, the Titan Prometheus stole fire from the gods to bring it to humanity. Our benefactor was later punished by the gods of Olympus, sent to the Underworld and continuously tortured for his transgression. The light he gave to us mythically is an important symbol. On the physical level, it represents the ability to cook our food and light our homes in the dark—a technological advancement. On the spiritual level, this light is the potential for enlightenment, not only knowledge, but wisdom and understanding. In many cultures and religions, the quest for light in times of darkness is a central mythological theme, showing us the importance and power of light.

In our modern metaphysical sense, light is information. Light is energy. In our holographic model of the universe, reality is a hologram, a construct of light and information perceived to be physical by our consciousness. Everything is affected by the power of light because everything *is* light. In the Hermetic principles, we learned that everything is a vibration. Light is the energy of vibration. Ultimately, everything, including matter, is a form of energy.

As living energy, we are constantly interacting with all forms of vibration, taking them in, releasing them, and processing them much like we process food and air. However, our minds do not understand subtle energy as easily as they do physical sustenance. We can see visible light, but as we stray from the visible spectrum, recognition becomes more difficult. We can feel energy, but our human minds use symbols, sensations, and feelings to describe the energy we experience. We do not recognize energy by a frequency or a wavelength. Instead, we feel warmth, coolness, tingling, heaviness, or peace. Those are all subjective experiences. Two energy-sensitive people can walk into a room and describe two different sensations, but come to the same conclusion about the energy.

In training the psychic mind, most people focus on the visual because we are used to working with visible light and color. As in a dream, we manifest our own source of light in meditation, creating images and symbols with our inner vision. And again, like the dream world, we can receive information from our other senses while in meditation. Voices, sounds, smells, tastes, and textures all give symbolic information, and such information comes from the same source as the visual input.

We use symbols to interpret, direct, and send our intentions with energy. Colored light is one such symbol. The vibration of light can carry an intention. In the next exercise, we will be visualizing "spiritual light." Although the experience can be quite vivid for some, we are not generating light from the visible spectrum. We are using the visible light spectrum as a symbol for activating our spiritual light and psychic intentions.

EXERCISE 21

Showers of Light

1. Start exercise 9: Counting Down to a Meditative State to get into your magickal mindset.

2. Visualize a cloud floating several feet above your head. The cloud can be white and fluffy, or dark and gray. It hovers a few feet over your crown.

3. The cloud will rain down drops of light. At any time, if you feel uncomfortable, experience the discomfort for a moment and, if you desire, change it to

a more comfortable color. If drops of light are causing the discomfort, you can change their form to snow, mist, bubbles, or a beam of light descending down upon you.

4. The cloud rains down drops of red light. Feel the ruby-red drops descend upon you, and flow from your crown all over your body. They cover you inside and out, even inside and around your protection shield. Feel the energy of red light.

5. After a few minutes, change the color of the drops, spending some time on each color in the spectrum. Use the following order of colors at first, but when you repeat the meditation, change the order as you see fit.

> **Red,** like a ruby
>
> **Red-orange,** like the embers of a fire
>
> **Orange,** like the fruit
>
> **Gold,** like the metal
>
> **Yellow,** like a lemon
>
> **Lime,** like the fruit
>
> **Green,** like the grass or an emerald
>
> **Turquoise,** like the stone or warm seawaters
>
> **Blue,** like the sky
>
> **Indigo,** the color of a clear, midnight sky
>
> **Purple,** like a grape
>
> **Violet,** like the flower
>
> **Black,** like a windowless room
>
> **Brown,** like the earth
>
> **Rust,** like metal
>
> **Pink,** like a flower
>
> **Silver,** like the metal
>
> **White,** crystal white like a prism or opal

6. After you spend some time with each color, end on crystal-clear white light to clear out any remaining energies that you do not want to carry with you.

7. Return yourself to normal consciousness, counting up, and giving yourself clearance and balance. Do any necessary grounding.

Write down your impressions. By going through the spectrum of colors, you cleanse your own body and protection field, and help re-balance yourself. I like to start with the more rainbowlike colors at first and then add in the mixtures at the end, or mix them together, using the order of black, brown, rust, pink, red, red-orange, orange, gold, yellow, lime, green, blue, turquoise, indigo, purple, violet, silver, and white. Sometimes I just use the seven colors of the rainbow for a quick and fun re-balancing exercise.

Psychologically, colors can have a personal effect on us. Some colors feel empowering, and others peaceful. Everybody has a color they absolutely love. Most of us have a color that makes us very uncomfortable. If we were attacked by someone who wore green clothing, green might kindle those feelings in us. If our mother always wore yellow, that color would generate whatever feelings we strongly associate with our mother.

Other times, colors seem to induce physiological responses, due to their energetic vibration. Generally, yellow is said to provide energy or induce agitation. My family used to have a kitchen painted yellow, and more fights took place there than anywhere else, so I'm inclined to agree. People will react differently to color due to their own psychological and physiological makeup.

Magickally, each color has certain correspondences, relating to different elements, planets, and deities. The following are some generally accepted magickal meanings of the colors, but I think it is always important to get your first impression through the previous exercise. Release your expectations about each color's energy. Try to qualify the feeling or sensation of each color in your body, mind, and heart. As you grow spiritually, your likes and dislikes of particular colors will change, and you will see the value in all colors. The ultimate goal is to be comfortable with all colors of the spectrum, because like a painter, they are all tools in your magickal palette.

Red—Red is the color of fire, bringing the properties of warmth, energy, and passion. The energy is very physical, but not grounding. For some, red is too intense and brings feelings of aggression or is associated with anger. Red is powerful for honoring and releasing anger, rather than suppressing it.

Red-orange—Red-orange combines the best of the colors of red and orange, like the spark of life in the ember of a fire. I was taught to use red-orange in critical healing.

Orange—Orange is another high-energy color, used to bolster energy and the immune system. Orange also clears the mind and strengthens the will. Orange is associated with the planet Mercury, and the powers of the mind, memory, and communication.

Gold—Gold is the divine masculine color, associated with the Sun. Like the Sun, it indicates good health, success, prosperity, and internal power. Gold can be used to overcome fear, and to contact divine will and unconditional love.

Yellow—Yellow is associated with both fire and air. In some, it is associated with fear, but it also helps clear the mind and aids in spiritual communication.

Lime—Lime is very cleansing, particularly for emotional problems or repressed issues. It brings issues to the surface to be cleared.

Green—Green is the color of life, growth, and healing. I associate it with the love of the Goddess, and the Earth, and I use it for healing on both the physical and emotional levels. It is also the color of money, and can be used for prosperity. Green is also the color of the heart, used for love.

Turquoise—Turquoise is a great all-purpose color, used for unconditional love and balance, communication, protection, and healing. When in doubt, use turquoise.

Blue—Blue is for peace, prosperity, spiritual healing, and dream work. Try visualizing blue around you on restless nights. Blue and purple are colors of Jupiter, which is the planet of expansion and abundance, so it is a strong color when you want your resources to expand.

Indigo—Indigo is the color of psychic energy, usually associated with the third-eye chakra, or psychic-seeing chakra. Indigo helps develop visualization skills and trust in psychic ability.

Purple—Purple is the color of spiritual peace and balance, bringing tranquility not only for the mind, but also for the soul. Shades of purple are great colors when you are feeling spiritually unbalanced or out of control.

Violet—Violet is one of the highest vibrational colors, and is used to cleanse lower vibrations from an area. Like purifying incense, the color can remove unwanted energies by raising the vibration of an area. It mixes the properties of red and purple. Some visualize it as a violet flame burning away harm. I visualize violet light before and after all my meditations and rituals. Violet is another color used to increase psychic and magickal abilities.

Black—Black is a highly charged color. People either love it or hate it. Some fear black because of cultural associations with evil, but psychologically black is the most relaxing color. When you close your eyes and your optic nerve is relaxed, all you see is black. When the nerve is agitated, you see all sorts of color flashes. Black is a very healing, soothing color. Black is the color of the dark goddesses and the Underworld. Physically, black and all dark colors are very grounding.

Brown—Earthen tones are for physical healing and alignment. They are particularly good for healing animals. Like black, brown is grounding and does not have some of the negative cultural associations that black does. The brown earth is the provider and sustainer of life.

Rust—Rust is another purification color, helping release and shed unwanted energy and thoughts, like rust. The next time you need to release something, visualize a symbol of what you want to release. If you want to quit smoking, picture the pack of cigarettes. Then imagine it filling with rust light, breaking apart.

Pink—Pink is the color of happiness and self-esteem. Use pink light when feeling down and out. It centers, calms, and brings uplifting thoughts and feelings. Pink is another color of the heart chakra and love. Pink is used to express love to yourself and others.

Silver—As gold matches the divine masculine, silver, like the Moon, connects with the divine feminine. Silver is for intuition, psychic ability, and going with the flow. Silver is great for realigning your internal cycles, particularly for women, but in general it helps you adapt to changes.

White—White is the spiritual color used by most traditions. Some associate witchcraft with black, but the White Goddess tradition is strong in our European roots. The Druids were said to wear robes of white, although that's under debate. White is the all-purpose color, containing all colors. Many use white light for protection and healing. When in doubt, use prismatic white light, what I call crystal-white light, since it will contain the energy you need.

If you want to bring the qualities and intentions of a color into your life, do another light shower meditation, as in exercise 21, but only focus on that particular color or imagine the light surrounding you, filling your aura. Many people use color to effect healing on all levels, and prevent illness in the first place. During the winter months I fill myself with green light every chance I get, and usually cold and flu season passes me by. Use your instant magick trigger to access any color magick any time. You don't have to be in a deep trance to feel its effects.

SENDING LIGHT

Not only does color affect you personally, but, like all vibrations, it can be sent out to affect the environment around you and even other people. Colors in a room affect the mood and setting, and the colors you broadcast also affect the people in your life.

In the physical world, we tend to think of things in terms of distance, space, and range. In the spiritual reality, we know that all things are one, all are thoughts in the divine mind. There is no distance or separation between us, just a perceived distance. If we can overcome that perception, our energies can affect anything at literally any place or time. The more you do this work, the more you will discover that there is no distance limiting our thoughts, intentions, and magick. We perceive that we are reaching out to someone or something, like when we reached out to the orange on our mind's screen. We can reach out and spiritually "touch" other people and objects, and we can also "send" them energy, intention, and thoughts. The difference in reaching or sending is only our perception.

Using meditation or your trigger, you can send light and intention to a recipient. Once you reach a magickal mindset, think about the person, place, or object you wish to connect to. Like the orange meditation, your recipient appears on the screen of your mind, regardless of how defined your image is. You can create a "gateway" using the symbol of the pentagram. "Open" the connection by drawing the invoking pentagram (figure 19) and repeating the name of the recipient three times. Then intend to send light and energy. Think about your intention and choose a color, or intuit what color is correct. Feel the recipient fill with the color, bathed in it, filling with light. You can use the image of laser beams, mists, colored water, or bubbles. Coming from an art background, I imagine painting the recipient with colors, like dipping into an imaginary paint can or picking up a crayon. Many people "breathe" out the color. Hold the intention and image as long as it feels intuitively correct, usually a few minutes, and release the image, erasing it from the screen of your mind. If you strengthened the connection by using the invoking pentagram, close it by drawing the banishing pentagram and release the connection with a blessing.

It is important to always keep the intent of "the highest good" when sending light. You want to "check in" prior to sending the light, and ask, from a non-ego point of view, is this the right thing to do? You are asking the divine mind, the Goddess and God, for permission to send light. If you feel affirmation, continue. In the best case scenario, ask the recipient's direct permission. If a friend is sick or unhappy, ask to send light. If your friend is not open to this, you can say something like "Pray in my own way," for it is the same thing, implying a different method. Witches live in a subculture that commonly asks, "Can I send light?" when being told of a problem. We have a "light network" instead of a prayer circle, where groups will send light to those in need. But if you can't ask directly, ask the divine mind.

In the next exercise, you are going to choose two recipients and send pink and blue light to them. The first recipient will be a person. Pick someone you see fairly regularly, who is unhappy and wants to be happy. Send him or her pink light. The best

Figure 19: *Invoking (top) and Banishing (bottom) Pentagrams*

thing to do is send light a few days in a row. The first time I did this meditation, I picked the most depressed person I knew. She was our aforementioned energy vampire from the previous chapter. I saw her five days a week every morning, so I tried this out one night to see if it "really worked." I asked permission from the divine and felt the answer was yes, and sent her pink light. The next morning I saw her come into the room positively glowing. I talked to her for a bit, and she told me she didn't know why she was happy. She had slept really well and had gotten up ready to take on the world. The difference was like night and day. The shift was not permanent, but I was impressed. I later told her about my studies and what pink light was supposed to do. I don't know if she used it herself or not, but she did eventually make a change in her life for the better.

The second target will be a place of confusion and chaos in your life. For most people, that place is work, but it can be home, or a relative or friend's house. Pick a place you will visit the next day. You can even repeat this part of the meditation before you depart for your destination. You will send this place calming, peaceful blue light. Notice the difference. Nurses have tried this trick before going to the hospital, and although still filled with stress and obviously sick patients, the usual frenzied pace is much quieter all around. Try this at your places of stress and tension.

Exercise 22

Sending Light

If the pink and blue associations do not work for you, choose the colors that you feel are most appropriate for the person and place. Let your intuition guide you.

1. Start exercise 9: Counting Down to a Meditative State to get into your magickal mindset.

2. On your mind's screen, call up the image of the person to whom you want to send pink light. Draw the invoking pentagram and state the person's name three times. Let the image appear. Ask the divine mind if you have permission. If yes, continue on and visualize the person surrounded by and filled with pink light. Hold the image and the intent of happiness, self-love,

and self-esteem. When the light feels complete, erase the image or draw the banishing pentagram, releasing the connection completely. I usually release by saying "Blessed be."

3. Now think of a place to which you want to send blue light. Draw the invoking pentagram and name the place three times. Call it to the screen of your mind. You can picture the outside or the inside of the place. Again, ask permission of the divine. If affirmative, visualize the place filling with blue light. For locations, I use the image of mist filling the space completely. Use whatever form of blue light feels appropriate. Hold the image and the intent of peacefulness and tranquility. When the light feels complete, release the image and draw the banishing pentagram, closing the connection. Say, "Blessed be."

4. Return yourself to normal consciousness, counting up, and giving yourself clearance and balance. Do any necessary grounding.

Take notice of this person and place the next day. Do you notice any changes? It can take several attempts of sending light to make a noticeable change. And remember, some people and places are beyond our influence. If they don't want to change, no amount of light will make a difference.

Sending light is a powerful technique. This is one of the most amazing tools I've ever learned, and I still use it on an almost daily basis. It effects great change in the individual and the environment around us all. You are not draining your personal energy, although you are using your mental energy to concentrate and hold the intention. You are using the abundant light of the holographic universe. Even if you can only send light for a second or two with your trigger, I suggest doing it. Every bit helps change a situation. Do not underestimate the power of intention.

Witches are often accused of seeing things strictly in terms of black and white, wearing dark robes and practicing much of the craft at night. These are times and colors of power for us. Black absorbs energy, drawing what we need to us, and white reflects energy. There are scientific properties of the physical colors. Black is only black because it absorbs the light spectrum, and white reflects it. The night is the time of the Moon and the Goddess, the divine aspect many witches favor. Some systems of magick break it down into "black magick," "white magick," and even "gray magick." Magick is the full spectrum of color, light, and life. In essence, witches are true light workers, because we use not only all the shades of gray in between the two extremes, but we also find the rainbow between black and white.

NEW ASSIGNMENTS

- Exercises 21 and 22—Complete and record your experiences in your Book of Shadows.

- Continue to send light to yourself, other people, places, and the world, as a part of your regular practice. If you cannot meditate regularly, still take a few moments to work with light and intention. You don't need to be in a deep meditative state to feel the power of light. Use your trigger.

CONTINUING ASSIGNMENTS

- Daily journal—Write three pages a day.
- Focus on a regular meditation practice, at least three times a week if not daily.
- Honor and recognize your intuition. Continue to ask it questions.
- Use instant magick in your daily life.
- Neutralize unwanted thoughts and intentions.

TIPS

- Pay strict attention to your feelings when you send these colors of light. Even if you don't see anything, don't get frustrated. Notice how you feel. As I said, this light is not physical, so you do not necessarily have to see it for it to be there, affecting you. With the Principle of Vibration, you asked to vibrate in harmony with an abstract concept. There were probably very few visuals, only feelings. You can do the same with the vibrations of color. Ask to vibrate in harmony with a color if you have difficulty visualizing it.

- Watch sunrises and sunsets. Not only will they inspire and influence your use of color magick, but recognizing, honoring, and taking time to be a part of the natural cycles is a fundamental part of witchcraft.

LESSON 7
ENERGY ANATOMY

Human beings spend most of their lives identifying with the physical body. We identify the face with the person and personality. We equate the brain with the mind. We equate the body with our only self-image. This is untrue. We are more than our physical body.

As you may have noticed, a basic premise of witchcraft, and almost any metaphysical discipline, is the belief there is more to reality than the physical. Humanity is well versed on the physical body. Less well-known is information on our nonphysical bodies, our energy anatomy. Some information survives in the form of ancient texts and disciplines. Other wisdom is being recorded as modern nontraditional healers chart unknown territory.

THE AURA

What's on the inside counts, but what's on the outside is just as important. I am not referring to the physical body as being all important, but the energy field that interpenetrates and surrounds the body. This field of energy has many names, but is most often referred to as the aura. The kundalini yoga tradition calls is it a "psycho-electric field." I love that name because it implies the relationship between your psyche and this energy. Your thoughts and intentions directly influence it, consciously or unconsciously. If you learn to be more conscious, you have greater control of the aura and your physical and psychic health.

This auric field draws to you the thoughts and vibrations you put out. It plays a very important part in magick. If you have strong energy in this field, it can reach out and bring to you whatever experience you desire. If your energy is weak, you are not going to attract the resources and vibrations you need to manifest your desires. Even worse, if you unconsciously put out harmful thoughts, you will manifest harm in your life.

The aura is generated through the interaction of your physical body's energy with other forms of personal energy, called subtle bodies. They are subtle because they are not necessarily physically visible, but they can be felt. The different layers of the aura correspond to the energies of your mind, your emotions, and spirit. When you did exercise 4: Feeling the Aura, you probably felt different levels in your partner's aura, some denser than others. Without even knowing it, you were instinctively feeling the various energy bodies. Repeat this exercise later, and look for more subtle information. You may feel the different levels more distinctly.

Many people can see the aura and receive information about a person from looking at the aura. Some see it naturally, and have since childhood, never realizing that others couldn't. Most of us forgot how to see auras if we were able to do so as children. We conditioned our mind to function only in the logical world, and didn't allow this "imaginative" experience to be ours. And that is exactly how it feels at first, like a burst of creative imagination. Like many meditations and exercises, it does not seem "real." You can't "prove" it. But once you start to have experiences that are meaningful for you, you won't need any physical proof.

When you start this exercise, don't expect too much and you will be pleasantly surprised. If you are looking for *Star Wars* special effects, you will probably be disappointed. If you are aware and open for a subtle experience, you will be amazed. We all have some unrealistic expectations about the aura. Due to Kirlian photography, and other forms of aura photography, available at many New Age centers and psychic fairs, we expect to see bright and vibrant colors like in the photographs. Some people do see that, but often it is more of a ghostlike image overlaying the physical reality, at least at first. When I first discovered auras, I could see plant auras really well. I felt I was really seeing the energy of newly growing leaves in the springtime, but I struggled to see the energy of people. Then after letting go of my desire and frustration, it just happened and I could see people's auras. This is a skill that comes with a combination of practice and relaxation. Have fun with it. Over months the abilities can develop even more, though some forget about aura viewing until it is needed for healing work or psychic readings.

EXERCISE 23

Aura Gazing

For this exercise, find a partner and take turns guiding one another. If you can do this in a small group, that is even better. Dress in solid colors, no flashy patterns. Blacks, whites, and dark blues are the best. A black cloth will also help, in a size roughly that of a napkin. Have a few plants on hand. You will also need a taper candle and a sentimental or power object, like something charged on your altar. Everything has an aura, not just living things.

1. Light a candle and place it somewhere in easy view. If you can have it up against a neutral background, like a white wall, do so. Such backgrounds make the exercise easier. If you find using a white background difficult, hang a black cloth behind the candle. Do your instant magick trigger. Take a few deep breaths. Stare at the candle flame. Do not focus on the flame or wick, but on the glow of light like a halo around the flame. Focus on this glow until you can see it. This is the first step of aura viewing. Blink as needed so you don't stress your eyes. Remember, you'll be looking with your spiritual eyes, not your physical ones, but we are giving your physical body a point of focus. Act like you are looking "through" the flame. Your eyes may go into a soft focus, or feel like they are crossing. That's fine. Do not force it.

2. Gently bring the halo of light down to the base of the candle. See and feel the light at the edge of the candle, below the flame. As you gaze, slowly bring this glow around the edge down the candle. If you lose it at any point, go back up at the flame and start again.

3. Bring the glow not only around the candle itself, but also around the candlestick holder. This will probably be fainter than the candle, which was fainter than the flame. This glow may come in flashes and not hold continuously. That is normal. Close your eyes and rest for a few moments.

4. Now pick an object of power, something you have consecrated. Place it where the candle is, up against the neutral background. Let your soft gaze fall on the new object, and look for the same glow or halo around it. I usually see it as a fuzzy white outline a half inch above the physical object.

5. When that feels comfortable, repeat step 4, but with a plant. My first experience with a plant felt like I was looking into its cells as patterns of energy.

6. Now take the black cloth in your lap and hold your hands over it. Rub your hands together and perform exercise 2: Feeling Energy, and exercise 3: Ball of Energy. Let your soft focus fall between your hands. You may see wisps of smokelike energy trails. Others describe it as cotton candy. The black background makes it easier to see the energy, and the more practiced you get, the less you will need the cloth.

7. Finally, have your partner stand up against the neutral background. Start by looking at the crown and allowing the soft halo to come into focus. As if the crown is the candle flame, bring that halo down along the head and shoulders, and around the entire body. Again, it will probably appear as a haze an inch or so away from the physical outline. Allow that experience to happen, even if only for a moment. Get comfortable with it.

8. As you continue your aura gazing, you may start to notice more than just the first layer of the aura, what is called the etheric body. You may see a whole egg or sphere shape around the person. At first it will probably be the edge of it, but you may see an overlay of color, from very faint to very

vibrant. Think about the colors of light and what they mean to you as you gaze. You may be drawn to a particular location in the body and notice some imbalance there. Ask your partner if there was an injury or upset in that body part. The injury does not have to be recent. You will be surprised at how many "hits" you get, letting your intuition and gaze naturally take you to the part of the body needing attention.

9. Ask your partner to think of very specific things while you aura gaze, in order to notice the differences. Try thinking about "home" first. The word home is charged with many emotional meanings, and could be a childhood home or the current living space. Take note, and then ask your partner how he or she feels about home, and match your observations with his or her thoughts. Try again with thoughts of "mother," "father," "job," and "some-one with whom you have strong feelings," and see what reactions you get. Happy and unhappy associations may cause different color shifts in the aura.

10. Switch roles and guide your partner through this exercise.

When you start gazing at the entire aura, the colors you perceive give you certain clues as to the person's energetic condition. Remember your own personal color associations. In general, the warmer colors indicate energy levels. The green range is often about emotional well-being. The blues and purples are about the mind and spirituality. Dominant colors give an indication as to personality, awareness, and current issues the individual is dealing with. Some colors remain stationary, while others change over time. Students usually see my aura as a mix of green and purple, which also happen to be two of my favorite colors; no wonder I am attracted to them. Yellow, gold, and blue have occasionally drifted through my aura as certain issues surfaced.

Different shades or intensities give us different indications. A bright yellow may mean a strong mind and will. A pale, sickly yellow may mean low metabolism and energy. Emerald green may indicate good physical health and vitality, while olive green may not. It all depends on your associations with colors. Unlike aura photography, two gazers may see different colors and come up with the same conclusion. They are seeing spiritual light and energy, not physical light, so it is open to interpretation, but in general, most will see similar colors. I may see blue and feel the person is very mental. To another, yellow and orange might be the colors of the mind, and he or she would see those brighter colors, but come to the same conclusion.

As you continue with aura gazing, the information you get will be more detailed. Some people see little homemade "movies," what we will later discuss as thought-forms, playing in the aura, usually around the head level. In these movies, the gazer sees or hears events in the past that still influence the person in the present. Some practitioners can see the images of current loved ones and family members in the aura. Others can see images from past lives in the aura. Healers focus on seeing the energetic state of the aura—if it is healthy and whole, or damaged. Your psychic mind will speak to you in the language of symbols that is most comfortable to you.

Auric Cleansing

Care and maintenance are essential if we want anything to work properly, including the aura. As you can see, the aura contains a lot of important information for us, and aids in our magick. Knowing how to control and heal it is a very important step in self-empowerment. You have already begun exercising control over your energy body. The affirmations help program your energy field to manifest your intentions. When you created a protection shield, you were programming your aura with the intention of protection. When you work with color and light, you are infusing these new vibrations into your aura. Try repeating the aura-gazing experience just described after your partner fills his or her aura with a different color of light. Also try it after exercise 6: Earth Walking. By changing your energy, you'll change the way others perceive your energy.

We do not learn how to keep our aura healthy in our traditional education. In fact, our society does not even promote energetic health. The edge of our aura is like a sphere or egg. The energy of thoughts, intentions, words, and arguments, our own and those directed at us, can damage this edge, allowing in unwanted vibration (figure 20A). With colorful phrases, we often refer to our relationships in terms of war: "She cut me to the quick." "His words are abrasive." "They stabbed me in the back." All of these images are truer than you know. We rip and tear our auric field, and through the cracks come unwanted vibrations. If you are easily overwhelmed by the energy of other people and places, your auric field may be letting in too much energy. You may not have a strong boundary, energetically or personally. This damage heals over time, but can heal much more quickly with our intentions.

Another sign of an unhealthy auric field is an abundance of unhealthy thought-forms. Thoughtforms are basically constructs of energy we create with our thoughts and intents. Thoughtforms are neither good nor bad. Like any piece of equipment, the label depends on how they are used. These constructs are like little computers we create that broadcast certain thoughts and vibrations. When we do a spell, or an act of instant magick, in many cases we are creating a small thoughtform with our intent and releasing it to fulfill its programming. In a detrimental sense, we create thoughtforms all the time and reinforce them with our "negative" self-programming. When you feel shame, anger, hate, or fear, and reflect that back on yourself, or accept judgments about yourself from other people, you create harmful programs, or heavy energy. These programs are often worded in such terms as, "I am not good enough," "I am not happy," "I am not pretty," and "I am not smart." These statements create thought-forms in your aura. They replay these harmful tapes, like a broken record, subconsciously speaking these messages, even when the situation does not warrant them. The use of affirmations creates helpful thoughtforms and programs. Neutralizing keeps us from creating new unwanted programs, but it does not remove the unwanted programs from years of living. Some even feel that our programs stay with us between lifetimes. If so, imagine how many old issues you are dealing with from these programs.

Harmful thoughtforms often appear as gray or black masses, little blobs floating in your auric field. If you are feeling the aura, they are usually experienced as packets of density. If the aura is a globe of water, the unwanted thoughtforms would be the murky sludge. Self-created thoughtforms lie on the inside of the field. Ones we accept from others might cling to the outside, unless they enter through the holes in the aura.

The last main issue of auric imbalance is unhealthy energy cords. A cord is an energetic connection, a circuit, that connects you to something else in an inappropriate way. Think of the cord as a straw, and you are either letting something or someone drain your energy, sucking it through the straw, or you are sucking energy from something else. The cord can act like a chain, preventing you from letting go and moving on.

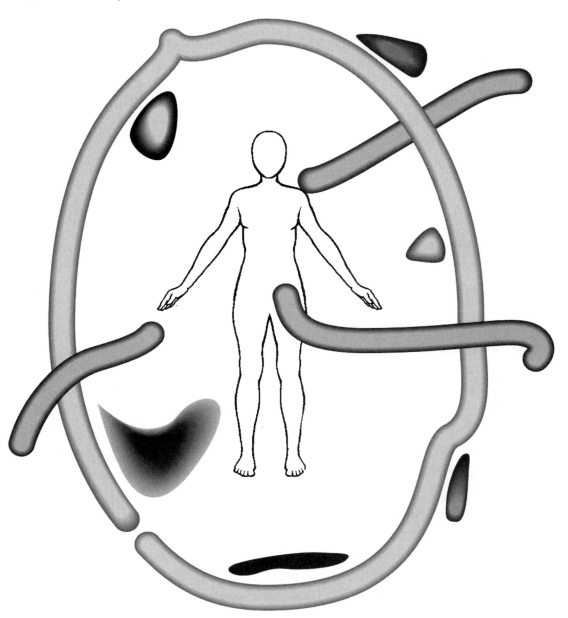

Figure 20A: *Damaged Aura*

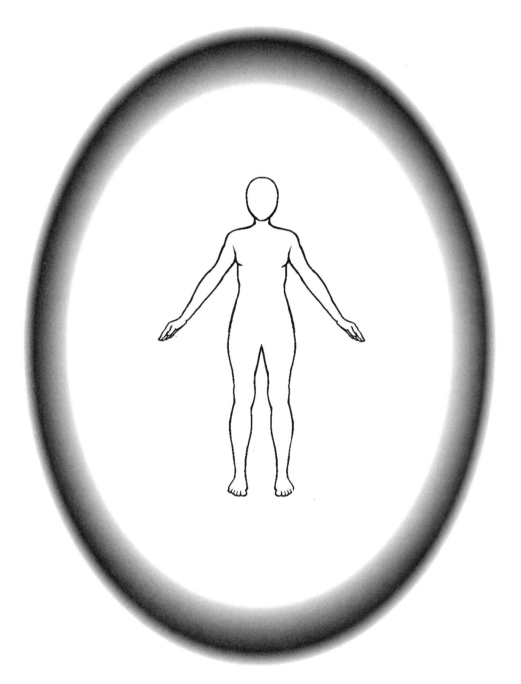

Figure 20B: *Healthy Aura*

Most cords tie us to someone in our lives with whom we have unresolved issues, and often an inappropriate relationship. By inappropriate, I mean no moral judgment, but a relationship that was not based in your own heartfelt joy. These people can be friends, family members, coworkers, or past lovers. You may even have some cords to current friends and lovers with whom things are great. But in the past, there was probably an issue that created the cord. They naturally dissolve, much like how scar tissue eventually goes away, but you can speed up the process yourself, with no scarring!

Cords can also be formed to places in your life, or moments in the past where you released a lot of energy. If you dwell on a certain location or time, you lose energy to it, because you are not using that energy for your present time. Memories and nostalgia are fine, but not if they prevent you from creating new memories. Some cords are connected to places of past abuse or violence.

In any case, the gentle dissolution of the cords and healing any damage they have created is paramount in living a responsible magickal life. When you heal them, you may know what the cord is connecting you to, or you may not. Usually knowledge brings awareness, but sometimes we don't know. The cord still heals. For particularly old or strong cords, the process may be repeated several times. You will only be guided to clear the cords you need to work on now. Just because you can't see them doesn't mean that there aren't more there. The first time I did this meditation, I had three cords, and I thought to myself, "Hey, that's not bad at all." I did not do this exercise as regularly as I should have, and when I did it again over a year later, I had eighteen cords. They were there before. I didn't create all eighteen in a year's time, but each one represented a different issue I was ready to handle at that moment. I wasn't ready when I first did the exercise.

EXERCISE 24

Aura Clearing

This meditation may bring up some difficult feelings for you to process and clear as you continue on your magickal path. You may have an emotional release. It is not uncommon to find people crying tears of pain or joy, making noises and tones, giggling, or feeling light headed. During the meditation, you may feel like toning or making some type of noise as a form of release. Please do so. Follow your intuition. Some blank out the experience entirely and wonder if they fell asleep. I truly feel that as we have guardian spirits, we have healing spirits as well, coming to help us in these situations, through events that are difficult to bear at this time. Sleep indicates that they are working with us on a deep level. Spirit guides will be explored in detail in chapters 13 and 14.

If this experience is difficult for you, please seek healing facilitation from a qualified practitioner. Your journal work and daily meditations can be very therapeutic, but sometimes we need outside assistance.

1. Start exercise 9: Counting Down to a Meditative State to get into your magickal mindset.

2. Be aware of your own aura, an egg or sphere shape around your body. Everyone perceives it differently. You can feel the energy of the aura moving around you, particularly in terms of temperature or magnetic resistance. You may psychically see it around you even with your eyes closed. What color is it, and what does that color mean to you? Do you notice any unusual patterns of color, or places that seem out of balance? Allow the information to come. Be aware of the energy around you.

3. Ground yourself by visualizing a beam of light, any color that feels right to you, descending down from your spine and into the center of the Earth. Your aura will look like a balloon being tied down, preventing it from going far. This sense of grounding is very important before doing the rest of this meditation.

4. Put out the intention that you wish to "completely cleanse the aura of any harm," and ask that this cleansing come with "ease, grace, and gentleness." Ask your healing guides to aid you. Ask for the love and guidance of the Goddess and God.

5. Look closely at the aura. Scan it from top to bottom, sensing any rips or tears. Look for leaks in the aura where you are releasing vital life force or allowing other energies to come in to infect you. They may feel like cold or "windy" spots. The event that created this hole might pop into your mind, allowing you to deal with the feelings associated with it. When you find this area, imagine it filling with a ball of white light. The white light fills the space like plaster over a hole in the wall. Allow the white light to change to whatever color is appropriate for that section of your aura. Continue this process until you have sealed all the holes in the aura.

6. Again scan the aura from top to bottom, this time searching for any unwanted thoughtforms. They will appear as areas of density, dark unhealthy-looking masses floating in the auric field, like garbage floating in water. When you find one, psychically reach out and "grab" it. When you do, the program, or thought creating it, becomes apparent, allowing you to mentally and emotionally release it. Fill the thoughtform with white light, push it out of the aura, and dissolve it in a burst of energy. Intend and order the thoughtforms outside of your aura as they dissolve. Continue this process until you have cleared all the harmful thoughtforms in the aura.

7. For the last step of the auric cleansing, scan the aura and body for any cords, beams of energy connecting you to someone or someplace else. Psychically reach out and "grab" the cord, and the connection is often revealed to you. Notice where the cord is in the aura. The location will be a clue to the type of harm it is doing to you. Cords in the heart indicate emotions. Cords in the belly are often fear or sexuality. Cords in the throat are communication issues. Cords in the back mean trust issues. When they are on the right side, it indicates masculine issues, and the left, feminine issues. When you find a cord, pull it out gently. The cord may be lodged in your body or in the aura, in the space around your body. Bless and release whatever is attached to the cord. Do this in love and healing, not anger or malice. Resentment is a common feeling, particularly when disconnecting

from an abusive relationship, but you are coming into your power now. Let it go as much as you can. Pull the cord out, and send white light down the tube, dissolving it safely, causing no harm to you or anyone at the other end. Release them by saying, "Blessed be." Fill in any holes created in your body or aura with white light, allowing it to change to the appropriate color. Continue this process until you have cleared all cords. The cords revealed to you now are the issues you are prepared to clear. Check on all sides, above and below you.

8. Change your aura's color through intention, choosing a color with qualities you desire. Do whatever feels good to you. You can even arrange colors in layers. Many people put a violet layer on the outside, for additional protection. If your aura is tight around your body and contracted, expand it to a comfortable size. If your aura is large and diffuse, bring your boundaries into a comfortable space, roughly a bit wider than arm's length.

9. Reaffirm your protection shield: "I charge my protection shield to protect me from all harm on any level, and reflect love back on the source of the harm." Repeat this three times and end with "So mote it be."

10. Return yourself to normal consciousness, counting up, and giving yourself clearance and balance. Do any necessary grounding.

The days after the meditation may be difficult. As we flush out these emotions and energetic toxins, their physical correspondences release from our body as well. Just as fasts and cleansing diets can bring up emotional issues, this meditation is the same process, starting with the subtle body rather than the physical. Drink plenty of pure water to flush the toxins out of your system and try to take it easy until you feel better.

CHAKRAS

Chakra is Sanskrit for "spinning wheel," referring to the spinning wheels of light within the energy body. As your physical body has physical organs, your spiritual bodies have spiritual, or energetic, organs, points of light, that process energy in much the same

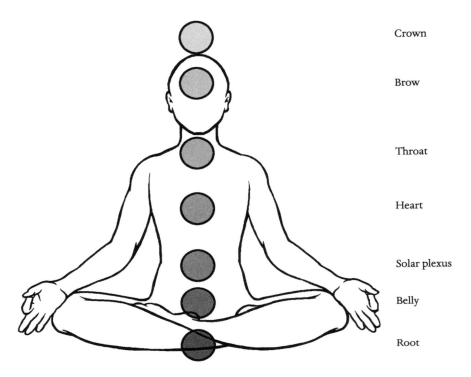

Crown

Brow

Throat

Heart

Solar plexus

Belly

Root

Figure 21: The Seven Chakras

way physical organs process food, water, and oxygen. Each works on a different level of reality. The word *chakra* is used universally in the New Age movement, although it is believed that many ancient cultures in addition to the Hindu knew of these energy centers. Unfortunately, their names for these energy centers were lost. Hopi dolls have been found with markings where each of the seven chakras exists. Myths of halos, "fire in the head," "wheels within wheels," and "tongues of flame" descending on the brow are possibly references to chakras.

Although there are many adaptations to the chakra system, the most commonly accepted model contains seven points running along the axis of the spine (figure 21). Each chakra contains one of the main colors of the spectrum, starting at the bottom of the spine and ascending. They are connected through a "central core channel," like a tube, through which energy flows, as well as spiraling kundalini channels. Each chakra is associated with a different function of consciousness as well as particular body systems, glands, subtle bodies, and gemstones. Consecrating and carrying the associated gemstones, or laying them on the chakra, will help alleviate any imbalances or issues you have with each.

Root

The root chakra is found at the base of the spine, often visualized as a ball of red light at the perineum point, between the sexual organs and the anus. In Hindu traditions, the root is called *Muladhara*. The root is considered the first chakra because it deals with our most basic functions and earthly needs, "rooting" us in the physical world. Our physical bodies relate to the root, because its function is to keep us alive. Our survival instinct, our sense of grounding or being "in the body," and the desire to procreate and carry on our genetic identity are related to this chakra. Because of this genetic identity, the root also relates to our immediate family or tribe, the people from which we originate. The glands associated with the root are the sexual glands, the gonads in men and the ovaries in women. It is also related to the excretory system, purging physical toxins out of the body to allow us to live. Dysfunctions of the root chakra can manifest as illness in those systems, sexual dysfunction, lack of pleasure and enjoyment in life, particularly from any physical sensations, ungrounded feelings, depression, or suicidal impulses. Betrayals from immediate family / tribe members, especially sexual abuse, create dysfunction in the root. Red stones, such as rubies and garnets, are associated with the root.

The root stores the energy of kundalini, which means "coiled serpent." Kundalini is part of our personal energy, our life force that lies dormant at the root chakra. It spirals up the body through the kundalini channels, the ida and pingala, as a double helix, through the seven chakras. The helix looks like the symbol of the modern medical associations: the caduceus, or staff with two coiled serpents. It also looks like our DNA (figure 22).

In many Western magickal traditions, the root chakra is not at the base of the spine, as in the Sanskrit literature, but between the feet. This variation comes from the different executions of Eastern and Western magick. In Eastern mysticism, meditation with the chakras is usually done sitting down with the base of the spine touching the

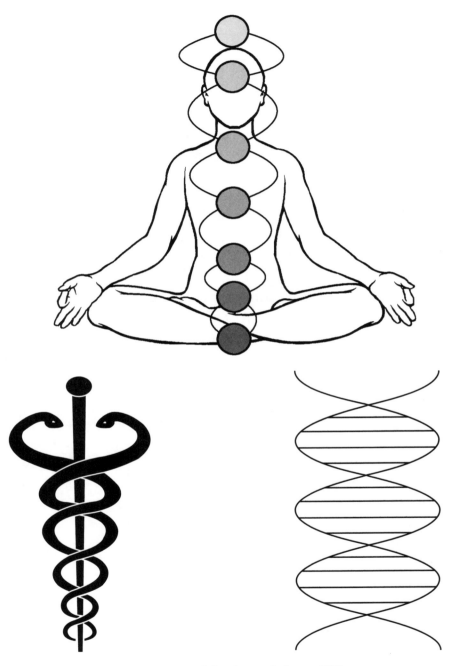

Figure 22: Kundalini Rising, Caduceus, DNA

ground. In Western magickal traditions, particularly in ceremonial magick, the practitioner is usually standing. To me, both examples further testify to the fact that energy will take form in any way we intend and perceive it to.

Belly

The belly chakra is also called the sacral chakra, relating it to the lower sacral spine, abdominal chakra, or *Svadisthana* in the Eastern texts. As there are many names, the location tends to vary according to the tradition and teacher. Possibilities include slightly below, above, or at the naval point. Personally I think it is because people have different body types. Certain individuals have longer arms, bigger heads, or smaller feet. Some have a lower or higher naval point, and these differences reflect the range of possibilities. When you activate the chakras in the next exercise, you will be able to feel where this point is for you, and visualize it as a ball of orange light in the belly area. Carnelian is the stone associated with the belly chakra.

As the second chakra, it moves beyond the physical needs of the root and into the realm of primal instincts and emotions. This energy relates to our basic need to reach out and commune with another being. While the root is our relationship to self, the belly is the relationship to others, symbolizing our recognition that there is more than just "me." Sexual and social relationships and one-on-one relationships are related to the belly. When you follow your instincts about a certain person, to trust or not to trust, many say you "follow your gut." That is why there is almost a physical sensation to our instincts. We are, in reality, following our own body's wisdom. Also, our ability to trust ourselves and relax relates to the belly. Inhibitions and freedom, tension and relaxation, are the tides of the orange chakra.

Physically, the belly chakra relates to the kidneys, intestines, lower digestive system, spleen, and pancreas. I have heard it referred to as the spleen chakra. The skeletal system could be connected, too. The etheric body, the energetic template to the physical body, relates to the belly. This level of the energy body holds our shape. The material of the physical body is regenerated every seven years, but illness and scars can last longer because the physical matter is filling in the associated damaged sections of the etheric body.

Disorders of the second chakra include digestive disorders, particularly ulcers, hypertension, mood swings, an inability to trust one's instincts, and difficulties communicating and relating to others as individuals.

Solar Plexus

The solar plexus is located right below the diaphragm muscle, beneath the rib cage. This yellow chakra is called *Manipura* and relates to a basic human desire to exercise control over the things that are beyond us. With the belly, we reach out to others, and now we seek to exercise our will on the outside world. Our sense of power, on all levels, from physical power, health, metabolism, and energy to our strength of will, mental control, and even spiritual energy, is tied to the solar plexus. The lesson of this chakra is to learn about our power and our fear.

Our self-image is related to the solar plexus. How do you view yourself? Through the lens of fear, or through self-control and trust? A healthy self-image relates to your sense of security in the world. The astral body, the next of the subtle energy bodies, is linked with the solar plexus, as are the powers of astral travel and psychokinesis, the ability to move matter with your mind, the ultimate act of willpower and control.

The musculature system, the power to move, is the main body system associated with the solar plexus, but it also relates to the stomach, liver, gall bladder, and adrenal glands. When you feel fear, these glands activate to give you a boost of adrenaline. We also say "butterflies in the stomach" when feeling fearful. The liver cleanses and stores toxins from the body, and harmful feelings are the biggest toxins we have. In Chinese medicine, the liver is called the "throne of anger" because our anger is stored there. Cleansing the liver releases old angers and pains. Imbalances in any of these organs, including hyperactivity or chronic fatigue, indicators of energy level, are signs of solar-plexus issues. Issues with power, control, and addiction are in the realm of the third chakra. Citrine is the healing stone of the solar plexus.

Heart

The heart, called *Anahata*, is located at the sternum and is usually viewed as green, sometimes with a pink center. The heart is the middle chakra and, as such, the bridge between our lower and higher selves. Associated with emotion, the heart chakra's true purpose is to bring us to a state of unconditional love, or perfect divine love. The purpose of our emotions is to bring us spiritual awareness through the connections we

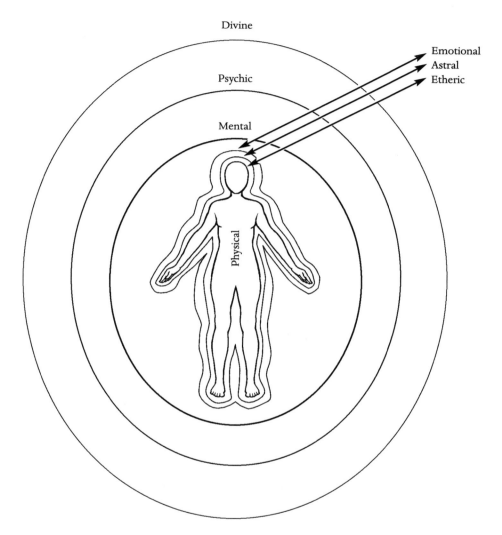

Figure 23: Layers of the Aura

feel to our family, friends, community, and eventually the entire human tribe and all of nature. Our sense of balance between our needs and desires and our feelings of compassion are associated with the heart. Any green or pink stones are associated with healing and opening the heart chakra, including emerald and rose quartz.

Energetically, the emotional body is linked to us through the heart space. Physically, this chakra is naturally associated with the heart muscle and circulatory system.

The skin, immune system, and thymus gland, often called the high heart, are also related to the heart chakra. When you suffer from heart and circulatory disorders, the heart chakra is in need of healing. An inability to form loving relationships, to trust others, to express your emotions freely, and feelings of guilt and shame are other signs of dysfunction. Love must start with the self before it can move out to others. Although anyone can suffer from a heart attack for a variety of reasons, the Western world tends to associate heart attacks with older men in a society that generally does not encourage them to be emotionally open, available, and affectionate, because it at one time clashed with society's expectations of men. Hopefully, as we change our expectations, heart disease, both physical and emotional, will decline.

Throat

The blue sphere at the base of the neck is the throat chakra and relates to the ability to express ourselves and communicate. Through the heart we have learned trust and compassion, to relate to others without a need for control. The throat chakra encourages us to express these higher thoughts and feelings to others. Strangely enough, the throat chakra represents not only expression, but also its opposite, listening. One must be able to take in and understand the expressions of another as well as send them out. The throat chakra is like a message-relaying system, taking in and sending out signals on all levels, for the throat chakra also relates to our spiritual and psychic hearing—listening to the inner voice, nature, the song of the universe, and our spirit guides. Psychic hearing is called clairaudience, and many people receive information this way. On this psychic level, the throat chakra rules our higher willpower. As the solar plexus is our need to control what is already there, our throat helps us manifest our will. Spells are often spoken. The ability to speak up and state what you desire to happen is part of your magickal abilities. Magick words have a long tradition because they manifest our will, and we use the energy of the throat chakra to send them off into the universe to return to us what we desire. Because of its relationship to our thoughts, words, intentions, and communications, the throat chakra relates to the mental body, the mind. The mind is not located solely in your brain, but throughout your entire body and energy field.

Physically, the respiratory system, including the vocal chords, larynx, tonsils, and thyroid, is related to the throat chakra. Our ability to take in breath is directly connected to our mind. Panic attacks and hyperventilation are triggered by thoughts that manifest as these immediate problems. Think of the people you know who have a thyroid condition—hyper being overactive, and hypo being underactive. It has been my experience that they have had some form of communication problem, usually speaking out too much and not listening, or not speaking up enough. Communication issues are all imbalances of the throat, including sarcasm, gossip, and a fear of speaking up.

The throat chakra is called *Vishuddi*, and its stones are turquoise, sapphire, and lapis lazuli.

Brow

This chakra is located between and slightly above the eyes. The Hindu texts call it *Anja*, although most refer to it as the third eye. The gland of this chakra is the pineal gland, found in the brain, and some evidence suggests that the structure of this gland is much like an eye that never fully developed. Although located within the brain, the pineal gland can sense light, which influences its ability to produce hormones. Metaphysicians feel that this eye is "looking" at the invisible spiritual light connecting us all.

The brow chakra relates to the function of seeing: physical seeing, seeing situations clearly, and seeing things psychically, our sixth sense. Through this chakra we learn to see things as they really are, to learn the spiritual reality that interacts with our physical reality. When we use our "mind's eye" to visualize something, we are using our brow chakra. Our powers of intuition, clairvoyance (psychic seeing), and most visually related tasks come from the third eye, relating to the psychic body. The psychic body brings us information and knowledge. In European traditions of witchcraft, particularly Celtic, this is called "the sight," and many people are naturally gifted with it, though anyone can learn to use it.

Besides the pineal gland, the brow chakra is associated with the lower brain and nervous system, how information is relayed to the entire body. Migraine headaches and nervous disorders are signs of imbalance, along with a "lack of vision" for yourself, or surrounding yourself with illusions and falsehoods about your life situations. Many metaphysical students suffer from what is now known as the "third eye headache" when opening to new abilities and energies. Classes with a lot of energies, such as crystal workshops or psychic development, tend to bring them on. They are temporary. Ground yourself and the troublesome energies and headache should dissipate. Indigo is the color of Anja, and indigo and purple stones like amethyst are used to help open this chakra.

Crown

The crown chakra sits not in the body, but at the top of the head, at the crown. Known as *Sahasrara*, it is visualized as violet, lavender, or dazzling white. It is the culmination of the chakra system, expressing our innate connection to the divine and all life. The crown chakra is the source of inspiration and divine wisdom. It opens the gates to spiritual epiphanies and insights, giving us greater spiritual understanding. This divine perspective, this spiritual sense of knowing, can be called the seventh sense, moving us beyond the simple intuitive and psychic flashes of the sixth sense. This chakra is our connection to the Great Mother Goddess and Father God, the Great Spirit and source of all that is. Our sense of divine love and a higher power springs from the well of the crown chakra and flows through to the energy centers below.

The crown relates to the pituitary gland. This is the master gland of the endocrine system, controlling hormonal levels throughout the body, though some traditions associate the pineal gland with the crown. The higher brain is also linked to the crown, our higher realms of consciousness. As the heart and love are connected to the immune system, so is the crown. In fact, body-wide disorders or illnesses are often related to the upper chakras.

The opal, diamond, and clear/white quartz are the stones of the crown.

Notice how the chakras, from one to seven, demonstrate a developmental cycle of consciousness, from simple physical needs to the spiritual.

Now that you have an overview of the chakra system, remember where your cords were in the aura-clearing meditation. Does knowledge of the chakras help refine the lesson learned when removing each cord? Illness in a certain area of the body indicates a problem with the associated chakra. Be open to the message. The colors of the chakras may also play a part in your light magick.

If you have been keeping up with the exercises and homework, you have already been working with the chakras without even knowing it. Just as you can breathe, digest, and metabolize without understanding anatomy, you use your chakras with or without knowledge of them. Although we are focusing on the seven major chakras, there are also points of energy in the hands, feet, and major nerve clusters in the body. All the energy exercises have involved some form of chakra work. Connecting to the Earth and sky ran energy through your central channel. You may have intuitively felt the chakras activating and aligning. Now you have the conscious information.

EXERCISE 25

Chakra Opening and Balancing

The following meditation opens and clears all seven chakras and can be used prior to any deep magickal work. Ideally the whole exercise should be done regularly. You can break the meditation into two parts. The first part works with opening and cleansing the chakras. The second part is the Earth and Sky meditation, as in exercise 16, but instead of letting the energy flow up and down, we will focus attention on each chakra point for a moment. I try to do the second half of this meditation every day to keep myself open, connected, and clear.

Prior to exercise 25, you must choose a symbol to represent balance. You will be visualizing this symbol over the chakras. Some possible symbols are shown in figure 24.

1. Start exercise 9: Counting Down to a Meditative State to get into your magickal mindset.

2. Be aware of the energy around you, your aura, and the flow of energy up and down the spine.

3. Focus your attention on the base of the spine, the root chakra. Be aware of this bright red disc. Feel the chakra start to spin open and activate as you inhale. Feel it spin open, cleansing any blocks you have to the physical world and to your sense of community. Release any anger you have for anyone or anything in the world. The chakra spins open like a red water lily or lotus flower revealing a fiery ruby within it, clear and energized.

4. With the next inhale, focus your attention on your naval area, at the belly or sacral chakra. Be aware of this glowing orange wheel of light. Feel the

Figure 24: Symbols of Balance

chakra start to spin open and activate. Feel it spin open and cleanse any blocks you have to your instincts and your relationships. Release any sense of betrayal. The chakra spins open like an orange lotus flower revealing an orange carnelian stone within it, clear and energized.

5. With the next inhale, focus your attention below the diaphragm muscle, at the solar-plexus chakra. Be aware of this shining yellow disc. Feel the chakra start to spin open and activate. Feel it spin open and cleanse any blocks you have to your personal power and will. Release any fear you have. The chakra spins open like a yellow lotus flower revealing a yellow citrine stone within it, clear and energized.

6. With the next inhale, focus your attention on the sternum bone, at the heart chakra. Be aware of this pulsing green wheel. Feel the chakra start to spin open and activate. Feel it spin open and cleanse any blocks you have to unconditional love, perfect love, and perfect trust. Release any grudges and forgive. The chakra spins open like a green lotus flower revealing an emerald within it, clear and energized.

7. With the next inhale, focus your attention on the thorax, at the throat chakra. Be aware of this spinning blue light. Feel the chakra start to spin open and activate. Feel it spin open and cleanse any blocks you have to communication, including psychic communication. Release any judgments you hold. The chakra spins open like a blue lotus flower revealing a blue sapphire within it, clear and energized.

8. With the next inhale, focus your attention on the brow, at the third-eye chakra. Be aware of this deep-indigo point of light. Feel the chakra start to

spin open and activate. Feel it spin open and cleanse any blocks you have to your psychic and magickal gifts. Release any blinders you have to the truth. The chakra spins open like a purple lotus flower revealing an amethyst within it, clear and energized.

9. With the next inhale, focus your attention on the top of the head, at the crown chakra. Be aware of this dazzling light, violet or white in color. Feel the chakra start to spin open and activate. Feel it open and cleanse any blocks you have to your connection to the divine, the Goddess and God. Come into your joy. The chakra spins open like a white lotus flower revealing a dazzling diamond within it, clear and energized.

10. With all seven chakras open and cleared, visualize your symbol of balance above the crown. Intend that it balance the energies of the crown chakra. Hold it there. Let it descend to the third eye with the same intention. Bring it down to the throat. Then bring it to the heart, solar plexus, belly, and root. When you are done balancing all the chakras, let the symbol descend from the base of your spine, down into the Earth, creating your grounding cord, a beam of light grounding you to the center of the planet.

11. Ask Mother Earth to send you this energy, and feel it ascend through this grounding "straw" or taproot to the root chakra as you inhale. Feel it energize the root, and with each breath, feel it move up through the belly, solar plexus, heart, throat, third eye, and crown, rising out of the crown and connecting you to the sky.

12. Ask the Sky Father to send his energy down, and feel it descend down through the crown like water, flowing down through the seven chakras and into the earth. Pause a moment at each of these points to feel the energy flow through. Feel the balance in each chakra and in your entire body.

13. When done, slow down the energy flow with your intent, and then stop it, allowing the remaining earth energy to flow upward and out, and the remaining sky energy to flow down and out into the Earth, helping ground you.

14. Return yourself to normal consciousness, counting up, and giving yourself clearance and balance. Do any necessary grounding.

Scan your aura and chakras often. As your awareness of the energy anatomy grows, you will perceive the location and reason for imbalances. Such information will help you pinpoint problem areas in your life that need to be addressed.

NEW ASSIGNMENTS

• Exercises 23 through 25—Complete and record your experiences in your Book of Shadows. Notice changes in yourself after the aura-clearing exercise and repeat as needed.

• Try aura gazing in your daily life, looking at the energy of people, plants, objects, and areas.

CONTINUING ASSIGNMENTS

• Daily journal—Write three pages a day.

• Focus on a regular meditation practice, at least three times a week if not daily.

• Honor and recognize your intuition. Continue to ask it questions.

• Use instant magick in your daily life.

• Neutralize unwanted thoughts and intentions.

• Continue using light in your life and meditations.

TIPS

• If you have difficulty perceiving the aura, pick a point six to twelve inches above the crown of your partner. Look at your partner only through your peripheral vision.

• If you want a physical exercise to improve your visualization, stare at your third eye or brow. Look up at the brow, between the eyes, and count to twelve. Release and relax for a minute and then repeat. Practice it in moderation. This eye exercise improves your visualization skills.

- Remember that not everybody gets their information visually. I tried this experiment with two other magickal friends of mine. I taught them about seeing the aura, but neither really saw it. One "heard" the color in his head when he looked—no visual involved. The other "knew" the color, but did not "hear" or "see" it. She just knew. Most of the time we had the same color, and every time we had the same general interpretation. You could experience tastes, sensations, or smells when exploring the aura and chakras, each with specific associations. Find your own way.

- Be gentle with yourself, particularly when it comes to aura and chakra clearing. Don't push yourself too far too fast. Magickal training is much like physical training. You must build your strength slowly, even if you have natural talent. Honor your own limits and do not compare your experiences to others. Your experience is perfect for you.

RECOMMENDED READING

Wheels of Life by Anodea Judith (Llewellyn Publications).
Anatomy of the Spirit by Caroline Myss (Three Rivers Press).

LESSON 8
JOURNEY WORK

Witches take many journeys, traveling far and wide, but not always in the physical realms. Witches take journeys of spirit, learning to walk between the material world and the spiritual planes. One of the best definitions of a witch is "a walker between the worlds." Our modern culture still clings to the archetype of the old witch woman flying on her broom in the night sky. Traditional formulas of "flying" potions and ointments are found in modern witchcraft books. To the casual observer, one would think that these refer to physical events, not internal, spiritual travels. The flying broom is a misinterpretation of ancient fertility rites. The women would dance in a circle, broom between the thighs, jumping and hopping up in an act of sympathetic magick. They jumped up with these phallic fertility symbols, mimicking the upward growth of new plant life, doing magick to ensure a fertile crop. Flying potions were concoctions of herbs that would help induce visions and allow one to journey in the spiritual realms. Many perceive this experience as flying. Stories of these rituals and herbal formulas were exaggerated to the image of the witch flying around on a broomstick.

Inducing an altered state and focusing your perception on a nonphysical reality is the act of journeying. Your perception and awareness shift from one channel to another, like a television. You are traveling without your physical body, but you're with your subtle bodies. Because of this, you are not limited to the distances your body can travel. You are only limited by your own mind and will. Your physical body does not disappear, but remains quiet and focused. Most people are simultaneously aware of the journey and the physical body.

Believe it or not, you have probably done some form of spiritual travel before. If you dream, you journey, and everyone dreams even if they don't remember it. Journeying is as natural to us as breathing, though we have placed so much importance on the physical realm that we neglect other levels of awareness.

Many types of journeying exist, the only differences being technique, perception, and belief system. Spiritual travel can be easily divided into two main categories, those that focus on physical locations, and those that do not.

Astral Travel

For journeys of the physical realm, you are focusing on a physical location that your body does not currently occupy. If you believe the Hermetic principles, this is not as crazy as it would seem. If all things are part of the divine mind, then "barriers" of distance, or even time, are only perceptions of other thoughts in the divine mind. They are not real since we are all essentially the same being, the divine mind. Most people call this experience astral projection, but remote viewing, psychic travel, soul travel, outer journeying, and mental projection are other terms applied. The goal is to psychically retrieve information about the location. The proof is to actually visit the location to verify this information. With practice, one can get quite specific and detailed. If you have difficulty believing that such abilities exist, I highly suggest the book *Psychic Warrior* by David A. Moorehouse. It is a personal account of someone who was part of a U.S. government remote-viewing unit and the intense training involved. I believe that the governments of the world take the entire psychic phenomenon much more seriously that most people believe.

GUIDED MEDITATION

The second type of journey is not as goal oriented, at least in regard to physical verification. This journey focuses on your own personal experiences. If you have ever sat back, relaxed, and imagined yourself at your favorite place, perhaps a mountain, beach, or forest, then you have had such a journey. Imagination is the key to these realms, as well as allowing the experience to happen. You may feel that you are making it up, and in a sense, you are, but that does not make the journey any less real. When we stop focusing on an actual physical location, we enter a realm beyond form, a realm of energy and vibration. Since the human mind has difficulty processing pure energy, we drape symbols, such as fantastic locations, on it to make the experience easier to understand. The symbols come from our conscious and subconscious minds. If you feel you're making the experience up with your imagination, you may be choosing the symbols on some level, but the energy and experience are very real.

Any type of guided meditation, whether guided by yourself or someone else, is a form of journey. With a teacher, one is creating a group experience, suggesting common symbols and building a common journey, although each participant will perceive it individually. Although most journeys are led in terms of visuals, all the psychic senses are engaged. People will often smell, hear, taste, feel, and know information in the journey.

When I lead such a journey, many participants comment afterward that they were "ahead of me," doing things slightly before I said them. Perhaps they were anticipating me, or reading my mind. Or better yet, perhaps they were going along with a very real group journey. Others will go off and do their own journey, not following my words, and that is correct for them. The best thing is to go with your first perception.

Guided imagery is sometimes called pathworking, based on the Kabalah. The Kabalah, spelled many different ways, or the Tree of Life, is a map of reality, a map of the spiritual planes in this system (figure 25). Each sphere represents a dimension, or level of consciousness. The lines connecting them are paths. Paths and spheres are associated with colors, sounds, angels, planets, tarot cards, and ritual tools. Many personal meditations are based on these images, moving from one sphere to the next via a path, hence the name *pathworking*. Now the term is applied to many types of meditation, since Western magickal traditions, including modern Wicca, have borrowed elements from the Kabalah.

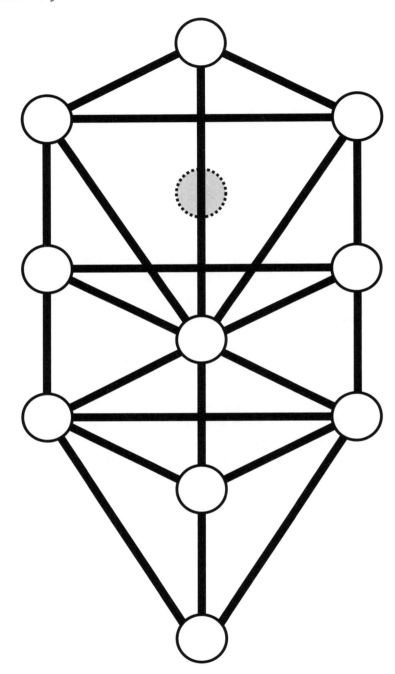

Figure 25: Kabalah

DREAMING

Dreams are another way of interfacing with a nonphysical reality. So many people believe that dreams occur solely inside one's head, but as we are learning, the mind is not limited to the brain, so why should dreams be? Magickal cultures believe that dreams are an opportunity for your spiritual body to travel to the spiritual realms for learning and rejuvenation. Everyone needs sleep and everyone dreams, even if they don't remember it. That is why sleep deprivation is so dangerous. You are not giving a part of you the necessary freedom to explore and heal.

With dreams, we obviously let our subconscious translate the messages we receive, using symbols. These symbols are sometimes obvious because they are also a part of our conscious mind, and at other times they are veiled, needing to be decoded and understood by the conscious self. If you survey the general populace, the majority of people would say that they cannot control their dreams. Dreams simply happen. Although that is true, there exists a small minority, particularly those practicing forms of meditation and mysticism, who can control their dreams and use this time in very unusual ways. They experience journeys to physical and nonphysical locations, speaking with spirits, learning new information, solving problems, and actually controlling the dream itself, like an extremely vivid guided meditation. That is why I encourage you to keep a dream journal. You never know what will come out as you train and explore these untapped abilities.

Controlling a dream is called lucid dreaming. As the dreamer, you are clearly aware that you are in a dream. Realizing it is a dream, and not "real" or physical, gives you a certain amount of control in the journey, as in a meditation. Unlike meditations, where you can be easily distracted if you do not allow yourself to go deeply into an altered state, with lucid dreaming, you are already in a deep altered state and cannot be easily distracted. The key to lucid dreaming is to program yourself to be aware that you are having a dream. This is particularly useful if you suffer from nightmares. It gives you a measure of control and tools for dealing with the feelings manifesting as nightmares.

Try these dreaming exercises on your own and experiment to find what works for you. Since you are working with the subconscious, don't be discouraged with the initial results—keep trying. Think of dream work as a wonderful tool to use if you have it, but don't let any difficulties hold you back from continuing your studies.

When faced with a problem or perplexing situation, write out your desire to easily solve this problem. Write something like "I, (state your name), ask in the name of the Goddess and God, to solve (name your problem)." Fold it up and put it under your pillow. Let it go. Do not try to figure it out again before you fall asleep, simply let it go, knowing that it will be taken care of. Keep your dream journal by your bed. When you wake up, you will have your answer in your dreams, though you may need to think about the symbolism in your dream, or share it with a close friend, to understand it.

A second dream exercise involves meditating for a few moments before bed. Count yourself down to your magickal mindset, or do your trigger, and program yourself, like an affirmation, so that you will see a certain object in your dream, such as a particular type of tree. When you see that tree, you will realize it is a dream and be in conscious control, a lucid dreaming state. Remember to keep your dream journal by your bed.

SHAMANIC JOURNEY

The last form of journeying is the shamanic journey. Shamanic trance is an altered state of consciousness entered through a variety of means, but most often involving drumming or music. This is an exhibitory form of altered consciousness to induce trance and open the veil between worlds. Some traditions involve the use of various plants, sometimes of a psychotropic nature, to facilitate the process. The old witch's flying potions are part of a long tradition of European shamanism.

In the practice of core shamanism, otherworldly journeyers had a basic map of reality. Like the Kabalah, the shaman's worldview was also often associated with a tree. The World Tree is seen as a giant spire, a universal axis or axis mundi, a ladder of sorts, connecting all the levels of reality (figure 26). At the base of the tree and its trunk, one finds the Middle World. The Middle World is our commonly accepted physical reality, the realm of time, space, and matter. Everyone lives in the Middle World while in body. Middle World travel is to move in time or space, like remote viewing or astral travel. In the roots of the tree, below the Earth, lies the Underworld. The Underworld is not a place of torment, punishment, or retribution, but a place of healing, power, and the ancestors. The Underworld is associated with our subconscious, unconscious, and psychic mind. The experiences can be dreamlike. In the branches of the World Tree is the Upper World. The Upper World is a heavenly realm, where information is more for spiritual growth and given directly, unlike the veiled Underworld symbolism.

Upper World

Middle World

Underworld

Figure 26: World Tree

Think of the conscious mind, or middle self, as the Middle World. The Underworld is represented by the psychic mind, and the Upper World is the divine mind, or super consciousness.

In shamanic journeys, the practitioner uses the tree and these three areas as a guide for further adventures, influenced by the mythology of one's particular culture or personal experiences. Although most use the World Tree image, some traditions use a world mountain, rising in the sky and rooted firmly in the earth. Any image can be used to represent the cosmic axis, like a ladder, beanstalk, or skyscraper.

LEVELS OF REALITY

Mystics act as psychonauts, explorers of the vast, unknown spiritual realms. Each explorer's experience is unique and personal. There are many common, archetypal experiences found all over the world, and these are encoded in the myths and traditions of mysticism, and as a result there are many ways to view the various levels of reality. The Kabalistic Tree of Life and the shamanic World Tree are but two. It is important when you study these models that you understand they are just that, models. They are not absolutes. They are human interpretations and symbols of energies that are vast and unknowable in three-dimensional terms. Each model is as valuable as the understanding or experience it gives you. Each is a map to guide you through journey experiences, but many different kinds of maps exist, from streets to topography, depending on what you need for your journey.

One model I have found to be very helpful is the concept of seven levels of reality, based on the chakras (figure 27). Each chakra is associated with a subtle body, as discussed in chapter 11. Each subtle body, each layer of the aura, is also associated with a level of existence, of consciousness. It is important to remember with this model that we are "multidimensional," capable of existing in many realms simultaneously, not just one. We focus on a small area at a time, but are always part of the great vastness of all levels in the divine mind. Think of these levels as the subtle bodies of the Goddess and God.

The first layer, associated with the root chakra, is the physical realm (figure 27). The physical realm is analogous with the earth element and the shamanic Middle World. This is the level of reality with which most people are familiar. Anything that is physical exists in this layer.

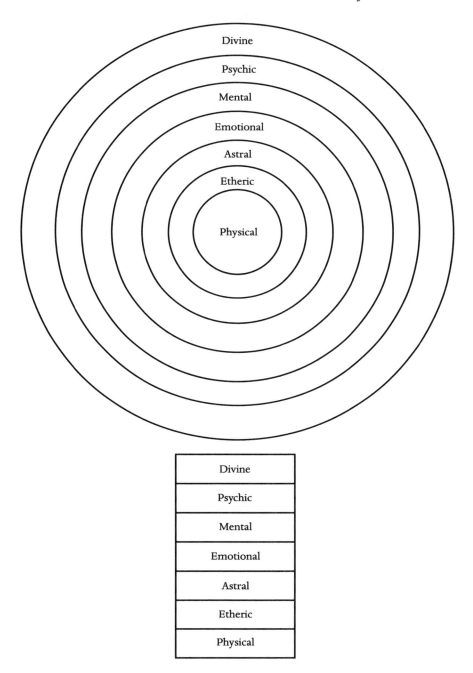

Figure 27: Planes of Reality

The etheric realm is the one most closely associated with the physical. Anything with a physical body has an etheric template, a duplicate. The first edge of the aura, closest to the human body, is the etheric body, providing the energetic and structural blueprint for matter. The etheric is also associated with the belly chakra, the element of earth, and the Middle World. Think of it as the energy background to the physical world. Since it is so closely associated with the physical, practitioners do not perceive themselves as journeying in the etheric.

The astral plane is the level that people are usually very interested in. The astral plane is a plane of shape and form, but not matter. It is said that everything physical has an astral counterpart, but not everything astral has a physical counterpart. The astral echoes the physical plane, but is not bound by the same sense of space in the physical, so one can use it as a medium to connect to physical locations, as in remote viewing. Here is the lower astral plane. The higher astral plane is less dependent on the physical and is much like a collective shared space for reality. Some speculate that our dreams occur on the astral because it is very reactive to our thoughts and emotions. Because of this reactive nature, it is linked with the element of water and the shamanic Underworld. Guided meditations in the astral take on the characteristics suggested by the journey's guide, whether a teacher, a tape, or yourself. Intimate groups of people, such as covens, will create a group space through a shared thought-form, creating an astral temple.

Some texts openly discourage astral travel because some practitioners have been frightened. The astral plane manifests your thoughts into forms, and these practitioners manifested their subconscious fears and anger into a vision of a frightening creature while on the astral plane. Clearing and healing your consciousness of unhealthy patterns is paramount to a magickal practitioner. Once you realize that you have created something, you can banish it. Even if you come across something that is not of your own making, if you are centered in your power, such astral entities will not be able to harm you. Remember your protection magick. There is also a fear that if your astral body is harmed or separated from your physical body, you will die. I call this the "body and soul fear" because it is based on the old notion that one part of you is physical, and the other is spiritual, or your soul. There are no other layers of body. If the body "loses" the soul, you are dead. When you realize that you have multiple spiritual bodies, you realize that astral travel is projecting a portion of your energy, your awareness, to another location. You are not separated, though it often feels that way and sudden shocks can be very disconcerting. They may cause a headache or discomfort, but certainly not death. Archaic texts warn you not to let anything sever your silver cord, linking your soul to your body, through the solar-plexus area. I think that image comes from the astral's association with the solar plexus. Though most perceive themselves as projecting up and out through the crown chakra, if there is a sensation of direction at all, it is perfectly acceptable to perceive it as projecting out of the solar plexus, the chakra associated with the astral body. Such a projection might be "seen" as a cord of energy. Don't let such notions scare or control you.

Strongly associated with the astral is the emotional plane, the level of our emotional body. The heart chakra is associated with the emotional level, as well as the element of water. Water is the element of emotion, mystery, and, most importantly, unconditional love. This is what other models call the "higher" astral plane, although I view it as a separate level. The "lower" astral plane is associated with the lower solar-plexus chakra.

The mental place is the next layer. I do not mean to imply that the mind is above the emotions, but that the mind is in some ways less dense in vibration than the emotional body. We feel emotions more strongly in the dense physical body than we feel thoughts. The mind greatly influences the emotions and vice versa. The mental plane is the place of thought and creation. When we think about what we want to manifest, we create the thought before we bring it into form. The mental plane is strongly tied to the element of air and the throat chakra, where we speak our thoughts.

Linked to the third eye is the psychic plane, where we receive and send out knowledge and information. Think of this psychic plane as a vastly connected relay station, linking not only all people, but also all things, animate and inanimate. Here we send out our desires, our intentions, to manifest into form. This plane, sometimes called the higher mental plane, is associated with the element of fire, our willpower, desire, and passion.

Lastly, the crown chakra is associated with the divine plane. Our divine selves represent the highest level of consciousness, our complete knowing and understanding of all. The crown is associated with the fifth element, that of spirit or akasha. Together, the mental, psychic, and divine planes are part of the shamanic Upper World, where insights and information are better understood and less symbolic. In this model, however, the layers go from the most spiritual and the least dense to the most dense in terms of vibrational energy.

Think of the different levels not as floors in a building, but as layers of water in the ocean. Each layer has a different pressure, temperature, clarity, and marine life, but it is difficult to distinguish where one layer ends and another begins. They blend into each other. Think of these levels of energy in the same way.

These names and attributes have helped me greatly, but other systems exist. Some people divide them into four, based on the four elements. Others use names such as upper and lower astral planes and upper and lower mental planes. I've heard the higher spiritual planes referred to as Buddhic planes. Such names may serve a Buddhist well, but less so for those of us not on a Buddhist path. Understanding more than one perspective gives you added insight into many systems and keeps you from being too attached to "your way" being the "right way" for everyone.

EXERCISE 26

Psychic Travel

The following meditation is an experience in psychic travel. First pick a place you have never gone to, but are capable of going to soon. I like using a store that I have never visited. Don't pick a distant place that you plan to travel to later in life. You want immediate access. For the moment, indoor locations, usually in public, are better for this exercise than outdoor locations. Have some paper and a pen nearby before counting down.

The best advice I can give for psychic travel is not to focus on your expectations. Do not expect the experience to be what you imagine an out-of-body or near-death experience would be like. Our expectations are often more vivid than reality. Don't be alarmed if you can still feel your body, or if you can't feel your body. Think of it less as leaving your body and more as sending out a part of your awareness and senses, as mental projection. Focus less on the physical sensations and more on the impressions. For many, it is much like the mind projection in exercise 13 than what they imagine a full out-of-body experience would be like.

1. Start exercise 9: Counting Down to a Meditative State to get into your magickal mindset.

2. Feel the energy of your body, and feel your perceptions and awareness in your body. Form the intention that you would like to psychically project your consciousness beyond your body. You may feel a slight sensation at your crown or solar plexus, or feel your awareness expanding outward in one direction. You can even imagine yourself standing outside of your body and your awareness "jumping in" to this duplicate image.

3. With your physical eyes closed, psychically take note of the room around you. Do not try to remember it, but allow the information to come to you. The information could be visual, or a psychic knowing of what is in the room. Take note of all the details, including the grain of wood on the door frame, the texture of the floor, your meditation altar, and anything else that catches your attention.

4. Now think of a location you do know well, such as your workplace or a friend's house. Intend to go there now. Imagine your presence leaving your meditation room, either through the conventional door, or floating out through the ceiling and roof. Let yourself travel to this location. If you are not sure of the actual direction, in relationship to your physical location, don't worry. Visualize a doorway of light, a portal, that will connect you to your intended location. Open this portal with an invoking pentagram. Go through it, count from five to one, and at one, the tunnel ends and you are at your destination. Such astral gateways can connect any two points, physical or nonphysical.

5. Look around this location, and let the details come to you. Most you will be familiar with it, but be aware of anything out of the ordinary. Make note of it. Return through the tunnel of light, counting five to one, and return your awareness to your body. Close the gateway with a banishing pentagram. If you wish to continue, do not count back up.

6. Repeat steps 2 through 5, but intend to go to your new location, the one where you have not yet physically been. Again, look around this location and let the details come to you, including colors, sounds, sights, and general layout. Even though you may be doing this at night, the location could appear to you in daylight, meaning you have shifted in time. Don't worry about this. Gather as much information as you can, and intend to remember it all. If the location is dark, ask to see it in the light.

7. Return yourself to normal consciousness, counting up, and giving yourself clearance and balance. Do any necessary grounding. You may need more grounding than usual, so go slowly and make sure your awareness is fully back.

8. Write down all the information you remember about this location. Sketch a little diagram. Get as much detail down on paper as you can, but do not try to fill in the gaps. If you don't know what was in the corner, don't try to force it with your conscious mind. Often things that do not make logical sense turn out to be right.

When you have a chance, check out the location and see how well you did. Remember, things can change by the time you get to the location. If you "saw" in the meditation a blue blur distinctively to the right, and go to the store and see blue shirts on the left, ask someone who works there. You may find that the shirts were on the right on the day you "traveled," and were moved. Go with your first intuition, your gut instinct. Remember that you do not have to be 100 percent right to make significant "hits."

I first did this psychic projection on a well-known bookstore that opened a branch in my area. All these stores are laid out similarly. When I projected out, my first impressions did not make any sense. The registers were in a funny place. The magazines were not in the right place. There was no little café that I could see. When I checked it out, things were fairly accurate and it was not set up like any other store I had visited. If I had tried to make it fit my conscious information, I would have been wrong.

Sometimes psychic travel in the physical occurs in the dream state. My student and friend Robin planned to visit her daughter in Italy. Before she went, she woke up with a vivid dream of Italy, a particular building, the layout and landscape, including a river running near it. She later got online to find the website of her hotel and saw the picture of her dream building. When she visited it, things matched up very well. She has a knack for this particular kind of work, and often checks in psychically with her sister. Although that is perfectly acceptable, you must use your own discretion with these abilities to avoid violating anyone's sense of boundaries or privacy.

My covenmate Ginella and her husband Scott had both studied with me, but at different times, and each had an interesting experience with psychic travel. In Ginella's vision, she saw many brass bars or rails in the restaurant she chose to visit. When she visited the restaurant, she was upset that there was only one brass rail when she had seen so many. She didn't realize that the restaurant had been damaged by fire, and her description fit the older decor much better. I only knew this because I had eaten there years ago. Sometimes we shift in time as well as space, since these realms connecting us are beyond such concepts. In these cases, intention is very important. Intend to stay in this time.

Scott was initially discouraged at his experience of psychic travel. His vision had many images, but his things did not match up with his physical visit. Then he turned around and looked at the area from a certain perspective and things fell into place. While not perfect, his new perspective gave him a significant amount of accurate "hits." Like any skill, it takes practice. You must determine if this is a skill you wish to develop further. Sometimes one small success helps build the grander picture of our magickal abilities, and we choose to focus on those abilities that we are drawn to use in our daily life. Everyone does not have to be perfect at everything.

NEW ASSIGNMENTS

- Exercise 26—Complete and record your experiences in your Book of Shadows.

- Start a dream journal. Affirm that you will remember your dreams when you wake up. And keep an open notebook and pen on the nightstand. You can even use a tape recorder if you like. When you wake up, write down or record the first thing you remember. The first few times might be blank, but you will be training yourself to write down your dreams. A fragmented sentence can make the whole thing come back to you. Dreams are important to unlocking the inner world. Dream recording helps you remember meditations more vividly.

CONTINUING ASSIGNMENTS

• Daily journal—Write three pages a day.

• Focus on a regular meditation practice, at least three times a week if not daily.

• Honor and recognize your intuition. Continue to ask it questions.

• Use instant magick, neutralization, light, and aura reading in your daily life.

TIPS

• Sometimes insomnia is a gentle sign to do introspective work. Though we must balance our daily health and sleep needs, if you find yourself in a period of insomnia, it may be time to do a little introspective work, journaling, or meditating. Once you receive your message, your body will settle down and sleep. Listen to your body and find a balance that suits your life and health. Extended periods of insomnia are unhealthy for the body and psyche.

• If you suffer from difficult dreams and nightmares, and suspect an external psychic attack, surround yourself and your bed with a protection shield, as done in chapter 9. Using the color blue is very powerful for this. If you continue to have nightmares, really pay attention to the images. Your higher self may be giving you a message or pointing out a fear you need to overcome.

• If you have trouble with the psychic projection exercise, start out by visualizing a bright cloud of smoke or vapor being released from your body, usually via one of the chakras. The cloud floats before you and takes shape, forming a perfect, idealized duplicate of you. Project your senses, mind, and sense of self-awareness into the duplicate. Imagine "jumping" out of the body and into the duplicate. Then continue onward in this astral double.

LESSON 9
SPIRIT WORK

As walkers between the worlds, witches make allies in the spiritual realms. Whenever you visit a new land, physical or otherwise, it is wise to make contacts in this land, someone trusted to give information and lead the adventure on safe paths. In essence, you need a guide. As a spiritual traveler, you need a spirit guide.

Spirits and guides are not exclusive to witchcraft. References to invisible allies are found in cultures all over the world, although mythologies and belief systems differ as to exactly who and what spirits and spirit guides are.

In general, a spirit refers to a nonphysical being existing beyond normal space and time. This entity could have been physical at one point, living in a body, and after death transcending the physical plane but still keeping in contact with it. Stories of ghosts and hauntings refer to spirits not only in contact with the physical, but somehow *bound* to it. The general theory is that these spirits did not have a peaceful death, left some business unfinished, or had an unhealthy attachment to someone or something that remained in the physical world. Other spirits were never physical, but always existed on other planes of reality, the beings of folklore and legends. Many spiritual systems assign spirits and their areas of influence to hierarchies. Certain beings, often called goddesses, gods, elementals, faeries, angels, or demons, have the ability to aid humanity under certain conditions. However, most have no interaction with humanity because they are at a different vibrational level and a different plane of existence.

Spirit guides are nonphysical beings. They aid humanity by offering personal advice, mystical knowledge, and magickal partnerships. Although assumed to be very altruistic, most traditions also assume that spirit guides are learning something from the process, or need this link to humanity for their own spiritual growth. Some feel that guides serve out of love for humanity. They give us information and insights that we do not consciously possess. Like a good friend and counselor wrapped into one, they tell us the things we need to hear, in a way we can understand. In some spiritual hierarchies, guides are believed to come from the same "soul group" or "soul family" as their human contacts, meaning a group of souls who remain together to learn and grow in a very familial manner. At some point, souls incarnate, or take physical form through birth, and some of their soul group remains in the spiritual realms to guide, consciously for those on the mystics path, and subconsciously for most others. Everyone has some sort of guide beyond the veil, but most people are unaware of this. In this paradigm, it is just as likely that at some point you were the guide and your current guide was in a body. You may both have been incarnated at the same time, sharing physical existence together as other members of the group were your guides. This system of exchange gives the relationship a wider perspective. Just because your guide is a spirit does not mean it does not understand basic human needs, emotions, and thoughts.

Other spiritual systems feel that spirits become guides once they have mastered the human level of existence and move on to the next plane. Still others feel that spirit guides are powerful spiritual beings who never were human and who exist beyond our understanding. As with any of my teachings, I do not tell you that this is the way the universe always operates and everyone else is wrong. My beliefs and viewpoints have changed over time, and have encompassed all the material here, so I present several possible viewpoints. Use what works for you. It is important to remember, in terms of nonphysical existence, that we have difficulty understanding it because it is beyond where we are existing at the moment, so we create symbols, systems, and viewpoints to understand it better, but they are just that: symbols, not absolute truth.

Regardless of origin, spirit guides serve as intermediaries between your conscious self and the higher self, and ultimately the divine mind. The divine mind can seem vast and unknowable, thus the need for an intermediary. In witchcraft, we perceive the divine force, the Great Spirit, as I call it, as embodied by the Goddess and God through the Principles of Polarity and Gender, helping us make a personal connection. Sometimes our guides are the goddesses, gods, and heroes of a specific mythology.

Other times they are ancestors, those who have passed before us in our genetic or spiritual lineage. Although you may not be Irish, your guide could manifest as an old Irish wise woman because you have adopted a Celtic path. This woman is in your spiritual family, if not in your bloodline. She could be part of your soul group, utilizing her appearance from a previous incarnation.

Animal spirits can also act as guides, and are most familiar to those following a shamanic or tribal path. Since our connection to the natural world is pivotal in the practice of the craft, animal teachers, or even plant spirits, are obvious manifestations for our guides.

Some students view guides as the familiar winged angels. Angels are viewed as safe and comfortable for those fearful of spirits. Some traditions of Wicca work closely with the archangels. Conversely, a segment of people drawn to witchcraft often shy away from angels, feeling that they hark from Christian beliefs, but in truth the mythology of angels goes far beyond Christianity. The bulk of the information comes from Judaism, but roots can be found in Egypt, Sumer, and Tibet. Older sources of angels paint a portrait that is not exclusively that of winged cherubs. Some are wheels of fire or fearsome beings with many eyes.

I have found that spirit guides typically manifest in ways the person is comfortable viewing. If they are spirit, they are greatly beyond shape and form, at least in the manner in which we are used to shape and form, and accordingly have a measure of control over their form. They may be based in the spiritual realms of the astral planes or above. With direct contact, our awareness of new realities opens up. Spirit guides seek to facilitate that process by choosing shapes that we are comfortable viewing at first.

Other guides manifest in forms that we have difficulties with, not to scare us, but to confront us with our fears and prejudices. I have a student who always works with female guides and goddess energies. Whenever a masculine presence appeared, she would turn it away or use the protection magick exercises to banish it. Soon all the guides coming to her were mostly masculine and she did not accept them until a female guide explained to her that they were not bad, but that she needed to face her fear of men and male energy. Such advice opened a whole new world of wisdom for her.

Why Call on Spirit Guides?

Why should I call on my spirit guides? What exactly do they do? "Serving as intermediaries with our divine selves" might seem like a nebulous answer. Practically, they have a great purpose: they serve as mentors. They can be called on to answer questions, help solve problems, point out our behavior patterns, give greater insight, provide confirmation to intuitive flashes, and ultimately to give us spiritual support. Guides are available to aid us in the physical and spiritual worlds. We can call on their wisdom for our personal problems and family issues. They act in many ways as a spiritual counselor would. Although spirit guides are not a substitute for any professional care you may need, I must say I've had my own personal breakthroughs and insights while meditating with my spirit guides. They can point out information and patterns we commit that are unhealthy, and we are more likely to accept this from a spirit rather than a physical person because our ego is more defensive with a physical person. During such inner spiritual conversations, you may feel like you are talking to yourself, but they allow you to cut through many of the games you may play with others. These personal breakthroughs lead to a greater awareness of self and ultimately help you along your spiritual path. Although we tend to divide our personal lives from our magickal selves, they are really intertwined.

Our guides are ever ready to lend support in our specific magickal works, be it daily meditation or spell crafting. They are great advisors as to when to do magick, and when not to do it. They often give tips on ritual and spell work, possibly drawing from past incarnations. They can give advice about the magickal properties of plants and crystals and be present with messages when you are doing any psychic work, including healing and things like tarot readings. Some psychics, as mediums or channels, basically let their own guides or their clients' guides speak through them via various techniques, such as trance work or automatic writing. Spirits can literally guide you on your psychic-projection travels and guide you on meditative journeys.

Many practitioners of spirit work believe that you have not one guide, but several guides, working in one or more teams. Different guides assume different roles in your spiritual development and welfare, and often new guides have to be requested or invoked into your life to start an active relationship with them.

Spirit guide—Spirit guides are those who are there to help and direct you, like a good friend or counselor, to be there to speak when you need them and to be there to listen when you need to talk. They act like spiritual therapists and good friends. They may cross over with any of the other following roles, and are the most common to interact with during a shamanic journey or meditation.

Protector—Protector spirits are concerned primarily with your physical welfare, but also with your spiritual protection. Different spirits may be in charge of different aspects of protection for you. Angel and animal spirits are often viewed as protectors.

Gatekeepers—Gatekeepers are not physical protectors, but protectors of your consciousness, guardians of your mind and spirit. They may simultaneously assume the role of protector as well.

Healer—Healers are spirits who are available for your healing on all levels and to aid others in healing. When you desire self-healing, call on your healers and ask for instructions. Once you have called on them, lie down and they will align your physical and subtle bodies, just like when you visit a witch or any other kind of hands-on healer. Your guides will put their spiritual hands on you and create balance. Ask them for any special instructions. Intuitively, you may feel like you have to change your position to facilitate their work. They will also let you know when the session is complete. When it is over, thank and release your healing guides. They can act as internal alchemists, healing body chemistry. If you do any other healing work, call on your healers before you begin, to guide you. Call on your client's healers, and both of your higher selves. I've been blessed with several healing guides, including one that looked like an ancient practitioner of Chinese medicine. He gave me information on several pressure points in my body to stimulate healing after an injury. I later found out that they were used in acupressure.

Joy guide—A joy guide is said to help you remain in contact with fun, laughter, and your inner child. Also known as a laughter guide, tricksters, faeries, and other mischievous spirits take on this role, sometimes hiding things from you. A joy guide is at times related to the gatekeeper function, guarding your consciousness from energies that would harm the inner child.

Runner—Runner spirits are those who help you manifest and find things in the physical world. Elementals and nature spirits are usually the embodiment of runners.

Master teacher—A master teacher is concerned about your spiritual development and the course of your study. A master teacher will provoke you not only to learn, but also to practice and develop your skills. Think of this spirit as a mentor, who will often be connected in some way to your chosen life profession.

Patron—A patron usually refers to a patron deity, a goddess or god whom you serve and for whom you act as an agent in this world. Your learning and development is directly tied to the patron whom you choose, or who chooses you, and can sometimes change with time as your path changes. A patron may also act as your master teacher.

My first experience with guides was in a meditation led by a teacher of mine. I was introduced to two guides, a female who was a cross between an elf and an Arabian princess, named Asha, and a tall, pale, lanky man, also reminiscent of an elf, named Llan. They were not what I expected at all. Asha aided more in the feminine, intuitive, and healing realms, while Llan seemed a little colder and mental, giving me more facts and figures. As I reconciled my own inner masculine and feminine, he warmed up and started teaching through story, something I soon adopted in my own teaching. Later I had a visitation in my meditation with the goddess Macha, an Irish goddess associated with crows and horses. She became my patron in the craft. Years later I had an experience with the Welsh god Gwydion. These four have been with me ever since, along with the Crow and Spider animal spirits. Many other spirits, angels, and deities have wandered in and out of my practice. They come and go from my life as needed. They present the information or experience they hold and then continue onward. As I've studied different paths and belief systems to expand my knowledge and experience as a teacher, these new guides have conformed to the new paradigms I've adopted, further demonstrating to me that spirit is ever changing and mutable to the form you need at the time.

It has been my experience through teaching this material to many different people from different backgrounds and beliefs that everyone has at least one guide at all times. Sometimes contact is not immediate, but guidance is available, and often comes through intuition and flashes of messages rather than direct conversation or visuals. Witches, shamans, and other mystics seem to have more guides than the average person because they spend more time than most people contacting the spirit realms. The more you travel, the more you make contacts, friends, and guides in foreign locales. These contacts will come in very handy as you develop your skills as a walker between worlds.

ARE THEY REAL?

One of the most frequently asked questions I get in regard to spirit work, and witchcraft in general, is "Is this real?" People will pull me aside after a lecture and ask, "Now really, was that real? Are spirits and guides really there, or did I make the experience up?" And that is the 64-million-dollar question. Are spirits real? Do they exist independently of the people who perceive them? The obvious answer picked by most people is no. They are figments of your imagination. At worst, they represent a psychological imbalance in which you are talking to people you think are real, who are not physically there. At best, they are a device used by your consciousness to have an internal dialogue. Your belief in a spirit facilitates the process of the inner conversation where insight and knowledge you already possess can be woven into a more complete picture.

In chapter 5, we discussed the three minds used in magick, the conscious mind, the psychic mind, and the divine mind, corresponding to the middle/ego self, the lower/psychic self, and the higher self, respectively. Many proponents of the internal dialogue will say that the spirit guide is a manifestation of the lower, psychic abilities to make an easier contact with the higher, divine self. In essence, you are talking to yourself, but a higher, wiser part of you.

In psychological terms, these intermediary personas are known as the anima and animus, the inner female and male aspects of each individual. At the first stage of this work in modern psychology, every man contained an inner feminine called the anima and every woman contained an inner masculine aspect called the animus. Today, practitioners feel that everyone contains both aspects, regardless of physical gender. The anima/animus helps us contact the higher mind and gives us a balanced perspective of the masculine, logical point of view and the feminine, intuitive point of view. When in contact with both, we make balanced, well-informed decisions. It's like using both sides of your brain to determine the next course of action, instead of letting one dominate. Ancient alchemists writing about the hermaphrodite, a composite of male and female, were writing about this spiritual truth, and not necessarily the physical.

I can't disagree with this viewpoint, as it was my own for quite a while. Although I believed in the power of the mind, psychic abilities, and, through those abilities, magick, I was not ready to believe in the existence of spirit guides. When I met Asha and Llan, I thought they were my anima and animus given a colorful voice. Llan especially looked like someone I knew in college. I felt that I gave his image to my animus because this person was the only male witch I knew, even though we were never introduced. After studying the work of Carl Jung, the idea of talking to a wiser part of myself was not as intimidating as speaking to spirits, so I went with it.

Later I had experiences with my guides that made me doubt this theory and made me look at the possibility that I was interacting with separate, distinct entities. Their personalities seemed to be complete and beyond simple aspects of myself. At a point when I was doubting myself and the craft, feeling overwhelmed by peer and societal pressure, I asked my guides to give me proof, some sign that this was all real and they were real: "If I am not talking to another part of myself, tell me something I don't already know." Asha told me, "Steve's mother is blind." I had just met my life partner,

Steve, a few months earlier and had not yet met his mother. When I did, she wasn't blind; she saw better than I did. All my hopes were dashed and I felt very disconnected. I continued with basic meditations and energy work. I could feel the energy exercises, so I thought energy was real, but I thought spirit guides were my imagination, and I did not journey or speak with my guides until a few weeks later. I met up with an old friend, also named Steve, and he told me about his mother. She had recently been declared legally blind. I immediately meditated with my spirit guides to apologize. Asha just laughed, and I thought it appropriate that they had helped me "see" by using the symbol of eyesight, a recurring issue in my life.

Since then I've had many different experiences that reaffirmed my belief that spirits guides are real. In class, I've felt the presence of particular spirits or deities and have had other people in the class describe them. During one ritual I felt the energy of Wotan, or Odin, the Norse father god. I particularly felt him in the south. A woman standing in the south, who was not a pagan but someone open to exploring new practices, said she felt a Viking standing behind her and proceeded to describe the one-eyed Wotan. I've also had students describe my spirit guides before I've discussed them in class.

A good friend of mine, one of the people who first got me involved in witchcraft, met an obscure Celtic goddess, dressed in full Celtic garb. She gave her name, which my friend had a hard time pronouncing. She had never studied the Celts before this point in time and would never have subconsciously chosen such a deity because she had no prior knowledge of myth. She later discovered that same goddess in a book. Many people report being met by different gods and goddesses they never knew existed, but later found in a book. Even if they did not believe in individual spirits, at the very least each of these people tapped into a collective consciousness containing these entities, the archetypal beings, and not their own personal subconscious.

In one meditation, the same guide presented itself to two different people. As we went around the room, one person described a guide, and when he spoke to it, the guide said, "I'm not here for you. I'm here for someone else." I then noticed the look of shock when the next student realized that it was the guide he saw. I've seen my students' guides at times. One experience in particular that stands out in my mind was during the same meditation. I saw a Roman centurion standing behind my friend

Scott. He, too, saw this figure, and described the bristle helmet but did not use the word *centurion*. We saw the same being, and that experience convinced him that spirits are "real."

With these experiences in mind, it is easy to believe that spirit guides are separate and distinct individual entities, but I fear that is not the whole truth either. I struggled with the concept for a long time, wanting to separate fact from fiction. What was real? Were they separate, or a part of me? The more I struggled and needed proof, the less productive it was. When I let go of needing to prove anything, I had more worthwhile experiences. We can look at spirits from the psychological perspective, or the more traditional entity perspective, but when you keep the Hermetic principles in mind, most importantly the Law of Mentalism, we are all connected and part of the same one spirit. We are all waves in the ocean. Is a separate entity in reality any different from my higher self? Not really. Am I any different from anyone or anything else, physical or nonphysical? No, not really. The only difference is perspective. Currently, I have the perspective of being a separate person, and that is the experience I need right now. When that need changes, my experience changes. By understanding that mysticism in part is based on a personal viewpoint, we create a better foundation for our own spiritual work. We also become more tolerant of other people's beliefs, realizing that it is all a point of view.

Fear and Discernment

One of the most interesting aspects of teaching spirit work is observing the various levels of enthusiasm or fear related to the experience. On one hand, you have people very interested in meeting their spirit guides and actively working with them. Often people who do not particularly want to become witches take my witchcraft classes to learn to work with spirit guides and journey. They are excited at the prospect of opening up to a brand new world. On the other hand, a small number of students express fear of working with spirits. They fear what spirits they will conjure up and the possibility that the spirit will be evil. Our popular culture, from folk tales to Hollywood thrillers, depicts the spirit world as a hostile place, filled with demons out to get us.

The word *demon* most likely comes from the Greek work *daimon*, meaning an inter-mediary spirit, one who connects humankind to the gods. That sounds like a spirit guide or angel, doesn't it? Historically, the gods of an existing religion become the demons of the conquering religion. That doesn't make one evil and the other good, it just means that one tribe is better at waging war than the other.

If you research demonology, you will notice the similarities of the demons' names to old pagan gods. Though some would argue from a fundamentalist Christian point of view that the pagan gods were demons, they are only spiritual entities who are the vic-tims of bad press and a smear campaign. The only demons you should worry about are those of your own making, the personal addictions and unhealthy attitudes you bring into life.

Although one should exercise caution when doing any spiritual work, it is no more dangerous than physical travel and interacting with real people. Most spirits mean no harm, some desire to help, and others may not have your best interests at heart. With a little practice, you can avoid harmful spirits entirely.

Some people fear that once they start talking to spirits, the spirit will never stop talking and will drive them crazy. My good friend and former covenmate Christina, who has always had a hard time with the concept of spirits, asked, "What's the differ-ence between spirit guides and schizophrenia?" We came to the conclusion that witches and shamans speaking to spirits can "turn off" the experience and focus on the material world whenever they want. Think of it as a radio with an off switch, or at least a button to change the station. Those with various types of illness can't turn it off. They may be talking to spirits, or they may be talking to themselves, but often due to a physiological problem, they cannot turn it off. Do not worry about "going crazy." With a basic foundation in meditation and metaphysics as presented in this book, you will al-ways be able to turn off your radio. You may have certain initiation experiences that are difficult at the time. Many shamans go through the "wild man" or "wild woman" initia-tion, where they seemingly go crazy and live alone in the woods to learn from the spir-its, but modern witches do not lose their faculties or create a physiological illness. I think that some people subconsciously don't want to talk to their spirit guides. They fear what the guides will say. Many people are unhappy with life, but are more frightened to change than to keep suffering, and a spirit guide will urge you to change if you are not living in a balanced manner. Change can be a frightening prospect.

When working with a new spirit or guide, use your discernment. Does this feel right intuitively, in your heart, mind, and body? If something is making you uncomfortable, what is it? Is it your own feelings reflected at you, or is it the entity? Various traditions feel that if a spirit can tell you its name three times in a row, then it is not lying to you, but sometimes a name does not prove anything. Others ask a spirit to send them the feeling of unconditional love along with the name. A spirit that means harm cannot exist in the vibration of love. You can use the banishing pentagram and ask all spirits who are not in "perfect love and perfect trust" to be banished now. If that spirit remains, then you can work with it. The protection techniques in chapter 9 are great preparation before working with any spirit.

Making Contact

This section is a series of exercises designed to facilitate the process of connecting with your spirit guides. To some, these are used as systems of divination, but we will be using them like an oracle. An oracle goes in a different direction from divination of the past, present, and future. It uses divination as a medium to connect with various spirit guides. We shall use these exercises to receive answers from our guides, often in a yes/no format, and then move on to more detailed messages.

Spiritualists from many traditions talk about spirits and guides existing at a different vibration. We know through the Principle of Vibration that all things vibrate, all things are energy, even the nonphysical. When we describe spirits as existing on other planes, like the astral, emotional, or mental planes, they are in a different vibration than the physical. These vibrations overlap, since we, as physical beings, have astral, emotional, and mental components. The event of contact is a process of both beings changing their vibration enough to "tune in" to the right frequency. Some use ritual, meditation, or lifestyle practices to achieve and maintain such vibrations. We know we can change our vibration through intent. Through intent, we can "tune in" to our guides, even when we are not seeking direct guidance, but only their presence to subtly guide us.

When I have a healing client or a tarot session, I tune in through my intentions and ask to be guided to say and do the correct thing. Sometimes I receive a direct message, and other times, it is just a flash of intuition, but I know my guides are present. I think that many teachers and healers do this, some consciously and others unconsciously.

Before doing any of the next exercises, sit quietly and say this or similar words:

"I ask my highest and best guidance to be present. I ask to vibrate in harmony with the highest and best guidance and understand all messages given to me."

Sometimes a slight tingle or shift in energy will follow, but if you don't notice anything, don't worry. They are present. Now you are ready to begin. When done, always thank and release your highest and best guidance. You can do so by saying, "Hail and farewell," by which you honor and release.

EXERCISE 27

Pendulum

The pendulum is a time-honored device used to divine yes or no questions. In this application, we are going to ask our guides to give us yes or no responses to questions posed. The item itself is a string with some sort of weight on the end. It can be as fancy or as simple as you like (figure 28). Silver and gold chains with crystals or metal beads are available. You can create a homemade pendulum using a piece of string and a metal washer or nut. Marilyn, a friend and fellow flower-essence consultant, uses a piece of thread and a sewing needle. More intellectually focused practitioners stress the necessity of using a properly weighted, professionally made pendulum, but I prefer the homemade ones. I avoid plastic because I feel that tools made of plastic give deceptive and incorrect answers. Plastic is a substance influenced by the planet Neptune, and although Neptune has many wonderful spiritual attributes, it is also the planet of illusions.

By dangling the weight, you receive an answer indicated by the motion of the pendulum. Traditionally, clockwise motions mean yes and counterclockwise motions mean no, but you should check in with your guides to find your own yes or no response. For instance, I know of cases where a circular motion means yes and a linear motion means no.

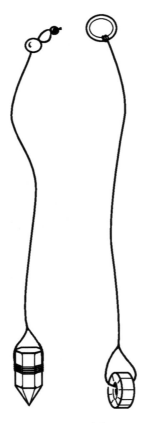

Figure 28: Pendulums

The original theory behind the pendulum is that your guides are influencing the motion of the pendulum psychokinetically, giving you their answer. When you hold the pendulum and bring it to a still point, you know that you are not deliberately moving it, although to others it may appear that you are. Something else appears to be moving the weight. Many people speculate that you are subconsciously moving the pendulum with very subtle movements from your hand muscles, or that you are even using your own natural, latent psychokinetic abilities to move it. If that is true, I feel that perhaps your guides are tapping into your subconscious or your own abilities to give their answer. When the mind is as centered and clear as possible, I've found the pendulum to be a very effective method of communication. I'm still not certain of the mechanism, but as long as it helps, I am happy to use it. I often use exercises 27 and 28 when choosing flower-essence remedies for my clients, asking their own guides what is best for them, and allowing those guides to answer through these divination techniques.

1. Get out your pendulum and prepare a list of yes/no questions. The first questions should be "What is a yes response?" and "What is a no response?" Once you know that, you can ask any other question.

2. Activate your trigger (as programmed in exercise 12). Once you feel sufficiently open, you can release the trigger, but still maintain a light meditative state.

3. Hold out the pendulum with the weight dangling. Keep your hand steady. Stop the weight from moving and let go. Tune in to your guides.

4. Ask your question and close your eyes.

5. Visualize a happy, peaceful place to clear your mind. Do not worry about getting an answer. Relax for a few moments.

6. Open your eyes and take note of the motion of the pendulum for your answer.

7. Thank and release your guides when done, saying, "Hail and farewell."

Don't be discouraged if this doesn't work at first. Contact is not always instantaneous. It can also take awhile to figure out what is yes and what is no. Keep practicing. Start with questions to which you know the answer, like your name, address, and age. When comfortable with the responses, start asking questions with unknown answers. You can ask for advice on anything, from the types of foods you should eat for optimum health to the veracity of someone's story.

EXERCISE 28

Muscle Testing

Muscle testing, also called applied kinesiology, is becoming more and more popular in holistic medical professions. Although not initially used to contact spirit guides, the underlying principle is to connect with the body's own intelligence and wisdom regarding health decisions. Various points in the body are strength tested with certain substances to see if they strengthen the body system or weaken it.

My first experience with muscle testing was to determine which metals were best for our overall health and vibration. Although we used gold and silver, you can use anything, such as herbs, flower essences, food, or crystals. I've even done it with a bottle of vitamin C and a bottle of rat poison, just to really test it.

If you have a partner for this preliminary muscle test, gather a small amount of gold jewelry and silver jewelry. The next exercise for muscle testing and spirit guides does not require a partner. Have your partner stand up and place his or her dominant arm out at a ninety-degree angle straight out from the body. Ask your partner to hold the arm locked in that position. Have your partner close his or her eyes while you test the level of strength by trying to push his or her arm down on the count of three. The goal is not to actually push the arm down, but to measure how much normal resistance it has. Then, with eyes still closed, place one metal in your partner's dominant hand. Count to three again and apply the same pressure. The arm will either stay equally strong, get stronger, or get noticeably weaker. Don't let your partner look at the metal, and try it again with the other metal. Switch it around several times. Usually, one metal will strengthen and another will weaken.

If that's not the case, try this exercise with different metals, such as copper and iron, or use an entirely different family of substances: crystals, herbs, or vitamins. As a last resort, try the bottle of vitamins and the bottle of poison. The only exception I've found to this exercise is when one person is radically stronger than the other, the stereotypical ninety-eight-pound weakling versus the bodybuilder. But for two people of normal strength, it almost always works. Switch roles and try it yourself. If you are alone, you can hold the substance with both hands at the heart level, standing straight,

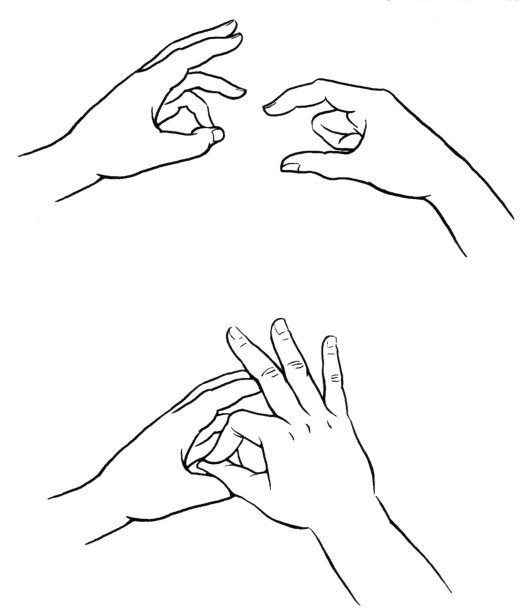

Figure 29: *Muscle Testing Hand Positions*

feet fairly close together. If you feel yourself sway forward slightly, it is an affirmative reaction. If you sway back, you are seeking to get away from the substance, a no response. It's a great trick to know when buying herbs or vitamins.

Muscle testing when communing with spirit guides does not necessarily require a partner, but it does require the use of both hands. Take your nondominant hand (the left hand if you are right-handed, and vice versa) and make a loop with your thumb and pinky. Take your dominant hand and make a pincer shape with your thumb and first finger. Place the pincer fingers into the loop (figure 29). Ask your question. With all your strength, you will try to keep the loop closed tight while simultaneously using all your strength to open your pincer fingers. If the loop of your thumb and pinky breaks, the answer is no. If the loop holds, the answer is yes.

The idea behind this type of muscle testing is that your body is an electromagnetic system. Your guides place a small charge into your system that will either weaken it or strengthen it. The test allows you to determine their response, although I've noticed that extended use of this technique during a single period eventually tires out the hands and gives less accurate results because the muscles involved are fatigued.

1. Prepare a list of yes/no questions. Again, start with simple questions to which you know the answers, and then move on to questions with unknown answers.

2. Activate your trigger (as programmed in exercise 12). Once you feel sufficiently open, you can release the trigger, but still maintain a light meditative state.

3. Get your hands into position, placing the dominant hand's pincer (thumb and first finger) into the nondominant hand's loop (thumb and pinky).

4. Ask your question, and then simultaneously try to open the pincers and hold the loop. It will almost immediately break or hold. Do not struggle with it. Note your answer. Repeat the process with all your questions.

5. Thank and release your guides when done, saying, "Hail and farewell."

EXERCISE 29

Automatic Writing

Automatic writing is a process of letting go of your conscious mind and allowing your deeper, psychic mind to control your hand, intuitively guiding the writing. The idea is to allow the guides to seed their answers into your psychic mind, communicating through the writing process. Unlike muscle testing or the pendulum, automatic writing allows a greater scope of information to come through. You can ask for specific information, such as names, dates, and detailed answers.

With automatic writing, the personality and character of the guide come through much more. Though some feel the presence of their guides during muscle testing, writing lets the words and phrases give you an idea about the being who is guiding you.

To prepare for automatic writing, get out a stack of loose paper. I prefer paper with no lines because I don't pay attention to them anyway while in this state. You should number the pages beforehand, because you could find yourself flinging away each sheet as you are done with it. Numbers make the reordering process much easier. Have a supply of pens or pencils on hand. I prefer ballpoint pens because they do not drag as much as other writing implements. Prepare a list of questions to use. Questions can include, "Who are you?" "What are you?" "What is your name?" "Are you male, female, or neither?" "Have we known each other in a past life?" "What is your purpose?" "What is your message for me now?" Keep the first session fairly simple. If you have a partner, have the questions read as you go along, so you do not have to distract yourself with reading while in a meditative state.

1. Start exercise 9: Counting Down to a Meditative State to get into your magickal mindset. Have your partner guide you through this process. You can gently open your eyes at this point if they were closed.

2. Tune in to the vibration of your highest and best guidance, as noted previously. Wait a few minutes and allow the link to be established.

3. Hold the pen and put paper in front of you. You do not necessarily have to look at the paper. In fact, it may be easier if you don't. Start asking questions and allow the hand to move. In some cases, it is completely automatic and the

writer has no idea of what is being written until it is read back later. For most, the words pop into your head as you write them, or just before they are written. Go with whatever experience feels right, but don't try to control it.

4. Read the answers when you are done. They may provoke other questions from you or your partner.

5. Return yourself to normal consciousness, counting up, giving yourself clearance and balance, and perform any grounding that may be needed. Thank and release your guides when done, saying, "Hail and farewell."

EXERCISE 30

Clairaudience—Conscious Channeling

Clairaudience is the act of psychically receiving information in terms of audio impression. One hears things instead of seeing them. Up until now, most of this training has been geared toward clairvoyance because we exist in a very visual society. Ultimately, we want to engage any of the senses when needed and open to clairsentience, or psychic knowing, where the corresponding physical sensory impression is not necessary or as important. There is little practical difference between clairvoyance, clairaudience, and clairsentience beyond what the practitioner feels most comfortable with. Each technique can yield the same information.

In this exercise, we are tuning in to our highest and best guidance and asking to receive information in an auditory way, hearing a message. You will not necessarily hear it with your physical ears, but instead with your inner "psychic ears," just as you visualize with your inner psychic eye. For some, the message may feel like it is physical. If you heard your message as you did during the automatic-writing exercise, then this will be no different, except that you will not be writing as you go. It will be more like a conversation in your mind, but one of the speakers will be your spirit guide.

When such conversations are spoken aloud, repeating back the message given by a guide, it is often called conscious channeling. Channeling is allowing yourself to be a vehicle for a message, either for yourself or for others. Although many variations exist, the two main types are conscious channeling and full body, or trance, channeling. Trance channeling is when you let a spirit take over physical control of the body and directly give its message. We are not attempting that here. Both types of channeling have advantages and drawbacks perceived by their various champions and opponents, but for now we are focusing on your inner, personal conversation with your guide.

1. Start exercise 9: Counting Down to a Meditative State to get into your magickal mindset.

2. Tune in to the vibration of your highest and best guidance, as noted previously. Wait a few moments and allow the link to be established. Ask to speak to your spirit guide.

3. Start speaking with your spirit guide, internally or out loud. You can start by explaining a situation for which you need advice, emotions you are having difficulty handling, or you can jump right into direct questions. When stuck, the best question is "What do I need to know now for my highest good?" or "What message do you have for me now?"

4. Return yourself to normal consciousness, counting up, and giving yourself clearance and balance. Do any necessary grounding. Thank and release your guides when done, saying, "Hail and farewell."

With practice, you will be able to receive these messages in lighter states of meditation, even by using your trigger. If you are less auditorily inclined, this exercise may be accompanied by visions and images of your guide. Your message could be dreamlike and symbolic. Whatever happens, it is the experience you need at that time.

NEW ASSIGNMENTS

• Exercises 27 through 30—Complete and record your experiences in your Book of Shadows.

- Build a relationship with your guides. Before you meditate, invite them into the space to guide and protect you. When you are done, thank and release them. If you have questions in your life, seek out answers from your guides and highest knowing. If you find yourself in difficult situations, call on your guides for help.

Continuing Assignments

- Daily journal—Write three pages a day.
- Continue with a dream journal.
- Focus on a regular meditation practice, at least three times a week if not daily.
- Honor and recognize your intuition. Continue to ask it questions.
- Use instant magick, neutralization, light, and aura reading in your daily life.

Tips

- If the usual method of muscle testing does not work for you, there is an alternative method. Take your first finger and thumb on each hand and create a ring, but link the rings of each hand together like links of a chain. Ask your question and try to pull the links apart. If a link breaks, your answer is no. If they stay together, the answer is yes. This particular technique is difficult if you are prone to sweaty hands.

Lesson 10
The Inner Temple

We each have a sacred place within us that is the heart of our personal power because it is centered and grounded in our truth, our own authentic self. Here we feel comfortable being ourselves, no matter what. Here we recognize our true selves, since our true selves can get lost in the shuffle of other people's and our own expectations. Here there are no expectations other than to claim our personal power for the highest good.

The place I speak of is metaphorical for most people, a symbol of their innate divinity. A few have layered a real-world image over this sacred space, a memory from a time of joy or empowerment. This happy place can be a memory of a beach, forest, tree house, or cottage that exists in the physical world. Often the image comes from childhood, the last time and place where the individual felt truly empowered to be his or her authentic self. Stress-management programs tell us to imagine that we are "in our happy place" to attain a measure of comfort that is lacking in the current physical world.

For witches, this place is not just symbolic, but a real place to renew their sense of self and personal power. This place is the inner temple, a personal oasis located in the spiritual realms. This sacred temple confers a sense of centering, safety, and tranquility, often reflecting ongoing changes within the individual. The inner temple is a home base of sorts, a magickal launch pad from which to spring into other journeys and meditations.

As we subjectively perceive the subtle planes like the astral and emotional to be physically outside us, we perceive the inner temple to be within us. Truly there is no physical location to these realms. They lie in a direction that cannot be pointed to. Think of the inner temple as your personal interface between your inner reality and the outer planes. Here all journeys begin, and here all journeys end.

Although the inner temple is not the last topic I teach in my level-one witchcraft course, in many ways it is the culmination. Connecting to this inner power and actively using it for your own betterment is the crux of the class and, in my opinion, the practice of witchcraft. Although there are many traditions, paths, and techniques, finding and affirming your own personal power and sense of the sacred is the cornerstone of all mysticism. This temple can lead in many directions, but through its creation, or rather its rediscovery—for it already exists within you—you create a solid center upon which to grow.

All of the exercises, journal writing, and meditations prior to this were designed to aid your access to the inner temple. I've seen many talented people exploring different areas of the metaphysical world lose themselves to zealousness, depression, or disbelief because they lacked a basic understanding of the ideas and experiences. They did not start out with practices grounded in introspection, so they did not build a proper foundation. They did not recognize that all experiences spring from their own sacred space.

BUILDING YOUR PLACE OF POWER

The inner temple can appear in any conceivable shape or size. Remember that our physical descriptions of it merely symbolize the nonphysical experiences we have. By using symbols and visualization, our conscious mind can interact more effectively with our psychic and divine minds. Everyone's inner temple will reflect their experiences and personal tastes, not only from this life, but possibly from past incarnations. The description can be very lifelike, or completely surreal. Do not try to make things conform to your magickal expectations, for the best messages come with our personal interpretations. If you have an extensive background in mythology, the images could conform to classical mythology. If not, you could find yourself drawing on modern pop-culture symbols. They express the same things, but in different ways. If you are expecting something out of the Celtic *Mabinogion* and get *Star Trek* instead, disappointment and disbelief often result, but such science fiction is a new expression of the old myths.

More traditional temple settings include physical temples and monuments. Stone monuments like Karnak and Stonehenge, the sacred circles built by ancient people, hold an air of mystery for us. The womblike cave of the Goddess, descending into the Earth with many different chambers, is a wonderful archetype, particularly for those focusing on the Goddess aspects of the craft. The pyramids of Egypt, which often look shining and new or even metallic, are popular, as are the Mayan step pyramids and temples. European castles, old towers, Native American pueblos, faery mounds, and caverns hollowed out beneath great trees are other vivid images ripe with possibilities. More natural settings, without humanmade structures, may be better suited for the outdoor person, including mountaintops, waterfalls, deep forests, and secluded islands.

Some of the most intriguing images shared in my classes include a pyramid made out of plants, completely organic and containing no stone. This student is an environmental activist and works as part of an organic commune. A writer envisioned his place of power as an endless library. Another saw a teepee with a Native American spirit guide / shaman waiting for her.

Someone who was entirely upset with her temple saw a basic four-walled room, with only a folding card table in the center of it. The place was not fancy, nor romantic, but sparse. Although she wasn't happy with the image, it reflected some of the things going on in her life. More modern and pop-culture images flashed in her mind during meditations, upsetting her terribly, but containing valuable messages. At one point, she saw herself sitting at the table with a television watching a rerun of the show *Home Improvement*. She said she didn't even like the show and couldn't remember the plot. All she could remember was *Home Improvement*. I asked her if those words had any meaning to her and her current living situation, and I saw a light bulb go off over her head. She was definitely getting a message in the only way her guides and mind could tell her—through television shows. Pay attention to what your symbols are, even if they do not fit what you envisioned to be part of the witch's world. Although this particular woman struggled with much of the basic material in witchcraft, she continued her studies and had some major breakthroughs that led to wonderful changes in her life.

Another interesting case was the vision of a tract home. This particular person was studying real estate and considering a career move, but she did not want a tract home to be her inner temple. Through sheer will, she made it conform to a hobbit home from *Lord of the Rings*, a book she enjoyed. There she met a spirit guide much like Gandalf the Wizard, a character from the story. I myself was very interested in who would have been in the tract home. Perhaps they had a message regarding the career shift.

Although you *can* exert control over your inner temple—it is your own sacred space, after all—I find it more productive to take a look at the images we are first given and understand them before changing them. The inner temple not only reflects our current personality and our state of mind, but what we are becoming. When we find things based on stories, myths, or pop-culture icons, they are no less real, but a system of symbols in which we communicate. As we learn more symbols, our symbolic "vocabulary" widens. That is one of the reasons you are encouraged to study mythology.

The temple space I can describe to you best is my own, and it has changed many times over the years. Understanding that its very nature is fluid helps us go with the flow of change in our physical life. My inner temple is a volcanic island with a volcano in the center of it, though it took me years to recognize that it was a volcano. Your temple space can help you discover things for your entire life, not just during one meditation. I visualize myself coming up out of a tunnel and onto the island, near the base of the mountain. I used to think that the mountain had no top so that I could see the

Moon when inside it. Later, a healing guide gave me a code word to invoke healing energies when I was working with anger issues, and the code word was "volcano." At the time of my first visit, I had no idea that I would be working on anger issues later in life. At the base of the volcano is a wishing well and a giant boulder that rolls away to reveal a staircase. At the end of the staircase, at the bottom of the volcano, is a circular room. Around the room are several doorways.

Originally this room was a laboratory of sorts, with books, bottles, herbs, musical instruments, furniture, and surreal crystals growing out of the floor and walls. Anything I could possibly need could be found here or easily created. At one end of the room was a large red curtain, as in an old theater. This curtain covered my gateway of guidance, which we will discuss in detail later in the chapter. Opening the curtain was like looking out into the cosmos. Most of the doors were gateways to various levels of consciousness. Some of the doors led to other places on the island, including a garden and forest.

After the first major transformation, the items of the laboratory dissolved into a pool of silver liquid sitting at the bottom. This pool led to the ocean around the island, acting as a gateway to many different experiences. Any item I needed could be pulled out of the silver and shaped with my will. Later, all the doors around the room had an oil painting above them, but the face was obscured until I entered the room. Each doorway led to a different past life when I was focused on past-life healing.

You will notice that the inner temple reflects fundamental parts of your personality and experience. The character of the temple will change and develop as you go through your own personal transformations. Go with your first impression and don't get too attached to any one idea of your sacred space.

Even though all temples are individual and distinct, there seem to be some commonalities. The following are tools and locations that are useful for your own personal development, giving access to new energies, guidance, and meditation paths.

Center

The center refers to the center of the temple, a place that represents the center of the self and easily leads to all areas of the temple. Your inner temple could be very simple and contain only the center, like one room of an ancient temple or a clearing in the woods. Knowing the center is important for temples that seem vast and wandering. You go to the center to commune with your balanced, centered self, at the heart of your personal power.

Reflective Surface

A reflective surface is used to look at your spiritual self, to take stock of the changes going on within you. It could be a magick mirror or a still pool of water or something else entirely, like my own pool of liquid silver. Such a surface is also used for scrying, looking into the past, present, and future, like looking into a crystal ball.

Place of Water

Some source of water is found in the temple, like a wishing well, pool, stream, waterfall, river, lake, or seacoast. This is a place in which to commune with our deep unconscious and the things we seek to hide by casting them out to the sea and burying them deep. Such water could also be your reflective surface. Quite often one area will have more than one function.

Place of Earth

This is a place of grounding, to help you find your way when feeling lost or ungrounded. It is also a place of manifesting. It could be a forest or jungle you travel through to find your own path, to find the trail that will lead you to your power. At other times, it is a beautiful garden, wild or cultivated, where you plant seeds for your dreams and desires. As the plants grow in your garden, you manifest the goals in your life.

The other two elements, fire and air, could also be represented as areas in your inner temple. Although I've worked deeply with all four elements, these two do not seem to be a part of my inner temple. Candles, torches, and the Sun represent fire in the temple room, and air is present through looking up and seeing the sky. If you find larger areas of fire and air for your own temple, explore them thoroughly. They probably have strong messages for you.

Rooms of Play

These space are less defined, but represent areas of interest for you, both magickally and mundane. Objects from your hobbies and important mementos of your life experiences could be found here. These are places in which to entertain yourself as you explore the inner life.

Gates of Consciousness

The gates of consciousness represent different energies and levels of awareness that we experience. There are many different interpretations of the gates. The following system uses twelve gates. By opening these gates, you either invite these energies into your temple, or you have the opportunity to enter and explore the realms beyond the gate.

The gateways themselves can manifest as doors, curtains, holes, and caves, or as science-fiction-like star portals, like in the movie *Stargate*. If you are outside, the gateway could be between two large rocks or two trees, or between two carved columns, like the columns of Stonehenge.

Guidance—Opened to invite your spirit guides and spiritual helpers to your temple.

Creativity—Lends help in expressing your artistic and creative sides.

Learning—Opens the gateway to understanding teachings, both mystical and mundane.

Memories—Reveals past experiences, of this life and previous incarnations.

Purpose—Illuminates your true purpose at this time.

Healing—Leads to a chamber of healing, where your healing guides can work on you deeply in safety and comfort. Used for healing on all levels.

Peace—Brings tranquility and comfort when feeling stress or unease.

Transformation—Reveals parts of us that we have hidden, such as the shadow self, and urges us to transform ourselves, to take the next step in our evolution. Use with caution.

Journey—Leads to different lands and dimensions throughout time and space. Used for exploring and quests for knowledge of a personal and spiritual nature.

Ancestors—Used to connect to those who have come before us, to those from whom we descend, genetically and spiritually.

Harmony—Manifests an experience of unity and oneness with everyone. Helps create group consciousness.

Dreams—Opens to the realm of our personal and collective unconscious, the spiritual lands we visit when we sleep. Best to be used before going to sleep, to solve problems and have lucid experiences. Open the gate as you fall asleep and close it in the morning.

EXERCISE 31

Visiting the Inner Temple

In this meditation, you will be visiting the inner temple. The previous descriptions can prepare you for many possibilities while visiting the inner temple, but don't expect everything described to be present in your first visit. Release your expectations, and go with your first impression.

The vehicle to help us reach the cosmic axis is the World Tree, discussed in chapter 12. The tree is the cosmic axis, within the center of the universe and within the center of ourselves. Shamanic travelers would find burrows, holes, and tunnels in the roots, or climb the branches to traverse the spiritual worlds. The roots reach deep into the Underworld space and the branches touch the heavenly Upper World, home of the sky gods. The trunk is firmly rooted in the Middle World, the world of humanity, the physical dimension. Somewhere on the borders of this Middle World exists the entrance to your inner temple. As part of the journey, you will search for the path leading to your inner temple, your own personal space in the World Tree. You can continue to use the World Tree to reach your inner temple, and I highly suggest that you do. Familiarity with the World Tree will help in subsequent adventures, but know that any time you close your eyes and desire to be in your inner temple, you can be there instantly.

We ask to meet our guides in our own inner temple, because here we are centered in our power. Only those spirits for our highest good can enter. We will not allow any harmful or unwanted spirits in this place.

1. Start exercise 9: Counting Down to a Meditative State to get into your magickal mindset.

2. In your mind's eye, visualize the great World Tree, a gigantic tree reaching up to the heavens and deep below the earth, larger than any tree you have ever seen. It is a sacred tree and you may recognize it as oak, ash, pine, willow, or any other tree that has meaning for you.

3. Imagine that the screen of your mind's eye is like a window or doorway, a portal through which you can easily pass. Step through the screen and stand before the World Tree. Look up and feel its power. Touch the tree and place in it the intention of visiting your inner temple.

4. Look around the base of the giant tree, in the roots, and search for a passageway. It may be a hole or tunnel, or even a pool of water that gives you entry into the tree. As you enter, you find yourself in a tunnel, winding and spiraling to your inner temple.

5. At the end of the tunnel you see a light, and you move toward that light and step out into your inner temple. Look around. Take stock of all you see. Notice all the fine details of your sacred space. Let the images come to you.

6. First look for a reflective surface, a mirror or pool of some kind. Gaze into the mirror and see yourself, your spiritual self, as you truly are. Look at your self-image. Do you like it? Do you like yourself? More importantly, do you love yourself? Love is the foundation of true magick. Look yourself in the eyes and tell yourself that you are loved.

7. Leave the mirror and continue exploring, looking for your place of water. Here you bathe in the water of your own power. Think of all your worries, hopes, fears, dreams, and insecurities. Think of all the things that bring you unrest. Feel them rise out of your body and sit on the surface of your skin, and then wash them away. Wash away all that does not serve your highest good and release it, to be dissolved in the waters.

8. When you are done with water, look around your temple again. Look for your place of earth, perhaps a small garden. It may have grown wild or be fallow at this point. Do not worry. Feel yourself in the garden, grounded and centered, yet still present. This is your place of stillness. Think about the things you wish to manifest and materialize in the world. Think of your plans and dreams, your projects. Think of manifesting your creativity. Take those thoughts and feel them take form as seeds in your pockets. Take the seeds out and plant them with love. Water the garden and allow the seeds to grow. As your dreams manifest, this garden will flourish.

9. If you notice any of the other elements calling to you—fire, air, the Sun, or the Moon—visit with them and experience these energies for yourself.

10. Journey to the center of your temple, if you are not there already. Somewhere in the center, you will find the gateway of healing. Go to the gateway. Open the door and feel a chamber filled with healing light. The light could be any color you need. Enter the room and feel the light fill you up, healing you on all levels. Your healing spirits may join you there, but you will not necessarily see them or hear them. Such guides may lay you down as they do their work, releasing illness, filling you with light or power objects such as crystal and plant spirits. You could be wrapped in healing bandages, like a mummy, or placed in a healing chamber, like a sarcophagus.

11. When you feel the process is complete, thank your healing guides and exit the gateway of healing, returning to the center of the inner temple. Now you will search for your gateway of guidance. It could be the same doorway, leading to a different location, or another doorway altogether. Ask to see the gateway of guidance and you will be led to it.

12. Open the gateway of guidance, and look out into the vast sea of stars. Say, *"In the name of the Goddess and God, I call on my highest and best spirit guides, those correct and for my highest good, to come through and meet with me now."* You see a shape or two come out of the gateway, and with each moment, the figure comes into clearer focus. You see your guide or guides standing before you.

13. Speak with your guides. Ask each guide its name. Who are they and where are they from? Ask each guide's purpose and if they have any messages for you. If ready, ask your guides what your purpose is right now. If you have any other personal questions, take this time to speak with your guides and gain their wisdom and advice.

14. Thank the guides when done and see them back out through the gateway of guidance. Now that you have made contact, you can speak with them at any time, and all the exercises from the previous chapter will become easier and clearer.

15. Invite the Goddess and God, the forces of creation, into your inner temple. You may see the Goddess and God manifest in your temple, filling it with their perfect love for you and all life. Feel them bless and protect this sacred space. At this time, you may speak with them or be with them.

16. When done, thank the Goddess and God. If there is anything about your temple that you do not like, you can change it now by doing some inner spiritual decorating.

17. Once done, return through the World Tree tunnel that brought you to this place and stand before the World Tree. Step back through the screen of your mind's eye and let the World Tree gently fade from view.

18. Return yourself to normal consciousness, counting up, and giving yourself clearance and balance. Do any necessary grounding.

Your visit to the inner temple can be very intense and vivid, or just some vague impressions. The more you visit this place of power, the more your sense of true self will grow. I highly recommend you visit it often as part of your regular meditations. Use it as a starting point, visiting your temple and saying your affirmations in the temple. Do your basic energy work and chakra exercises while you visualize yourself in the temple, and any other meditations can be started with the World Tree or one of the many gateways in the temple.

When speaking with your guides, you may have difficulty seeing or hearing them. Do not worry. Such issues are fairly common and clear up with time. The age-old response is "You are not ready to hear or see them yet," which frustrates people to no end. I don't know if that is necessarily true, or if there is no reason to meet with them yet, but I do know that with intention and practice of meditation, your relationship with your guides will blossom.

When I first met my guides, I saw them in great detail, but I could not hear what they were saying. I saw their lips move, but heard no sound. I got very upset and put the whole idea of spirit guides on the back burner for a while, thinking, *If they can't talk to me, then what good are they?* Someone suggested months later that I ask them to speak up, and tell them that I can't understand. I did, and it was like someone suddenly turned up the volume of my television. I could hear every word perfectly. Through that experience, I learned that intention is very important. You get what you ask for, and if you don't ask, you might not get it.

Go to your guides when needed, or check in regularly with the question "What message to you have for me now?" They may lead you on individual journeys, or teach you meditations, rituals, and healing techniques. Guides are a wealth of wisdom and magick. Do not let such a resourceful relationship go to waste. And don't be surprised if the guides have favors or missions to ask of you, such as doing healing work or performing rituals at certain times. As always, follow your highest intuition in such cases, and do what feels correct to you.

New Assignments

• Exercise 31—Complete and record your experiences in your Book of Shadows.

Continuing Assignments

• Daily journal—Write three pages a day.

• Continue with a dream journal.

- Focus on a regular meditation practice, at least three times a week if not daily.

- Use intuition, instant magick, neutralization, light, and aura reading in your daily life.

TIPS

- Make the inner temple and contacting your spirit guides a regular part of your practice. Use it as a launch pad to discover yourself and your personal power. Use it to heal and renew yourself. Continue to build a relationship with your guides, calling on them as needed during meditation, magick, and in day-to-day situations.

- You can visit your inner temple anytime. Close your eyes, take five quick centering and relaxing breaths, and imagine you are there. Go there to relax and refresh yourself.

- Enjoy the experience. Learn to love the journey, and do not necessarily focus on the goals. You have everything you need with you all the time. As your perceptions deepen, your experiences will come with more clarity.

- As difficult as it may be to hear, sometimes we are not ready to have the experiences we want. Our ego may want what the body and spirit are not ready to experience. Such experiences often depend on our emotional, mental, and physical health, and our energy level, discipline, and willingness to release our attachment and truly listen. Practice quieting the mind, relaxing yet remaining focused, and find balance and health in your life in all areas. The previous meditations and energy exercises prepare you for deeper experiences. There's an old spiritual saying stating that the fruit will fall from the tree when it's ready, not before. It needs time to ripen.

- If you practice meditation in a group, you might find that it is much easier to do things in a group rather than on your own. When in a group of like-minded people, particularly with a teacher or leader, you create a group consciousness that helps propel everyone into deeper states of awareness. This is why many people gather together in groups to practice magick. Conversely, some people thrive only when they are alone. They have more meaningful experiences in private. Everyone is different. Do what is right for you.

Lesson 11
Healing

Western medicine focuses on the physical anatomy, the internal organs, bones, and blood vessels. All of our "traditional" cures are based completely in the physical, usually viewing the symptoms, the areas of discomfort, as the main problem. Witches, on the other hand, have an entirely different focus.

One of the greatest definitions of witchcraft is "healing," for those who practice the craft are truly practicing the healing arts, for the individual, for the tribe, and for the world. Ancient witches were the medicine people of their communities, fully addressing health through a wide range of techniques. Such witches were physical healers, using herbcraft, the plant's spirit medicine, to heal on all levels, but we understand herbalism today as an "alternative" way to treat physical illnesses. The witch's magickal potions, cauldron, and chalice were the vessels through which these healing remedies flowed. These healers did not focus exclusively on the physical illness and symptoms, but used these pains to trace the illness back to the source. Witches were counselors, psychological and spiritual. As religious leaders, they led each individual to a greater understanding of spirit, addressing issues and experiences that made their patients feel separated from spirit. They were energy healers, intuitively knowing the energy anatomy and addressing the imbalances within the mind, emotions, and spirit that manifested disease. Witches wore many hats in the days of old, and are doing so again. If most people knew that *witchcraft* is synonymous with *healing*, the word would have no stigma attached to it.

Because witches look at the world as a holistic system, we view healing holistically. Although taking care of painful symptoms is helpful, one must look for the reason behind the symptom. Illness can be thought of as a form of magick we practice on ourselves. Magick is manifestation, and we unconsciously manifest a disease to understand the message our body is telling us. We can use those same tools, intent and will, to restore a healthy balance. To do so, we look at the root of the imbalance, not the outward result. Like a weed, once the root is removed, the weed will not grow back.

The word *disease* is one of the most important clues to our magickal healing. Words and names hold power in magick. Everyone is familiar with the magician's magickal words that make things happen. The entomology of a word traces back to its true meaning and power. When you break *disease* down into basic components, you have "dis" and "ease." *Dis-* is a prefix that denotes a negative, opposite, or absence of, as in the word disrespect. *Ease* is exactly what it means: ease, comfort, relaxation. Disease is the lack of comfort. This is not our traditional definition of disease. Most people use the word to mean something impairing health. By looking at the root of the word, we discover its secret: impairing health is a lack of ease. Medicine generally accepts that tension and stress affect health and suggests that patients relax, exercise, and enjoy themselves. Modern medical communities are exploring the link between the mind and body, exploring how your thoughts and attitudes contribute to your overall health. Witches know that the connection not only includes the mind and body, but also the emotions and spirit.

The solution to combating physical illness is awareness and balance of the inner self. If you can resolve inner tensions and conflicts before they manifest physically, you spare yourself much physical discomfort. Your body does not want to be diseased. The natural state is health, but manifesting illness in the body is your inner self's last-ditch effort for you to consciously recognize you have a problem, an imbalance, and to take care of it.

We are all capable of denying our emotions and thoughts. In this society, it is quite common to do what is expected of us rather than what we intuitively feel called to do, but it is much harder to ignore a physical reaction. Often minor illnesses are messages from your body to take it easy and rest. You will not rest, so it forces you to rest. Every illness has a message for us, because each is based on an imbalance. Some are simple. Other messages are much more complex and personal. Although each person's disease delivers an individual message, certain types of illnesses manifest for basic reasons, having common points of imbalance.

Understanding the chakras is key to understanding the imbalance of the energy body. Many psychological functions are inherently tied to physical anatomy (figure 30). An imbalance in one often leads to an imbalance in the other. Energy anatomy can be as important as physical anatomy. When seeking to discover the message of an illness when doing healing work, first look at where the illness is or, at the very least, where the symptoms are manifesting. Ask yourself, "Is this body part associated with any chakra?" and "What chakra is closest to this body part?" Then think about the chakra, its meaning and lessons. Does the ill person have issues in these areas? If so, try to identify them. You started looking on the physical level, but now expand to the emotions and mind. Are certain feelings and thoughts influencing the energy of that chakra, causing the root of the disease? Discuss thoroughly and extend your look into the spiritual issues of that chakra and the person's own connection with divinity.

This is a difficult experience for those not used to introspective work. Ultimately this viewpoint is empowering because it means *you* created an imbalance, and now *you* can create health, but some may think such a holistic view is putting the blame on them, implying they created the illness. To the person experiencing the illness, it seems that the body is in a state of revolt and that he or she has no physical control over it. Any such conversation, with yourself or others, should be tempered with unconditional love and understanding. Remember that you cannot heal anyone else, you can only help them heal themselves.

As each chakra expresses imbalance through a range of physical and spiritual issues, so, too, do the sides of the body give clues. Illness on the left side often deals with the arena of home, family, and emotional life. The left is considered more receptive, feminine, and intuitive. Illness or injury on the right side usually falls under the domain of work, activity, and public life. The right is considered more active and masculine. For more information on the roots of illness, I suggest reading Louise L. Hay's *Heal Your Body*.

	Root	Belly	Solar Plexus
Function:	survival	instinct	power
Body:	physical	etheric	astral
Glands:	ovaries, gonads	pancreas	adrenal
Body Systems:	reproductive, excretory	lower digestive, skeletal	upper digestive, musculature
Organs:	sex organs, colon, anus, legs, feet, skin, DNA	intestines, spleen, kidneys	liver, stomach, gall bladder
Illnesses:	sexual dysfunction, infertility, genetic illness, colon cancer, venereal disease	ulcers, kidney infection/stones, pancreatic illness, hypertension	hyperactivity, chronic fatigue, stomach disease, liver disease
Imbalances:	ungrounded, depression, lack of pleasure, suicidal impulses, betrayal, sexual or gender shame	stress, inability to trust, difficulty relating to others, sense of not fitting in, nervousness	abuses of power, fear, poor self-image control issues, ego issues, giving away power, anger, addictions
Learning:	learn to be in the physical world, pleasure, grounding	learn to trust self and others, make societal and sexual relationships	find personal power, learn to control self, not others, learn to express anger in a healthy manner

Figure 30: Chakra Chart

Heart	Throat	Brow	Crown
love	expression	vision	spirituality
emotional	mental	psychic	divine
thymus	thyroid	pineal	pituitary
circulatory, immune	respiratory	nervous	nervous, endocrine
heart, blood, veins, arteries, skin, lymph nodes, arms, hands	throat, mouth, teeth, larynx, vocal cords, trachea, tonsils, lungs, ears	lower brain, eyes, nerve tissue	upper brain, glands, skin, spinal cord
heart disease, blood pressure imbalance, chronic illness, colds, flu, viral/bacterial infections, diabetes	high/low metabolism, hormone imbalance, throat, mouth, tooth and lung disease, asthma, laryngitis, loss of breath, bronchitis	visual impairment, headaches, nervous disorders	hormone imbalance, auto-immune and environmental illnesses, all body-wide illnesses
shame, guilt, fear, inability to form relationships, selfishness, dislike physical contact	fear of speaking up, gossip, silence, inability to listen	inability to see the world clearly, lack of vision, inability to realize potential, illusions, dellusions	feeling of separation, lack of spiritual experience, no belief in divinity, domination of the physical over all
learn to love, empathy, compasion, self-love	learn to speak and listen, creative expression, listen to guidance, act on higher will	learn to access visionary and psychic abilities, intuition	learn to connect to the divine, inspiration, bliss, wholeness, spiritual insight

Psychic Diagnosis

Diagnosis is an important first step in the healing process. You must understand the forces at play before you attempt to restore balance. Traditional medical doctors base their diagnosis on symptoms, medical tests, and extensive knowledge gathered in medical school that is continually updated in the medical journals. Nontraditional medics often diagnose using techniques such as pulses, tongue color, or the variations of the eye. Metaphysical healers use their intuitive and psychic abilities, what witches call magickal talents.

To find the true root of healing, we again trace the roots of the words used in healing. *Diagnosis* contains the word *gnosis*. Gnosis is knowledge, and in an ancient Greek context, such knowledge was usually of a spiritual, metaphysical nature. Gnosis is spiritual truth, and also refers to the meditative state when all becomes clear and illuminated. By entering a meditative state, you awaken to the true nature of the universe, a spiritual nature. *Dia-* means "through" or "across," suggesting that diagnosis originally meant to move through or across to reach the truth. A diagnosis is an analysis of the problem, and from the roots of the word, we know that diagnosis of illness was at one time as much a spiritual art as it was a scientific one.

It is important to remember that all forms of diagnosis that help us get to the truth are worthwhile. Medical and metaphysical diagnoses can be complementary, if an individual is open to both. Medical diagnosis can be more precise as to the exact nature of the malady, including chemical and cellular information, but intuitive skills are quite accurate when practiced and more importantly often point the way to the root of the problem. To confirm the physical accuracy of such psychic abilities, one exercise in this chapter will work with a doctor's diagnosis, but you will not have that prior knowledge.

Although I suggest that you take thorough stock of your own health on the physical, emotional, mental, and spiritual levels and work on your own healing first, if you choose to explore healing with others, it is important to know that *you are not legally authorized to make a medical diagnosis* without appropriate medical training and licenses. It helps to work with someone who has a medical diagnosis, but if not, make sure to phrase all your information in the form of suggestions, and qualify it with statements such as, "I feel the problem is . . . ," even if you are certain of the psychic diagnosis in your heart and mind. Always recommend that a client confirm such intuitions with a medical professional, and never recommend changes in medical treatments and routines prescribed by a doctor. You can suggest alternative practitioners and therapies, but realize that there is a distinction between a metaphysician and a medical physician. As psychic healers, witches must be sure to represent themselves as reputably as possible.

There are two distinct styles of psychic diagnosis, and, in fact, all healing could be broken into these two categories. One is hands-on, or more accurately, in person, since touch is not necessary. The other is distant. As we know that all beings are thoughts in the divine mind, from the Principle of Mentalism, there is truly no distance between us. All is one. Therefore, it doesn't matter how close or far away someone is to affect them magickally.

EXERCISE 32

Psychic Scanning

For the in-person diagnosis, you will be using the skills you learned in earlier chapters relating to feeling and perceiving energy. In chapter 5, exercise 4: Feeling the Aura, you learned to feel the aura of your partner, as a sensation of temperature or magnetism. Now the experience deepens with your knowledge of energy anatomy.

1. Start with your partner either standing before you, or lying down, preferably on a raised surface such as a massage table. Take a few breaths to tune in to yourself, reaffirm your protection shield, and ask your healing guides to be present. You do not have to count down into a deep meditative state.

2. Hold your hands out, palms facing your partner, and move closer, attempting to feel the aura. I like to start in the crown area. Once you feel the first layer of the energy body, slowly bring your hands down over the chakra line, from the crown, down the face, throat, and chest, and down the torso and legs. As you move, notice any inconsistencies. The information can be received differently each time, so you are specifically looking for areas of dissimilarity. If most of the body is warm, you could find pockets of cold. Other areas could be extremely warm. Certain spots might have a bumpy, rough, or abrasive feeling energetically. The layer of energy can sink at certain points, feeling weaker or like a hole.

3. Notice your intuitive feelings at each spot. Was the temperature or texture intrinsically healthy, or did it feel uncomfortable and unbalanced?

4. Repeat steps 2 and 3, at various distances from the body, exploring the different layers of the aura. If your partner is standing, you can walk to both sides and behind to feel the aura. Be thorough, but do not focus on minutia. One or two initial scans will give you all the information you need.

5. Now use your knowledge of the aura and energy anatomy to apply some of this intuitive information. Which body areas and chakras were affected? Then discuss with your partner the chakras and areas of concern. If you didn't feel anything, don't worry. If your partner is relatively healthy, both physically and energetically, you won't find many differences. This is a good exercise to do often, so you can notice the changes.

Once you feel comfortable scanning through your hands and sensation, add the following steps to the exercise, based on your experience with exercise 23: Aura Gazing. South American shamans state that the body can be seen through, like glass, to know where the disease is located. As you grow more proficient, one of these techniques may be more helpful than the other.

6. Gaze at your partner in a soft focus, starting at the crown. Again, allow the first layer of the aura, the etheric body, to come into view. Trace the outline of the etheric body, that thin layer of white, all around the body. Notice where it breaks or seems weaker. If the energy level is low in a certain area, it could indicate an imbalance or injury.

7. Allow your gaze to expand to the full aura, and scan the aura from head to toe, left and right sides. First notice the color impressions. Does any area seem different or discolored? Are the colors complementary, or do they clash? What parts of the body look like they are clashing?

8. Scan the surface of the aura for any rips or tears in the egglike sphere. They may coincide with any cold spots you felt. Scan inside the field for darker, thick spots, such as unhealthy thoughtforms. Look for any cords of energy. Scan the chakras for imbalances of size, shape, or color.

9. As in step 5, use your knowledge and intuition to gain more information about the nature of the imbalances and then discuss them with your partner.

Distance diagnosis works much the same way as the hands-on approach. I originally learned many of these techniques from Laurie Cabot, in her *Witchcraft as a Science One* class, and thought psychic healing was exclusive to more traditional witchcraft. I later found similar techniques from José Silva and his *The Silva Method of Mind Control* course, from author Caroline Myss, and from the healing arts of reiki, pranic healing, and shamanism. Professional practitioners in more mainstream settings call themselves medical intuitives.

The basic technique of distance diagnosis is to enter a meditative state and make a psychic connection to your target. Usually the name, age, and place of residence is enough. Most practitioners then call forth a psychic image of the person, in miniature, in the mind's eye, like a doll. This image contains all the information of the original, like a hologram. You may feel like you can reach out and grab it, like in the orange meditation. By scanning the body, as in the previous exercise, and even psychically scanning deeper on the physical level, a diagnosis is made. The scanning process can be sensory, physically running your hand over the image to feel the variations; visual, like viewing the aura; or clairsentient, knowing, where the answer pops into your head.

Another technique is journeying out to the target. Instead of bringing the image of your target to the screen of your mind in miniature, you psychically go to the target and perform the scan. I prefer the first method myself.

Scanning, in person or distantly, can offer the practitioner some common symbols for disease. It is important to remember that such symbols can be individual and unique, speaking solely to your creative mind, but some common symbols for illnesses have been reported. Scan over this short identification list and read through the next section on healing techniques before performing the distant-healing exercise at the end of this chapter.

Illness	Symbol
Arthritis	Redness or heat around the joint
Bacteria	Green or yellow masses of energy
Cancer	Black, brown, or gray lumps of energy
Chakra imbalance	Chakra color is darker, dense, or unhealthy looking

Chronic fatigue	General sense of fatigue or energy loss, energy is "spraying" out of the aura like a leaky balloon
Diabetes	White flecks in the blood and body
Heart disease	Redness, heat, or pressure in the heart area
HIV	Black spiked objects in the blood and body
Hyperactivity	Energy is buzzing around the aura like insects
Hypertension	Throbbing sensation in the blood vessels
Intestinal disease	Inflammation or darkness surrounding the lower digestive system
Kidney infection	Green, red, or yellow color in the kidney area, stonelike formations for kidney stones
Liver disease	Black, red, or yellow in the liver, feelings of fire or anger
Missing organs	A hole or void in the body, although in some cases you may still sense the energetic presence of the organ, and not feel a void
Nervous disorders	Strong "electric" feeling or image in the nervous system
Virus	Spiked or sharp "objects" in the blood and body

These symbols will hopefully spark your creative imagination and show you how psychic diagnosis can work. Some symbols are obvious. A broken bone will often appear like a broken bone. Disease usually appears as discoloration or inflammation. Remember to relate the colors and locations of imbalance to the chakras. If you plan to do detailed medical work as a healer, I highly suggest studying anatomy and investing in the reference book *Gray's Anatomy*. As you develop, you might psychically "see" organs and sections unknown to you.

Healing Techniques

The following are healing techniques using previous experiences from this book. Certain ones are more appropriate in person, and others are more helpful for distance healings. Always use the technique that calls to you.

Before attempting any healing, you must ask permission. Ask the person directly for permission first. If you receive a yes, ask his or her higher self. Quiet your mind for a moment. Be open. Affirm your protection shield and call on your guides and higher self and the guides and higher self of the person you are working on healing. Then ask permission and wait for an answer. If you do not hear or feel it, you can use muscle testing (exercise 28) or the pendulum (exercise 27) for a direct answer. If you cannot get direct permission first, in the case of distance healing or if someone is unconscious and unable to answer, meditate and ask the higher self for permission, as you would before sending light.

Use the scanning techniques and ask the higher self of your client for any additional information or techniques that should be used. The message could be something un-usual, such as to have him or her face north or hold a certain crystal. Even if it does not make sense to you, the message has a deeper meaning for the person involved.

Remember that you are not doing the healing, but facilitating the healing. The in-dividual and the higher powers—guides, gods and goddesses, the Great Spirit—are re-ally doing the healing work. Always ask that the work be for the "highest good of all involved." If someone is receiving something from the experience of illness, you should not stop it unless it is for the highest good.

Light

Visualize the healing recipient bathed in colored lights. Green is usually for general health and minor healing and red-orange is for critical healing. You can use any color for healing and soothing the mind and emotions, perhaps the most dominant and healthy color you scanned in the aura. Use your intuition and ask for guidance when choosing (figure 31).

Visualization

Visualize the healing occurring. Visualize broken bones knitting back together. Imagine bacteria and viruses deteriorating. Cells become healthy. Wounds seal. Lungs and sinuses clear. Arteries clear. Healing water flushes out toxins. The immune system devours can-cer. The images can be real and scientific, or mystical and otherworldly. The white blood cells devouring the cancer cells could be visualized as the wild dogs of the goddess Diana devouring the illness. Microscopic healers/doctors can go around maintaining your body systems, clearing clogs and infection, and sewing up wounds. Be creative.

Red   AIDS/HIV, anemia, low blood pressure, low energy, parasites, sexual dysfunction, venereal disease, viral infections

Red-orange AIDS/HIV, hay fever, infections, internal bleeding, loss of blood, low blood pressure, pneumonia

Orange Bladder infections, bowel syndromes, broken bones

Gold   AIDS/HIV, back problems, low metabolism, nerves, sore muscles, total health

Yellow Adrenal problems, bladder infections, indigestion, liver disease, low metabolism, sore muscles, stomach cramps

Lime   Cleansing, nausea, Ph balance, purging, stomachaches, toxicity

Green Blood loss, colds, eczema, eye infections, flu, heart conditions, infections, insect bites, rashes, ulcers

Turquoise All purpose, epilepsy, fevers, menstrual problems, pain, nausea, rashes, swelling

Blue   Anxiety, asthma, ear infections, fevers, high blood pressure, high metabolism, liver, stress, TMJ syndrome

Indigo Alcoholism/addiction, eye infections, headaches, hemorrhoids, high blood pressure, inflammation, Parkinson's, pnemonia, thyroid conditions

Purple Brain swelling, eye problems, liver disease, nervous disorders, nervous tension

Violet Abcesses, arthritis, bacteria, cancer, cleansing, cysts, infection, unwanted growths, viral infections, warts

Black Eye conditions, relaxation, stress, ungroundedness

Brown Animal healing, bleeding, open wounds, ungroundedness

Rust   Cleansing, grounding, removing unwanted material

Pink   AIDS/HIV, blemishes, breast cancer, menstrual problems

Silver Emotional problems, fertility problems, maternal issues, menstration issues, psychic blocks

White All purpose, cleansing, healing, soothing

Figure 31: Healing Light

Visualization is particularly good for physical illness. We have all heard the phrase "mind over matter," but we do not often witness people moving objects across a room through the powers of psychokinesis. Mystics believe we have greater control on a microscopic level, creating the term *cellular psychokinesis*, or CPK for short. Isaac Bonewits, in his book *Real Magic*, discusses this at greater length.

Hands-On Healing

Mystical traditions throughout the world, from witches to early Christians, used the laying on of hands to transfer healing energy from the practitioner to the recipient. The recipient's own body and energy systems use this power to effect the healing, stimulating the immune system and clearing out energy blocks and harmful thoughtforms.

Although there are many different systems of hands-on healing, the most important thing to remember is not to use your own personal energy to effect the healing. It will only leave you feeling drained and possibly feeling the symptoms of your client. You can draw energy from the energy around you, Earth and sky energies, and the divine. Do the chakra meditation, running energy up from the earth and down from the sky, and then move the energy through your arms and release it through your hands. Do not force it into your client, just allow it to flow. When the flow stops moving, stop this form of healing. You do not want to overload anyone. You could also project this energy out through your chakras, particularly the solar plexus, heart, or third eye, as colored light. After the first few times practicing this healing, stop and check in with yourself. Are you feeling tired, sick, or otherwise drained? Make sure that you are not using your own energy, but only the energy of the Earth and sky. Ask your guides for help, or discontinue if you are having problems. It might not be the healing technique for you.

Aura and Chakra Cleansing

Either by guiding your client through the meditations, or visualizing the effects yourself, use the aura-cleansing and chakra-balancing techniques you learned. Use white light to seal holes and tears in the aura. Smooth them out. Remove unwanted thoughtforms by reaching out to them and pulling them out, dissolving them in light. If you find ones that are stuck, imagine turning them upside down in your hands, reversing the polarity of the energy. It will then easily release and transmute. Remove and dissolve all cords. This work is akin to psychic/shamanic surgery, where harmful energy forms are released to effect healing.

Healing Guides

Call on your own healing guides, and the guides of the recipient. You can guide the client through a meditation to connect to his or her own healing guides and gateway of healing. Use your own gateway of healing and guides when sick yourself. Some people feel the presence of their guides as additional "hands" with hands-on healing, or see them delivering energy to the recipient with distance healing.

Before bed, invoke your healing guides by quieting your mind, asking them to be present and giving them permission to heal you while you sleep. In the morning, thank and release them.

Exercise 33

Healing Case

For this exercise, it is paramount to have a partner. Your partner must gather together information on three or more people who have been diagnosed with a physical illness or injury, not including mental illnesses caused by chemical imbalances. Your partner will need the name, age, and city of residence of each person, along with a general description of height, weight, hair and eye color, general build, and a list of their physical ailments and locations in the body. It is also extremely helpful if your partner knows these people well, including their general personalities and mental/emotional states. You must not know any of these people.

Your partner will only be giving you the name, age, and location of your case, guiding you through the steps of this exercise, confirming your intuition. If you make a "mistake" with the diagnosis of the case, your partner should avoid saying "No" or "You're wrong." Nothing shoots holes in your confidence more than to hear such statements, and they may not even be correct. Often we receive information that is absolutely correct, but our partner has no knowledge of it. If you feel that strongly about it, let your partner double-check later with the person. I've demonstrated this many times, and although I've sometimes missed major aspects, I've zoned in on the most recent illness or injury, which is probably in the forefront of the recipient's consciousness. Guidance from your partner should be phrased as, "I don't have that information," "Look closer," or "Look in another place."

Until you gain some confidence with this ability, your partner will be pivotal in your success. Make sure that your partner is familiar with the exercise, reading it over fully and understanding it before attempting it. Your partner does not necessarily have to be practicing witchcraft with you, but being open to this work is important. Don't pick someone who will scoff, disbelieve, or otherwise hinder you. Pick someone with an open mind and encouraging personality.

If you get stuck on a case, don't get frustrated, simply move on to the next case. Some people are difficult to make a connection with. Your energies don't mix. Others don't want to be healed. If you are not inclined to the medical, you may find your information more involved with the emotional and mental health of the recipient. We are focusing on the medical at this point to give our psychic abilities some real-world verification.

1. Start exercise 9: Counting Down to a Meditative State to get into your magickal mindset. Your partner can guide you down. Affirm your protection shield and invoke your healing guides to be with you. Follow your guides' intuitive prompting.

2. Your partner will give you the name, age, and location of the first case. Make the connection by repeating the name, age, and location of the target at least three times, more if necessary. Draw an invoking pentagram on the screen of your mind to open the link.

3. Call on your target's higher self and guides to be with you, and ask for their permission. If you don't have permission, intend to end this connection and move on to the next case.

4. Once you have permission, allow the link to occur and an image to form in your mind's eye. Let the first bits of information come to you, usually as a "knowing" in your mind. Or you may receive the information visually. Get a basic description of the person, including hair and eye color and general build. If you have no height reference, imagine someone whose height you know standing next to the person. Are they taller or shorter? Sometimes numbers pop into your head. If you have difficulty with the description, skip ahead to the next step.

5. Use the techniques of exercise 32 to scan the body. Physically pass your hand over the image. Notice any differences. Scan the energy field and the chakras. Get any intuitive flashes you can. Ask to see major health issues, and different body parts will attract your attention, often revealing the illness through the symbols previously discussed. If necessary, pick one and project yourself into the area for a closer look. Images and symbols, colors and sensation could occur. Diagnose the area to the best of your knowledge and intuition. If you do not know the name of the condition, a general description will suffice. Repeat this with all areas of interest.

   If your partner knows the recipient of this exercise, you can continue your scan of the energy field, seven chakras, and subtle bodies to give an energetic health reading, giving your intuitive impressions of this person's mental, emotional, and spiritual state.

6. Ask to send healing to the recipient, for the highest good. Use one of the healing techniques described in this lesson. Sending light, visualization healing, or asking the guides for help are the most effective techniques for distance healing. Send a blessing with the words "Blessed be." When done, thank and release all guides and your higher selves. Release the connection by drawing a banishing pentagram and imagining yourself wiping the image off the screen of your mind.

7. Return yourself to normal consciousness, counting up, and giving yourself clearance and balance. Do any necessary grounding. You may need more grounding than usual, so go slowly and make sure your awareness is fully back.

Potential Difficulties

Some practitioners intuitively gain information through feeling physical sensations, instead of receiving visual or auditory information. These witches are more physical and sensory with their psychic abilities. Such sensory techniques often lead to a harmful connection to the healing recipient, where the practitioner feels the pain and illness in his or her own body. Understandably, this is not often a pleasant experience for the practitioner. It can turn potential healers away from the path. Since these practitioners didn't intend to feel the pain, and the experience seems to happen automatically, they don't know how to stop it. Acknowledge the information you receive, and ask your guides to give you the information without further pain. This acknowledgment and request is usually sufficient to end painful experiences. You don't have to experience the pain of the target to diagnose and send healing.

Others get information that is too detailed, and their background does not allow them to understand complex scientific and anatomical images. Even worse, such images can be potentially graphic and overwhelming. If you experience this, ask your guides to give you the information in an easier manner.

Whenever you are uncomfortable and cannot banish a feeling, end the experience, count up, and take a break.

If you get stuck, or no areas attract your attention, begin a more methodical search. Although not a good technique for those with vivid imaginations and weak stomachs, ask to view each body system one by one and ask, "Is the problem here?" I start with the skeletal system, and move through the circulatory, musculature, respiratory, digestive, excretory, reproductive, and immune systems. You can use muscle testing or a pendulum to get a yes/no response. If no information presents itself, focus on the chakra system again and the layers of the aura.

For those less medically inclined, the information might be more like a shamanic journey, traveling through the body. Illness will be represented as monsters and creatures of myth. Healing is effected by defeating the creatures, who then reveal their true nature as an illness or injury.

The last step, which could also be the first, is to ask to commune with the recipient's higher self, getting not only the medical information directly, but the reasons behind it. This is always an important step for long-term healing work, to understand the cause and nature of the imbalance. You may receive direct messages from his or her higher self or guides. Follow any direction given here by the higher self to effect the greatest healing. It may give you specific instructions, visualization, or techniques.

New Assignments

- Exercises 32–33—Complete and record your experiences in your Book of Shadows.

- Regularly scan your body, aura, and chakras for imbalances and perform any healing needed. Find illness before it manifests physically. Get into an active relationship with your health.

Continuing Assignments

- Daily journal—Write three pages a day.

- Continue with a dream journal.

- Focus on a regular meditation practice, at least three times a week if not daily.

- Use intuition, instant magick, neutralization, light, and aura reading in your daily life.

Tips

- Notice your own thoughts, feelings, and impressions when doing healing. They might be giving you psychic information.

- If you have difficulty with a diagnosis, see if you can borrow and hold an object of personal significance to the recipient of the healing, such as a ring, watch, or key. You will make a solid link to the recipient through the vibrations of the object. This technique is often called psychometry, and works through the Law of Contagion, as mentioned in chapter 8.

- If you don't have a partner for exercise 33: Healing Case, you can do it alone and then later try to get verification of your impressions from the recipient.

- You can also use these techniques to heal and communicate with animals and plants.

Recommended Reading

Heal Your Body by Louise L. Hay (Hay House).

Lesson 12
Born Again

When I was a young boy, I remember watching television with my mother. We were watching a documentary on the Old West, specifically the Native Americans' Trail of Tears. We looked at each other with a spooky fascination. We are normally very close, but this was different. We watched each part with utter devotion, as if the secrets of life were being revealed in this program. I then turned to my mother and said, "Do you remember when we were there?"

That afternoon was my first introduction to past-life memories, but I didn't know it at the time. I was raised in a Catholic family, with no previous belief or discussion of past lives. The topic was just starting to surface in mainstream American culture, but the idea was not nearly as widespread as it is today. Strangely enough, I later learned that early Gnostic Christians believed in reincarnation. The patriarchal church, when codifying the Bible, struck out those books and passages containing such information, though some survived, including the following quotation:

"Because it was toward John that all the prophesies of the prophet and of the Law were leading, and he, if you will believe me, is Elijah who was to return. If anyone has ears to hear, let him listen."
—Matthew 11:14–15

Modern scholars speculate that this passage of the New Testament is one of the few obscure references left in the Bible regarding reincarnation, implying John was Elijah in a past life.

Since my Trail of Tears experience, I've heard similar stories. While a friend was passing through the area with her family, we visited America's Stonehenge, a sacred site near my home in New Hampshire. She brought her two children, both wonderfully magickal beings. Her son and I had a remarkable connection, and as we walked through the woods and a snake passed our trail, he said, "Do you remember when we were all here together, a long time ago?" We talked about how we just met that day and then he got indignant and said, "Not now! Long, long time ago!" His mother and I looked at each other in amazement. Another great student and friend of mine named Carin mentioned to me that her daughter said at a very young age, "You're a much better mommy to me than I was to you, and I'm so sorry."

Each time I discuss past lives, I hear another story, even the simple sensations of remembrance, what the French language calls "déjà vu," a feeling that one has been here or done this before. If places do not kindle our feelings, sometimes we meet someone so connected to us, emotionally, intuitively, even spiritually, that it seems we have known each other forever even though we have just met. It is the feeling of familiarity when there is no connection in this life that points us to another piece of the cosmic puzzle. Religions the world over have beliefs in the human soul, a distinct essence that continues on after death. Theologies and mythologies give us a guide to what happens to souls prior to birth and after life. Although atheists would argue that such fables are created to give us comfort or to control, the various faiths do seem to have similar threads woven into very different tapestries.

The myth of much modern Christianity is that "good" souls go to eternal reward in Heaven while "bad" souls go to Hell, a place of fire and torment, to be punished for their sins. Pagan religions are filled with similar upper worlds and underworlds, though without the moral context of Christianity. In the Celtic cosmology, there were not so many differences between the two worlds. The Underworld was a place of the ancestors, family spirits, guides, and guardians. Souls went to feed the World Tree, the great oak, and their power would emerge again in their tribe. Julius Caesar, the author of some of the few ancient texts we have on the Celts and their secretive priesthood, the Druids, asserted that Celts were so fearless in battle because they believed that if they died they would be born again. Unfortunately the Celts probably didn't subscribe to our modern, global ideas of reincarnation. The idea of a Celtic warrior or Druid reincarnating as a Roman soldier would not settle well with these people. The Celts most likely saw spirit passing through tribal or even blood lines, and there is currently great exploration of the idea of genetic memory passing from one generation to the next. Perhaps the ancient Celts were right after all.

Modern concepts of reincarnation stem from the Eastern traditions, particularly from India, but many of the fundamental Hindu concepts, such as caste systems, have been toned down. Considering that the Hindus and Celts possibly share a common ancestry, it's not surprising that both had strong tenets regarding past lives.

The basic concept is that the human soul is immortal. Aspects of our consciousness, our subtle bodies, continue on after the physical body perishes. This soul can then be reborn into another life, possibly a different culture, to continue spiritual development through new experiences. Most feel that this structure is an education system, making life a "school" for us to learn our lessons. To me, that smacks of too strong a moralistic tone. Personally, I feel that if we are all thoughts in the Divine Mind, like a hologram, then we each contain the information of everything. Each of our lives is a different experience to help us creatively remember ourselves.

To those who follow the cycles of the seasons, it seems only natural that we do not cease to exist, but instead enter a new cycle. The universe does not waste energy. All things are recycled in time. Even so, this opens up a whole range of unanswered questions and other possibilities embraced by sects of the spiritual movements. Opinions differ as to where souls come from, what happens when all the "lessons" are learned, and the nature of animal, insect, plant, and even mineral spirits. How does all of life figure into this system? As we touch on various views, please keep in mind that once a spirit passes the veil to the next world, concepts of three-dimensional time and space lose the importance we place on them. All of these systems are points of view, and none truly represent the entire picture. Life after death is something we only truly understand after we pass.

Although there is no "official" Wiccan view, most witches believe in the concept of past lives. The Wiccan belief in reincarnation most likely stems from the Celtic worldview influencing the modern craft, so many witches believe that the soul returns to the Underworld after death, to act as a guide or guard for family and friends. The Underworld is not a place of torment, but a zone of rest and regeneration. At the proper point in time, a soul will return to the waking world, reborn as a new child. Such reincarnations are not necessarily through family bloodlines, but groups of spirits will often incarnate together, knowing each other through many lives as family, lovers, and friends. Those who continue through the cycles and complete whatever goal is before them can remain in this cycle to aid others or continue onward to the upper worlds, the realm of gods, paradise, and the land of milk and honey. Here they are fully united with their divine, higher self and continue with new experiences. Some witches do not distinguish between the Upper World and the Underworld, viewing it all as the Otherworld, beyond the veil.

Although most reincarnation theories assert that everyone reincarnates, many witches feel that only those involved with the craft at some point in their lives undergo the process of rebirth. Those who are drawn to the magickal arts now practiced them in a past incarnation. Others are called "once borns" because they lack the multilife perspective. In my own work with past-life healing, I've encountered many people with no interest in magick who have successfully undergone a past-life regression, so I do not subscribe to the "once born" theory. Most likely this is a corruption of the Hindu concept of a twice born, which refers to "people who have taken a second birth, as it were, in spiritual wisdom."[1] A person focused on the spiritual is more likely to explore past lives. The priests and teachers of India, the Brahman, are called twice born. They fulfill much the same role as the witch.

Most occultists do not feel that you are limited to a particular number of incarnations. W. W. Westcott, one of the founders of the Golden Dawn, states one theory that

---

1. Sri Swami Satchidananda, *The Living Gita* (Yogaville, VA: Integral Yogi Publications, 1988) 254.

souls are limited to three incarnations. Students of the Golden Dawn have copied this information, though in other sources Westcott speaks about other theories of reincarnation. The three incarnations may come from a Bible passage regarding punishment for three generations.

Many "New Age" theories are very similar to the witch's view, minus the mythological references. Souls are seen as belonging to a soul group, a larger collection of spirits with similar goals and vibrations. Some souls in the group incarnate while those remaining act as spirit guides, keeping them on course. In fact, some believe that the soul group shares memories, so your past-life memories may actually be of someone else in your group.

You can look at reincarnation as a system of spiritual evolution. A soul continues to incarnate in a "lower" life force until it does a service for a "higher" life form, such as the lower life form being food for the higher. Only then does the soul continue on to the next level. In this paradigm, an ant might reincarnate eventually as a dog and then a human. Devolution in morals, consciousness, or spirit may result in taking a step "backward." Such beliefs engender a sense of compassion for all life, since you don't know what you were, or what you'll come back as next time. Other systems have no moral basis to incarnating as an animal, plant, or mineral. You learn a quality that your soul needs in that incarnation. You could learn about change and "shedding your skin" in the life of a snake, and bring that knowledge back to your next human incarnation. The power and significance of animals is important, because they remind us of the experiences, or "animal medicine," we learned when in that form. According to the Lurianic system, named for a famous Kabalist named Luria, one remains in a "lower" life form until being of service to a "higher" life form, even as food for that life form. Various believers incorporate other forms of life, including plants, microscopic organisms, minerals, and elemental/nature spirits, into the ladder of consciousness.

Another intriguing theory is that individual souls are not as separate and distinct as most people like to believe. Our ego's point of view gives us that perception, but ultimately we are all connected. The energy of the soul is like a lake. When we take a body, it is like pouring some of that water into a glass, and for the moment it is separate and distinct. At death it is poured back into the lake, back into unity, and is no longer separate. This system accounts for the reports that several individuals were famous figures in history. Although the experience is greatly exaggerated, people joke that everyone thinks they were Cleopatra. If souls are separate, one is right and the rest are wrong. If souls are like a lake, a little bit of Cleopatra's energy could end up in many different people, connecting each to the life experiences of Cleopatra. As cycles repeat in nature, basic elements break down to be reborn in new forms. Why would souls not do the same thing? Although this is a highly plausible viewpoint, it frightens many people because it threatens their sense of individuality. The principle of mentalism tells us that we all contain everything, so such a group existence is not any more threatening than the hologram theory. We are all waves in the divine ocean.

Akin to the water theory is the belief in a collective information bank to which we all have access. In fact, we, and all existence, are collectively the information bank. This sounds much like the hologram, doesn't it? Jung called it the Collective Consciousness. Before him, mystics called it the Akashic Records. Isaac Bonewits calls it the Switchboard. All are slightly different ways of describing the same thing. If we are all one, we each have access to every past life in existence. If such a life has meaning for our current situation, we can access that information. Rarely a regression will not reveal just a past life, but a future life or even a parallel life occurring at the same time. The Akashic Records account for this, because all information, past, present, and all possible futures, are contained within it.

Those who believe in psychic abilities but do not feel that past lives are credible call the regression experience an exercise in transtemporal telepathy. One uses psychic powers to reach beyond space and time, and as one reads the minds of those in the past. The participant so highly identifies with their plights that he or she feels that this is a past identity.

The view of the skeptical psychiatrist is that all this information is confabulation, but it somehow connects the deeper areas of the mind with the conscious to resolve and heal. Quite a few doctors practice regression therapy, but personally do not believe in it, at least not at first. Such regressions are another tool to aid the patient and if it works, they use it. For some, past lives are simple fantasy and nothing more.

For the longest time, I had great difficulty deciding exactly what I believed in regard to reincarnation. I had some enlightening experiences with it, but I questioned myself. Did I make it up? No, I had enough experiences that I did not think I could subconsciously devise them all. I knew too many people who had retrieved some facts, dates, locations, and historical information that they had not come across previously. I was convinced that there was something to the phenomenon, even if it was not completely verifiable. I was stuck between thinking of my individuality as a soul and my collective connection to all life. I struggled between theories and never found one completely satisfactory. Then I asked a spirit guide.

The guide gave me an example of plants, such as a blade of grass. The blade grows, matures, and dies at the end of the season, only to be reborn again in spring. The blade is like the body. The root is like the soul. Each blade of grass has an individual root, as each body has an individual soul. Sometimes the grass remains in the Underworld for a time, then reaches up into the daylight of the world, only to return again. When the root completes many cycles, sometimes it withers away and breaks down into basic minerals, which are absorbed by the other individual roots. Through this beautiful example, my guides told me that we are both individual and united.

KARMA

The concept of karma is one aspect of the Eastern philosophy of reincarnation that has become popular in the Western world. Though mainly a concept in Hinduism and Buddhism, karma has made its way into the world of the witch.

Karma is the Sanskrit term for the energy generated by our actions, particularly in relationship to future incarnations. Witches see it as an extension of the Law of Three: what you do will come back to you threefold. Seen from an ethical viewpoint, karma could mean that one who does "good" acts gets rewarded with good and one who performs "bad" actions gets punished with bad events. Similar vibrations attract each other, as in the Principle of Vibration. Sometimes karma is described in terms of money and accounts. One creates a karmic debit or credit, seeking to balance the cosmic books to achieve release from the cycle of death and rebirth. One who is free from karma reaches a level of spiritual mastery. The Hebrew tradition calls it *tee-koon*, meaning "correct." This most likely refers to a notion similar to karma, "correcting" mistakes of past behaviors.

Karma can be seen without moral subtext, as a divine experience exchanger. There is no judgment in the witch's world, but instead cause and effect. Energy will return to its source. If you act in a way that causes suffering, you receive an experience to understand the same type of suffering you caused. If you act in a giving manner, you experience what it means to receive. Some experiences are exchanged during a single life, and others manifest in future lives. Such experiences, or "lessons," help us truly remember our divine natures and higher selves. Karma helps us wake up to the spiritual truths of the existence and fulfill our part of the pattern. Karmic astrologers believe that your birth chart gives clues to past-life experiences and your soul's plan for this life based on those experiences.

Relationships are linked together through karma. People with strong past histories often have to resolve karmic energies between them and therefore continue to incarnate together. Powerful emotions and experiences are focused on, such as the bonds of family, the bonds of love, and the bonds of fear and violence. They are all links of karmic energy. Role reversal is common, where parent becomes child or killer becomes killed. All are part of the experience of karma. On a soul level, and not our ego, we seek to explore all the aspects of human existence to remember our true nature. Eastern religions seek nonattachment, to release those bonds of karma and receive freedom from the wheel of rebirth.

Past-life relationships are the most difficult. We often have vague familiarity with people in our lives when we first meet them, falling into patterns that we do not understand. Situations between lives change, and obligations from past lives are no longer appropriate in this life. In this life, your brother could be the soul who was your mother in a past life. If you feel intuitively that your brother in this life should care for, nurture, and protect you like a mother, this expectation is not appropriate. That relationship is over. This person is no longer your mother, but your brother, and you must work though your current roles. People have these unconscious feelings and expectations all the time, and get upset when others don't live up to past-life roles. You are forging new relationships and new ways of relating to each other. This is particularly difficult in romantic relationships, where we feel we have found our "soul mate." Because we feel a past-life connection, we automatically assume that everything will go flawlessly. We have found someone to complete us. This is not the case at all. Focus on your *life* mate, who you are meant to partner with in this lifetime. When we use the term *soul mate*, it brings unrealistic expectations to a romantic relationship. On a spiritual level, your soul mate is not necessarily someone with whom you will have a romantic relationship, and may in fact be part of your soul group on the other side of the veil.

The point of reincarnation is to wipe the slate clean, at least the conscious slate, giving you a fresh start. Karma does affect us, but we are never fated into events beyond our control. Magick has taught me that we are all capable of choosing and manifesting our own fate. We all have free will, though our soul and karma may be leading us in a certain direction to help us find balance and remembrance.

€XPLORATION

Why would you want to explore your past lives? The answer is difficult, but there are many benefits. People can suffer from emotional blocks and traumas that have no connection to this life. Traditional therapies do not help. Often fears from past deaths, such as heights, water, enclosed spaces, or weapons, translate into irrational fears in this life. Once the root is understood, the fear abates. On the extreme end of the spectrum, such energetic blocks in the aura can cause physical illness. One of the most significant experiences I've ever had was watching the transformation of a woman named Sue. Prior to the class, she was plagued with back pain and overwhelmed with her sense of responsibility to take care of her family. During the class regression she discovered a past life as a male farmer, where she lived on a withering farm, responsible for the needs of the family. When the animals died, she pulled the farming equipment herself. This past lifetime ended in both physical and emotional pain. While she was in the regression, unknown to her, I saw her shoulders and spine straighten and take a natural, healthy posture. Her memory of the past incarnation healed her current pain and gave her a greater awareness of her issues. We've kept in contact, and as far as I know, she has never had back pain like that since. When she starts to relapse, she realizes it is a pattern of past guilt and releases it.

Most past-life issues help you explore your own actions, motivations, and reoccurring patterns of unhealthy behavior. With this awareness, the cycles can be broken. Take responsibility for what is affecting you here and now.

Talents, knowledge, and skills from a past life can be retrieved with a regression. Esoteric, artistic, or technical information can be brought through, though it is not often accessible in the conscious self.

The main reason that reincarnation is included in witchcraft training is as an initiation experience. Those with knowledge of life after death are better prepared to walk between the worlds, truly knowing that life continues on after physical death. Such an experience opens you to the true magickal reality.

EXERCISE 34

Past-Life Exploration

Though most people are eager to start exploring previous incarnations, fear of the unknown can rear its head prior to this exercise. If you experience extreme fear before the regression, think carefully about whether you are ready to do this exercise. One woman in particular had a problem with anything tight around her neck, including jewelry and certain clothing. She truly felt it was related to a past-life experience and wanted to resolve it, but when the time came, she became very afraid and refused to do a regression. It was not her time for it. Honor your own boundaries.

Past-life exploration is another experience facilitated by a partner. Though it can be done individually, with the help of guides, I certainly don't recommend such solo adventures when beginning. A partner guides you through the process, moving you along when you are stuck, asking questions that you are not aware enough to ask while in your magickal state, and helping you process difficult situations.

Usually as you start the process, you will feel as if you are reliving the life, in the body of your previous incarnation. Some people identify so strongly with it that they hear the thoughts and feel the sensations that occurred in the past. When facing trauma, the experience is difficult. A great technique is to have your partner guide you out of the body and view the entire event as a movie, in your mind's eye. You are watching it, knowing it is you, but not necessarily actively participating in it. Although this gives you some distance to observe, the effects are still quite powerful.

Much of the information will be intuitive flashes and simple experiences of knowing. You may hear foreign languages, but understand them or hear them translated into your native tongue. You may hear your thoughts and know your feelings, and often pick up on the feelings of those around you. When looking into the eyes of someone in the past, you may recognize their individual spark as someone you know in this life. Remember the expression "The eyes are the windows to the soul." You may also move forward or backward in time, to the next important event.

The very best advice I can give you in this experience is to go into it with no preconceived notions and follow your first impression. You can feel a conscious call to a certain place or time, and since you do remember it, your regression may not need to go there at this time. I could have named ten different places and times that I felt a connection to when I first experienced this, and I was open to any one of them. I was drawn to England, Egypt, India, and South America, to name a few. But my first experience was in France. I felt absolutely no connection to France and the time period I was in. I studied French in college and absolutely hated it, and perhaps this was why. I thought I had no connection to France and the language, but I discovered a very unhappy, difficult life in France. I explored my lives in England and Egypt much later. Don't worry if you experience something boring and mundane. The majority of lives on Earth have been rather normal. Look to the personal relationships for your important experience.

As for the guiding partner, take things slowly. The deeper the trance state, the slower the spoken answers will come, and you will have to gently nudge the regressed person to interact with you verbally. Always ask the person how he or she is feeling. If something is causing great stress, give the option of stepping out of the body or even leaving this life and returning to the present time. Gently guide, and be reassuring and encouraging. Take notes and ask questions. A theme will often present itself. If the experience is not progressing, you can guide the person forward or backward in time, to the next significant event. Say, "I'm going to count from five to one, and when I reach one, you will perceive the next significant event in this life." When you reach one, tell your partner to take a look around. Try moving in time at several points, whenever you feel stuck at the current moment. You can return at any time by rising up out of this life, up through the sky and finding the stairs of your inner temple leading back. Or you can continue to the death experience.

1. Start exercise 9: Counting Down to a Meditative State to get into your magickal mindset.

2. In your mind's eye, visualize the great World Tree.

3. Imagine that the screen of your mind's eye is like a window or doorway, a portal through which you can easily pass. Step through the screen and stand before the World Tree. Look up and feel its power. Touch the tree and place in it the intention of visiting your inner temple to do past-life exploration.

4. Look around the base of the giant tree, in the roots, and search for a passageway to your inner temple. Enter it. At the end of the tunnel you see a light, and you move toward that light and step out into your inner temple.

5. Affirm your protection shield and invoke your guides to be with you. Remember that they are present to answer any questions and send you in the right direction. When in doubt, ask them to help.

6. Ask to find the Gateway of Memories. Ask for the past-life experience correct and good for you. Once you stand before the doorway, open it up. It leads you through a long tunnel with many doors.

7. One door in particular will stand out to you, perhaps by its color or a symbol. This door leads to the past life correct for you. Go to that door and open it up. See the staircase descending and walk down it, counting each of the twenty-two steps backward, from twenty-two to one.

8. Jump off the last step and feel yourself jumping into your past life. Immediately look down at your feet. What are your impressions? What do you

see? Are you wearing shoes? Scan the body upward and describe what you are wearing. Are you a man or woman?

9. Look up and around at your environment. What do you see? If there is a reflective surface around, look into it and describe yourself. Do you recognize the time period or location? Access the memories of this person. Who are you? Where are you? What is the season? What is the year?

10. How do you feel in this life, physically and emotionally? Are you healthy? Are you happy? If you are uncomfortable or in any pain, you can step out of your body and observe the events like a movie.

11. Is there anyone around you? What are the relationships between these people and you? Do you recognize them as people in your current life? What are they doing?

12. If you feel prepared to experience your last moments, move forward in time to your passing, as you count down from five to one. Look around and describe what you see. Where are you? How are you dying? Is there anyone with you? How do you feel about your life?

13. Watch your spirit leave your body and travel outward. Follow this passing spirit beyond the veil, where other spirits will greet it. You could hear their messages, and take this time to speak with your own guides to understand the significance this life is having on your current incarnation.

14. Before you are the stairs leading back to the inner temple. Count them up, from one to twenty-two. Walk down the hallway back to the center of your temple and close the Gate of Memories. Listen for any messages your guides have and ask any further questions.

15. When you are done, return through the World Tree tunnel and stand before the World Tree. Step back through the screen of your mind's eye and let the World Tree gently fade from view.

16. Return yourself to normal consciousness, counting up, and giving yourself clearance and balance. Do any necessary grounding.

When done, discuss the experience with your partner, because you may not remember the details that clearly. Notice how past-life experiences, patterns, and lessons are affecting your current life.

NEW ASSIGNMENTS

• Exercise 34—Complete and record your experiences in your Book of Shadows.

CONTINUING ASSIGNMENTS

• Daily journal—Write three pages a day.

• Continue with a dream journal.

• Focus on a regular meditation practice, at least three times a week if not daily.

• Use intuition, instant magick, neutralization, light, aura reading, and healing scans in your daily life.

TIPS

• If you have difficulty accessing past-life memories from the Gateway of Memories, try these alternate images and techniques: (1) Visualize yourself descending into a tunnel, like the birth canal, leading to your past life; (2) Instead of using stairs, some people identify with elevators, where each floor is another past life. Press the button of the past life and step out of the door; (3) Imagine rising out of your physical body like astral projection. Make a symbol, such as a pentagram, on the roof in white light as your "homing signal," and ascend up into space, into the space-time. Then descend down into the past life, counting from twenty-two to one. When done, reverse the process and look for your homing symbol, returning you to your present physical body.

• Very rarely a person encounters an existence that he or she cannot understand, such as the time between lifetimes. The lack of physicality can be upsetting. Some report lives in other planes of existence and on other planets. Starting with the intention of a physical existence on Earth can help weed out such experiences, unless, of course, you are comfortable exploring them.

Lesson 13
Initiation

The only task left to complete is initiation. Such a task is no small feat. Initiation is the culmination of your work and should never be entered into lightly. Before you do enter into it, understand what initiation means.

The word *initiation* has many meanings, depending on the context. Usually it is an induction into a special group or society. The induction process consists of some form of ceremony or ritual. The ritual may contain a task presented as a challenge to each potential member. Such tests must be passed. They can be as simple as giving the appropriate word, handshake, or symbol, as learned in preparation for the ritual, or a test of courage, wits, intelligence, or foolhardiness. Though they may seem to have nothing mysterious in origin, the infamous hazing initiation rituals of college fraternities serve the same purpose as occult initiations. Each member, through the history of the group, comes from a similar background and goes through an ordeal, facing the same rituals and consequences. Success from passing the trials creates a common bond, regardless of whether you joined last year or twenty years ago. The events themselves may change, but the general feeling is conveyed, a sense of camaraderie. This is why such relationships last well past college and members of a fraternity in the business world will help their younger "brothers." For those of us who don't belong to a restricted group such as a fraternity or sorority, the rites of passage in life, recognized in both civil society and mainstream religious groups, are initiations. Marriage, childbirth, retirement, divorce, puberty, menstruation, coming out, and religious rites of baptism, communion, and confession are initiations.

The rituals and sacraments of all religions are initiations, leading you into a new peer group comprised of those who have also experienced the same event. Marriage can bring you into a new group of peers. Having a child can do the same thing, giving you a new world to explore. Ultimately, initiations bring you into a new world, be it social, political, religious, or mystical.

For the spiritually inclined, the new world may simply be a new worldview. The ritual, trials, and tests might not come from a humanmade agency, but from life itself, from nature or the people we attract into our world. Sacred stories are filled with initiations, particularly the wild woman/man who goes crazy, running off into the forest. In reality, the wild one is opening to magickal ability, speaking with spirits. Living in the wilderness, so close to nature, is an initiation. This future shaman must get these abilities under control, learn from the spirits, and come back having mastered his or her magickal abilities. Magickal traditions from all over the world are marked by a cloistering of the initiate in isolation, and often include fasting to induce a spiritual awakening. Some go to monasteries. Others travel to the top of a mountain, go deep in the jungle, or take a pilgrimage into the desert. Initiations force one to look at the world through a different lens, seeing a magickal world beyond the mundane. Initiations are shifts in consciousness, bringing a new worldview.

Testing experiences need not be so prolonged or dramatic. Anything that confronts you with an unclaimed part of yourself is considered an initiation of sorts. St. John of the Cross used the words "dark night of the soul" to explain the feelings of darkness, depression, and loneliness that mystics feel prior to great spiritual revelation. From this we garnered the saying "It's always darkest before the dawn." One does not have to be considered a mystic to have had this experience. We have all had an experience of darkness. We all feel alone at times. We all question our self, our friends, family, and view on divinity. That is part of the human condition because it leads us to greater glimpses of awareness. The initiation process may be jumpstarted by illness, tragedy, betrayal, or the sudden realization that you are different. The way one handles the experience is the true test, and the true initiation. By understanding and experiencing this isolation, you can then feel the connection between all things. Suddenly things before you seem clear because you worked through your darkness. A new path is illuminated and things fall into place more easily than before, if you act on it. By using this as a growth experience, and making the changes necessary to transform your life, you have passed the initiation and joined the group of people who have seen beyond the dark night. In your own way, you have had your personal, spiritual epiphany. To take a lesson from the philosopher Nietzsche, "If it doesn't kill you, it will make you stronger." As the birthing process can sometimes be difficult, but ultimately brings the greatest gift of new life to the world, initiations are spiritual rebirths, granting you a new life. To initiate means to begin. With every culmination and ending, there is a new beginning. With every death there is a rebirth.

The initiations of witchcraft encompass these concepts and more. They are inductions into a special group and a new worldview. Your new fellowship is the ranks of the dedicated witches of the world. Known by many names and traditions, you are joining their ancient lineage. It does not matter if you are in a formal coven or are an eclectic solitary; in your spirit, you are joining all those before you in the craft of the witch, and honoring all those who come after you. You are passing the threshold, like Alice through the looking glass, and entering a new life filled with hidden knowledge and personal revelation. The word initiate can refer to one who holds secret knowledge, whether through personal experience or formal training. Until rather recently, the witchcraft "society" was secretive and closed off from the world.

As a walker between the worlds, you are firmly planting one foot in each world, the physical and the immaterial. The initiation breaks down a self-perceived barrier to allow free passage across to the mystical realms. Grant Morrison, a Chaos magician and author of the avant-garde comic *The Invisibles*, a story and spell about magick, revolution, and the coming age, states in that work, "All times are the same time. The initiation of a sorcerer reveals this. That is why they say a true initiation never ends."[1] Magick and initiation take place outside of time, and the initiation itself lets us perceive the world beyond time and space, where all things are one.

---

1. Grant Morrison, *The Invisibles: Apocalipstick* (New York: Vertigo/DC Comics, 2001) 133.

Ultimately, you are on the path of priesthood or priesthood. Each witch, after a period of training, is considered his or her own intermediary to the Goddess and God; in effect, a priest or priestess. Those claiming the roles of High Priestess or High Priest and Crone or Elder are respected members of the community, but each initiate has full authority and encouragement to perform all the rituals and rites whenever she or he desires.

The witch hunters of old spread perverse information about the practices of witches and their initiations. Contracts in blood, kissing the Devil, and performing the Catholic mass backward are only some of the more mentionable rumors. These have absolutely nothing to do with a modern witch's initiation, if they ever had anything to do with initiations in the first place. No one is asked to renounce Christianity or any faith. No one in Wicca recognizes a devil or Satan, let alone pays homage to him, and no person or animal is harmed. Although modern rituals can be intense and dramatic, they are not the stuff of Hollywood movies.

The induction into witchcraft can contain two aspects. Some experience one and not the other, depending on the background, but I like to focus on both. The first is the objective initiation. This is the standard function of the ritual. When you train with a formal tradition for a length of time and service, completing tasks and learning, you are granted an initiation ceremony. Here, the teacher or group declares you a witch, or at least a witch of that particular tradition. Everyone present agrees on what physically happens and bears witness to the proclamation. Even if you are alone, there is a set of events performed that could be documented. In the objective experience, you are letting the authority of another, or the authority you see in the ritual itself, define you as a witch.

The subjective experience is the second part of the initiation, an intensely personal, life-altering experience. For many, that occurs in the ritual itself, through thoughts, emotions, visions, and voices. Some of the rituals will stimulate such a subjective experience, though none can force it if the applicant is not ready. Some report difficulties with psychic work prior to the initiation ritual, and then a blossoming of abilities and a cleansing of the chakras after the event. Dreams often bring such transformative experiences and are taken as initiations. The personal subjective initiation could happen at any point during the training, or during life.

My own mind and narrow expectations of abilities were blown away after doing my first healing. The information I received staggered the skeptic in me, and since it was a personal experience, I could not doubt it as being fabricated. My whole world changed dramatically as I walked out of that class believing that I could do absolutely anything, as long as it harms none. I still carry that belief with me to this day. In effect, I was changed forever. I was truly initiated at that moment. Not everyone in the class had the same subjective experience, though our objective experience was very similar. That awakening was simply what I needed to change my life for the better.

All the exercises and rituals of this book are initiations of sorts. Certain ones will have meaning for you. The recognition of energy, psychic ability, astral travel, healing, spirit contact, and past-life regressions are all forms of initiation, breaking you away from the old life and thrusting you into the new.

Some long-standing witches may never have the subjective initiation. For those witches who do have a subjective initiation, the process is driven by their own inner divinity and guidance. The initiation comes with a feeling of belonging or "coming home." You feel a divine presence or blessing urging you on the path. Sometimes the subjective experience is not granted though ritual or training, but through spontaneous visions and experiences, akin to the previously mentioned wild man shamanic initiation. In fact, the subjective initiation is very shamanic in nature, since it occurs internally, allowing one to interface with the spiritual realm and higher powers.

What Makes a Witch?

Two schools of thought exist for proclaiming yourself a witch. For the solitary or eclectic, your own personal desire, self-initiation ritual, and subjective experiences make you a witch. In more formal traditions, formal initiation makes you a witch. Some take that to mean that it "takes a witch to make a witch." Both views believe that the divine powers, the Goddess and God, are guiding the potential student to the path and ultimately to be an initiate, but the first school believes in self-determination and proclamation, while the second believes in formal requirements by a practicing group and ceremony to facilitate the process. Both are absolutely correct and yet completely wrong. In the end, only the Goddess and God can truly initiate. Rituals, journeys, and the like are only vehicles for the wishes of the Goddess and God.

Just as you may have more than one "dark night of the soul" experience in your life, you may have more than one initiation into the craft. Witches actually encourage this, because each initiation marks the end of a time of training, study, and expansion of your abilities. To finalize this training, one claims the personal power and subsequent new "vision of the world" through an initiation ritual.

DEGREES OF WITCHCRAFT

In the more classic traditions of Wicca, such as Gardnerian, the levels of initiation are divided into three (figure 32). One starts as an initiate, with no formal rank or title. A basic understanding of the history, ethics, mythology, theology, and holidays is required. Some teachers demand that prospective students take a survey of world religions before any further training, to make an educated decision that witchcraft is the path they truly feel called to walk. Once initiates are accepted, training begins for the first degree. Each degree of training usually lasts a minimum of a year and a day, if not longer.

The talents of a first-degree witch include basic meditation, psychic and energy-work skills, starting a magickal journal, participating in ritual, training in a healing art, building a home altar, and learning to cleanse, bless, and protect the home. Most importantly is striving to live the Wiccan Rede as a day-to-day reality.

The first-degree initiation ritual has somewhat of a hazing feel to it. At various points, the initiate is blindfolded, spun around, startled by a bell, and bound loosely with three cords, of blue, red, and white, at the wrists, neck, knees, and ankles, which later may serve as a belt for ritual robes while at the first-degree level. In strict Gardnerian traditions, the initiator keeps the cords.

Challenge is an aspect of these rituals. The initiate asks for admittance into the circle, and promises at sword or knifepoint to only enter the circle in perfect love and perfect trust, and never with ill will. *Love* and *trust* are the passwords to enter the circle. Once spoken, the initiate jumps over a broom and/or blade, to cross the threshold, the doorway, and enter sacred space.

Coven members will then introduce themselves and give spiritual blessings as gifts. The initiate asks the Goddess and God to be a witch. Then, in response to the question "What are you?" the initiate declares in a mirror held by the High Priest or Priestess, "I am a witch!" Usually a male applicant is initiated by a High Priestess and a female by a High Priest. All three initiation rituals are often done skyclad, meaning naked, wearing only the sky. In family traditions, it is common for mother to initiate daughter and father to initiate son. The new witch is presented to the four quarters before the ritual is ended and the circle released. In the most traditional covens, scourging (light ritual whipping) and a vow to keep the traditions of the craft secret are used. This initiation is said to be "of the personality," for one is transformed afterward.

The second-degree witch is considered a priest or priestess, with the ability to lead rituals, cast a magick circle, and do spells.

The last degree of traditional witchcraft is the third, marking a High Priestess or Priest.

Other systems of magickal initiation use different symbols for initiation. Various ceremonial magick groups use ten initiations, based on the ten spheres of the Hebrew Tree of Life. Alex Sanders, a ritual magician as well as a witch, reportedly believed that the first three initiations of witchcraft were the same as the first three initiations of ritual magick. Some traditions base their degrees on the seven chakras or the seven magickal planets, using the qualities of each to determine the course of study. Others use the twelve astrological signs. Many modern Wiccan traditions use an elemental system.

As a teacher, I use a structure based on the five elements—fire, earth, water, air, and spirit—and, as I see it, the five branches of witchcraft and magick (figure 33). The initial chapters of this book include a basic understanding of witchcraft, similar to the unnumbered initiate level of the traditional three-tier system. The lesson work is the first degree, based on the element of fire, of energy, will, guidance, protection, illumination, wisdom, and personal power. I feel that an aspiring witch must claim personal power and experience a profound connection to all things as a foundation for deeper magickal work. True, anyone can do a spell if they follow a recipe book, but I emphasize an understanding of how and why witchcraft works. The lessons of this book are based on my level-one classes. This is the first spark of magick.

First Degree

Second Degree

Third Degree

Figure 32: *Traditional Degree Symbols*

Figure 33: *My Personal Degree Symbols*

Level two relates to the element of earth, creating sacred space and manifesting your desires onto the physical plane through spell work. Students of the second level are claiming the title of priestess or priest. Water and shamanic witchcraft is the focus of level three, with introspection and shadow work as the guiding force. At the fourth level we study aspects of ceremonial magick, deepen our relationship with the elements, breath work, and magickal symbols, and create individual "reality maps" to connect to the higher self, based on our own experiences and ideas. Air is the element of the fourth degree. The fifth degree and element, spirit, is the realm of the High Priestess and High Priest, learning to use all these skills to live a magickal life. The chakras and zodiac signs are studied in-depth as temples of initiation and areas of life to master as a servant of the universe.

Witches and magicians are not the only ones to use initiation systems. Initiations can be found in Eastern religions, including Buddhism and Johre. Martial artists pass tests in skill and knowledge to move to the next degree. In the practice of reiki, a healing system brought to the world from Japan, initiations, called attunements, are given for each level of training. The reiki master, or teacher, must be initiated to that level to be able to hold and pass the energy, like the old "It takes a witch to make a witch" belief. The Freemasons have long used initiation systems, having thirty-three degrees. Their rituals probably influenced Gerald Gardner in his development of initiations.

Look for the initiations in your life. Remember how each affected you and how the change manifested in your outlook and daily life. Reflect on all the tests and trials that have made your stronger and more aware. Now you will see unusual or difficult situations in your life as opportunities for spiritual advancement rather than hardship.

Magickal Names

If initiation is a symbolic rebirth, it can be marked with a new name, symbolic of this new life. This is considered your craft name, what some feel is your true name. You might take a new name once, and use it only privately, either telling no one at all, or only other members of the craft. You can also take a new craft name at every initiation, adding to or discarding old identities.

Many practitioners have public craft names and private, personal craft names used only in intimate settings. Secret names were used not only for initiatory purposes, but for practical reasons. Originally, in magick, knowing the true name of someone supposedly gave you power and control over that person. By using magickal names, no one would know your "true" name, depending on what you considered your true name. Later, during the persecutions, witches who did confess may have given out craft names, but not legal names, so hoping to spare their sisters and brothers of the faith from a similar fate. Even now, witch names can be used to protect the privacy of others when speaking without the luxury of an intimate setting, though usually it is polite to ask someone what they would like to be called. Witches may use their craft names all the time, and some even legally change their birth name to their craft name. When in doubt, asking is better than assuming, as long as you ask with respect.

The act of taking a new name is magickal in itself. At times, it is a returning to a core identity, shedding the skin placed over the individual's true self by society. More often, it is a claiming of new attributes, skills, and lessons one seeks to learn at this level of training.

Witch names can come from the mythic world, taking identities in honor of different deities, heroes, and creatures. Some are based in the plant and animal kingdoms. Foreign languages play a part, making the name seem more mystical by association. Latin was widely used in the prime days of the Golden Dawn ritual magicians. Random syllables that sound pleasing to the ear are just as suitable. Many names are a combination of several sources.

When researching a name, particularly one from a deity or hero in established mythology, take into consideration all the meanings and stories related to the name. All mythologies have been rewritten, and all have lighter and darker aspects, but be aware of what archetype you are invoking.

How do you get a witch name? There are several ways. You can simply decide on one, think about it, and once your decision is final, proclaim yourself with this name. Usually names feel right immediately or not at all. The proclamation can be a part of your self-initiation, or done at another time. Many choose a craft name before ever coming close to an initiation experience, and that's fine. Choosing the name was in a sense the first initiation.

A teacher, peer, or friend could suggest a name to you. Sometimes we are too close to see what really suits us and it takes someone else to point it out. Their choice can be based on intuition, or through systems such as numerology.

The last method, and my personal favorite, is through meditative experience, asking the Goddess and God to give you the name correct for you. Prior to your initiation, some teachers suggest an all-night vigil spent fasting, meditating, and contemplating your new name. If you would like to do a vigil, by all means, go ahead. You could wait for the shamanic experience I will detail in the self-initiation ritual. Quite a few of my own students have gotten their names during the journey prior to the ritual.

Though traditions vary, I feel that you do not have to take a witch name at the first initiation, or ever! Though I have a personal, private name that I do not share with anyone, for the longest time I was simply content with Christopher, and felt that was my true identity. Though my witch name adds to it, I did not shed my past name. Do what is right for you and your own eclectic tradition. I recommend *The Complete Book of Magickal Names* by Phoenix McFarland for more ideas.

Year-and-a-Day Preparation

If you have followed the course outlined in this book, you have done much of your training to prepare you for your first initiation. You have the talents and experiences of a first-degree witch. Look back into your magickal journal, to your first entry describing exercise 1, your intention ritual. Read and review it. Have you accomplished what you set out to do? Have your goals broadened?

If you have followed your own schedule, determine how many weeks you have left in your year and a day, as determined by your intention ritual. If you have passed the year mark for this work, you may want to use two years and two days to give yourself ample time to reflect, instead of rushing into anything immediately. You will know when the time is right for you.

Continue your studies, looking to other views on the craft. A true witch must be educated on the craft. If this is the first book you have read on the craft, peruse many others to get an overall view of this science, art, and spirituality. I recommend the following books because they each present a different view of the craft, but please go to the books that speak to you.

Power of the Witch by Laurie Cabot (Delta Press).

Wicca: A Guide for the Solitary Practitioner by Scott Cunningham (Llewellyn Publications).

The Spiral Dance: A Rebirth of the Ancient Religion of the Great Goddess by Starhawk (Harper San Francisco).

Wicca: The Old Religion in the New Age by Vivianne Crowley (Aquarian Press).

To Ride a Silver Broomstick by Silver RavenWolf (Llewellyn Publications).

There is a self-test in the appendix of this manual, for those who want to test their grasp of the material.

SELF-INITIATION

I definitely believe that only the Goddess and God can make one a witch, though many others may help along the way. Initiation is a process of self-discovery. Because of this belief, your self-initiation is divided into two parts. The first is the shamanic journey, a more subjective, internal initiation. The second is a ritual, an announcement of your intent and acceptance of this new role.

Even if you do not choose to call yourself a witch, or if you already consider yourself a witch, you can complete these studies with this journey and ritual, modified in whatever way will make you comfortable. Rituals are a part of closure, marking the end of a time of study and the start of a new phase of life, even if that phase takes you to a different path altogether. Each stone is a new part of your personal foundation.

On the last day of your year-and-a-day period, try to be as reflective and meditative as possible. If you can take the day off and spend some time in solitude, so much the better. You may prefer to do this initiation in the morning, at sunrise, or in the evening. I like my rituals in the evening, as close to midnight, the witching hour, as possible.

To prepare, you will need a few materials on hand. First, get out your intention slip from the first exercise. You will also need a flameproof container in which to burn it. I use a cauldron, and you can get them at New Age shops around the country, or you can use a metal bowl or a regular heat-resistant bowl with some sand in it to absorb the heat. Sturdy metal pots will also work. If you have to resort to an ashtray, use one that is bought specifically for this reason and no other. A candle is necessary to light the flame, and you can use the one on your meditation altar.

Obtain an oil for anointing yourself. You can mix together essential oils (I suggest ten drops of frankincense, ten drops of myrrh, and twenty drops of a base oil, such as apricot kernel or grape seed), buy a blessing or protection oil, or simply use kitchen olive oil. Also, get a small amount of sea salt.

Traditionally, witches do initiation rituals either skyclad or in black robes. Some witches buy robes, while others make them at home. They symbolize a separation from the mundane world and a journey into the magickal world, priming the consciousness to enter a meditative state simply by donning them. If you do choose to use a robe, you may want to keep with the older traditions and get three cords, of blue, red, and white, that are long enough to make into a belt or sash for your robe.

If you plan on wearing a pentacle, or do so already, have this piece of jewelry ready.

Most importantly, have your witch name prepared before this day, if you choose to take one. In fact, the evening before your last day can be used for an all-night vigil to claim a new name.

To start your self-initiation, light the candle on your altar. Protect the space and invite your divine protectors to be with you, as you usually do. Get all your materials out and onto your altar, including the items on this checklist:

> Incense (optional)
>
> Intention slip
>
> Flameproof vessel
>
> Anointing oil
>
> Sea salt
>
> Robes and cords (optional)
>
> Pentacle jewelry (optional)

THE JOURNEY

Announce your desire of initiation into the realm of witchcraft with these or similar words:

"I ask the Goddess and God that I may enter your service and the sacred traditions of the craft, to become a witch in fact and name."

You can play some music to accompany your journey, if you'd like, and then prepare for deep meditation and journeywork. The constant rhythm of the shamanic drumming as performed on Michael Harner's *Shamanic Journey Solo and Double Drumming* (Foundations for Shamanic Studies) is ideal, or you can use more dreamlike, relaxing New Age music. Perform the relaxation and countdown of exercise 9 and lead yourself into a meditative state. You have learned about the World Tree, the cosmic axis connecting the upper worlds to the lower worlds, the places of initiation, healing, and knowledge. In this meditation, guide yourself to your inner temple, your sacred heart of the World Tree, and call on your guides. Call on the Goddess and God, and allow yourself to journey, led by your guides and deities.

In this meditation, you will receive your initiation and complete your own individual and unique training. The experience could quite literally be anything, and will often surprise you. This is the lesson that no one can teach you except for the Goddess and God.

When the experience is complete, use the World Tree and your inner temple to return to the middle, conscious world. Count yourself up. When you return from this journey, take a few moments to reflect on it. You may want to write it down now, or save this for later and proceed immediately to the ritual.

Return to the altar and candle flame. Thank the Goddess and God for your spiritual initiation. If you would like, light some incense to set the tone of the ceremony. You can have the following ritual written out and before you, with your personal touches and instructions. It need not be memorized.

If you choose to wear a ritual robe, and do not have it on yet, wear it now, without the corded belt, signifying that the spiritual initiation into the craft has started, but is not complete.

THE CHOICE

This aspect of the ritual signifies that you truly choose, in full knowledge, to walk this path and accept all the responsibilities that it entails. From your training, you understand that the acts of witchcraft are real. You are awakening to the world that lies beyond what others call the "real" or physical world. You acknowledge that there are paths other than the ones traditionally shown in society. Say:

"I choose to walk my own path between the worlds, in the space beyond space, and the time beyond time. I choose my own path into the labyrinth of the mysteries. I choose to live a life of perfect love and perfect trust. I choose the life of a witch for this lifetime, here and now. So mote it be."

CLAIMING YOUR POWER

Read your intention slip aloud, and reflect on your original intent. Have you accomplished it? Has it changed? Restate your intent, with any modifications or an entirely new intention. Burn the paper and feel the power of your intention permeate the space.

Mix a pinch of the salt with your anointing oil, drawing a banishing pentagram over the mixture, and feel it fill with light. Anoint yourself while speaking these blessings:

Anoint the third eye. *"I anoint my third eye, so I may see truly in this world and all others."*

Anoint the throat. *"I anoint my throat, to speak truly and receive the truth."*

Anoint the hands. *"I anoint my hands, to heal myself, my people, and the Earth, to be a guardian and caretaker."*

Don the cord belt around your robe. You can braid the three strands together at this point, or knot them in three places. With each knot, a blessing, intention, or vow can be made as a form of knot magick. Traditional covens would take your measurements, meaning height, width, and the circumference of the head, and then keep the cords to prevent betrayal. If the new witch did betray the coven, the cords were used as a link to the betrayer for curse of retribution.

PRESENTATION TO THE GODDESS AND GOD

The presentation formalizes your relationship with the Goddess and God, and marks you as an initiate into the life of a witch.

"From this day forth, I shall be known to the Goddess and God as (witch name or birth name). I ask to walk hand in hand, in the love of the Goddess and God. I am a witch. I am a witch. I am a witch. So mote it be."

If you plan on wearing a pentacle, take it out now. Anoint it with the oil. Raise it up to the Goddess and God. Feel it burn with powerful energy.

"I ask the Goddess and God to bless this pentacle with their love. It is a sign of protection, of balance, and of magick. I manifest all three in my life now. So mote it be."

THANKS

Create a circle of thanks, thanking first and foremost the Goddess and God, and then all beings who have aided you on your journey, including spirit guides and people who have been supportive or helpful in any way. Giving thanks to the universe helps create more blessings in the future and energetically thanks those who have given their time and energy.

"I thank the Goddess and God for all gifts, and I thank all those who have helped me in my quest, including (name them). I send you all my gratitude, love, and light. Blessed be."

The ritual of self-initiation is complete! Congratulations and welcome to a new phase of your life. I wish you many blessings.

This ritual can be adapted to those working with partners, in groups, or with mentors. Statements can be rewritten as questions, asking the initiate to answer affirmatively. The anointing and blessings can be done by another, as a conduit for the deities' blessing. If you know how to cast a magick circle, the entire ritual can done within the circle, but such work is the training and initiation of the second level of witchcraft, that of the priestess or priest. Now that you have laid the foundation of your inner spiritual life, you are more able to bring the sacred out into the world, to build the Outer Temple of witchcraft, to do spell work, celebrate the rituals of the year, and claim your role as priestess or priest of the Goddess and God.

Blessed be!

Appendix: Self-Test

Answer these questions to demonstrate your mastery of this material. Use a separate piece of paper if you need more room.

1. Briefly define the following words:

Magick:

Witchcraft:

Personal energy:

Aura:

Book of Shadows:

Centering:

Degrees of witchcraft:

Grounding:

Healing:

Initiate / Initiation:

Law of Three:

Pagan:

Pentagram:

Pentacle:

Reincarnation:

Subtle bodies:

Wiccan Rede:

2. What are the differences between witchcraft and Wicca? What are the differences between pagan and neopagan?

3. What are the commonly accepted translations of the word *Wicca*?

4. Who is commonly credited with the modern revival of witchcraft?

5. Briefly describe the history of witchcraft, from Paleolithic times to the present.

6. What are some of the different traditions of witchcraft currently being practiced?

7. In your own words, how does magick work?

8. In your own words, what is a hologram and why is it important to understand?

9. What is the witch's pyramid?

10. Matching:

_____Law of Mentalism

_____Law of Correspondence

_____Law of Vibration

_____Law of Polarity

_____Law of Rhythm

_____Law of Gender

_____Law of Cause and Effect

A) Everything is dual; everything has poles; everything has its opposite.

B) Everything flows; everything has its tides.

C) Everything is a creation of the All, the divine mind.

D) Everything has its masculine and feminine principles.

E) Every cause has its effect, and every effect has its cause.

F) As above, so below; as below, so above.

G) Nothing rests; everything moves.

Briefly explain each of the Hermetic principles.

11. Colors: Fill in your personal correspondences to each color.
Pink:

Red:

Silver:

Orange :

Brown:

Blue:

White:

Black:

Gold:

Red-orange:

Green:

Purple:

Violet:

Yellow:

Turquoise:

Indigo:

12. Chakras: Fill in the blanks of this chart. Be able to describe the progression of the chakras, from bottom to top.

Chakra	Color	Location	Information
Crown	_____	_____	Divinity, higher self
_____	_____	Brow	_____
_____	Blue	_____	_____
_____	_____	_____	Love, emotion, healing
Solar plexus	Yellow	_____	_____
Sacral	_____	Belly	_____
_____	Red	_____	_____

13. In your own words, metaphysically, what is disease?

14. Describe the World Tree, its function, and its use.

15. In your own experience, what are spirit guides?

16. According to your own beliefs, what is karma?

17. What does it mean to be a witch?

Bibliography

Adler, Margot. *Drawing Down the Moon: Witches, Druids, Goddess Worshippers, and Other Pagans in America Today*. Boston, MA: Beacon Press, 1979.

Belhayes, Iris, with Enid. *Spirit Guides*. San Diego, CA: ACS Publishing, 1986.

Bentov, Itzhak. *Stalking the Wild Pendulum: On the Mechanics of Consciousness*. Rochester, VT: Destiny Books, 1988.

Black, Jason S., and Christopher S. Hyatt, P.h.D. *Urban Voodoo: A Beginner's Guide to Afro-Caribbean Magic*. Tempe AZ: New Falcon Publications, 1995.

Bonewits, Isaac. *Real Magic*. York Beach, ME: Samuel Weiser, Inc., 1989.

Bruyere, Rosalyn L. *Wheels of Light*. New York: Fireside Publishing, 1989.

Cabot, Laurie. *A Salem Witch's Herbal Magic*. Salem, MA: Celtic Crow Publishing, 1994.

———. *Witchcraft as a Science I and II*. Class handouts and lecture notes. Salem, MA: 1993.

Cabot, Laurie, with Tom Cowan. *Power of the Witch: The Earth, the Moon and the Magical Path to Enlightenment*. New York: Dell Publishing, 1989.

Cameron, Julie. *The Artist's Way*. New York: J. P. Tarcher/Penguin Putman, Inc., 1992.

Capra, Fritja. *The Tao of Physics*. New York: Bantam Books, 1975.

Choquette, Sonia, and Patrick Tully. *Your Psychic Pathway*. Audiocassette. Niles, IL: Nightingale Conant, 1999.

Conway, D. J. *The Ancient & Shining Ones*. St. Paul, MN: Llewellyn Publications, 1993.

———. *Moon Magic*. St. Paul, MN: Llewellyn Publications, 1995.

Cooper, Phillip. *Basic Magic: A Practical Guide.* York Beach, ME: Samuel Weiser, Inc., 1996.

Corrigan, Ian. *The Portal Book: Teachings and Works of Celtic Witchcraft.* Cleveland, OH: The Association of Consciousness Exploration, 1996.

Crowley, Aleister. *Magick in Theory and Practice.* New York: Dover Publications, 1976.

Crowley, Vivianne. *Wicca: The Old Religion in the New Age.* San Francisco, CA: Aquarian Press, 1989.

Cunningham, Scott. *Wicca: A Guide for the Solitary Practitioner.* St. Paul, MN: Llewellyn Publications, 1988.

Dyer, Dr. Wayne W. *Real Magic: Creating Miracles in Everyday Life.* Audiocassette. New York: Harper Audio/HarperCollins Publishers, Inc., 1992.

Farrar, Janet and Stewart. *Spells and How They Work.* Custer, WA: Phoenix Publishing, Inc., 1990.

Farrar, Stewart. *What Witches Do.* New York: Coward, McCann & GeoGhegan, Inc., 1971.

Freke, Timothy, and Peter Gandy. *The Hermetica: The Lost Wisdom of the Pharaohs.* New York: Jeremy P. Tarcher/Putman, 1999.

Gimbutas, Marija. *The Goddesses and Gods of Old Europe: Myths and Cult Images.* Berkeley, Los Angeles, CA: University of California Press, 1982

Grimassi, Raven. *Italian Witchcraft.* St. Paul, MN: Llewellyn Publications, 2000.

———. *The Wiccan Mysteries.* St. Paul, MN: Llewellyn Publications, 1997.

Grist, Tony and Aileen. *The Illustrated Guide to Wicca.* New York: Sterling Publishing Company, Inc., 2000.

Grolier Multimedia Encyclopedia. Grolier Interactive Inc., 1997.

Guiley, Rosemary Ellen. *The Encyclopedia of Witches & Witchcraft.* New York: Checkmark Books, 1999.

———. *Harper's Encyclopedia of Mystical & Paranormal Experience.* New York: HarperSanFrancisco, 1991.

Gurunam (Joseph Michael Levry). *Lifting the Veil: Practical Kabbalah with Kundalini Yoga.* New York: Rootlight, Inc., 2000.

Hay, Louise H. *Heal Your Body.* Carlsbad, CA: Hay House, 1988.

Harner, Michael. *The Way of the Shaman.* Third edition. New York: HarperCollins, 1990.

Hine, Phil. *Condensed Chaos.* Tempe, AZ: New Falcon, 1995.

Jenkins, Elizabeth B. *Initiation.* New York: Putnam, 1997.

Jong, Erica. *Witches.* New York: Harry N. Abrams, Inc., 1981.

Judith, Anodea. *Wheels of Life*. St. Paul, MN: Llewellyn Publications, 1987.

K., Amber. *Covencraft: Witchcraft for Three or More*. St. Paul, MN: Llewellyn Publications, 1998.

Kenyon, Tom. *Sound Healing and the Inner Terrain of Consciousness*. VHS. Anchorage, AK: Big Dipper Productions, 1996.

Kraig, Donald Michael. *Modern Magick: Eleven Lessons in the High Magickal Arts*. St. Paul, MN: Llewellyn Publications, 1988.

The Kybalion: Hermetic Philosophy by Three Initiates. Chicago, IL: The Yogi Publication Society, 1912.

Marshall, Ian, and Danah Zohar. *Who's Afraid of Schrödinger's Cat? An A-to-Z Guide to All the New Science Ideas You Need to Keep Up with the New Thinking*. New York: William Morrow and Co., 1997.

McFarland, Phoenix. *The Complete Book of Magical Names*. St. Paul, MN: Llewellyn Publications, 1996.

Moorehouse, David A. *Psychic Warrior*. New York: St. Martin's Mass Market, 1988.

Morrison, Grant. *The Invisibles: Apocalipstick*. New York: Vertigo/DC Comics, 2001.

Moura, Ann. *Origins of Modern Witchcraft*. St. Paul, MN: Llewellyn Publications, 2000.

Myss, Caroline. *Anatomy of the Spirit: The Seven Stages of Power and Healing*. New York: Three Rivers Press, 1996.

Pajeon, Kala and Ketz. *The Candle Magick Workbook*. New York: Citadel Press, 1992.

RavenWolf, Silver. *To Ride a Silver Broomstick*. St. Paul, MN: Llewellyn Publications, 1993.

Rheeders, Kate. *Qabalah: A Beginner's Guide*. London: Hodder & Stoughton, 1996.

Rhodes, J. Philip. *Wicca Unveiled: The Complete Rituals of Modern Witchcraft*. Glastonbury, Somerset, Great Britain: The Speaking Tree, 2000.

Richardson, Alen. *Earth God Rising*. St. Paul, MN: Llewellyn Publications, 1990.

Sabrina, Lady. *Cauldron of Transformation*. St. Paul, MN: Llewellyn Publications, 1996.

Satchidananda, Sri Swami. *The Living Gita: The Complete Bhagavad Gita*. Yogaville, VA: Integral Yoga Publications, 1988.

Silva, José, and Philip Miele. *The Silva Mind Control Method*. New York: Pocket Books/Simon & Schuster, Inc., 1977.

Starhawk. *The Spiral Dance: A Rebirth of the Ancient Religion of the Great Goddess*. New York: HarperSanFrancisco, 1979.

Stone, Merlin. *When God Was a Woman*. New York: Harcourt Brace Jovanovich, 1976.

Talbot, Michael. *The Holographic Universe*. New York: HarperCollins, 1991.

Thorsson, Edred. *The Book of Ogham*. St. Paul, MN: Llewellyn Publications, 1994.

Valiente, Doreen. *An ABC of Witchcraft Past and Present*. New York: St. Martin's Press, Inc., 1973.

Weiss, Brian. *Many Lives, Many Masters*. New York: Simon & Schuster, 1988.

Whitcomb, Bill. *The Magician's Companion*. St. Paul, MN: Llewellyn Publications, 1993.

Yin, Amorah Quan. *The Pleiadian Workbook: Awakening Your Divine Ka*. Santa Fe, NM: Bear & Co., 1996.

Index

affirmations, 89, 104–107, 110, 143, 198–199, 270

Akashic Records, 296

Alexandrian, 32, 39, 49–52

alpha, 87, 108, 117, 164

altar, 4, 70, 93–95, 97, 115, 135, 165, 174, 195, 233, 310, 318–319

altered states, 66–67, 96

Anahata, 210

ancestors, 8, 13, 18–19, 39, 41, 48, 57, 65, 72, 85, 226, 239, 266, 293

angels, 125, 177, 223, 238–239, 243

Anglo-Saxon, 9, 27, 30, 44

anima/animus, 244

Anja, 213

ankh, 1, 173–174

Aradia, 33, 35–36, 38

archetypes, 12–13, 19, 26, 37, 43, 98, 221, 261, 315

Asatru, 53–54

astral body, 210, 230–231

astral plane, 230–231

astral travel, 5, 210, 222, 226, 230, 309

Atlantis, 22, 36

automatic writing, 241, 255

autumn equinox, 47

belly, 149, 204, 209–210, 215, 217, 230, 276

Beltane, 46–47

beta, 87–88, 96, 105

Blavatsky, H. P., 34, 36, 56

Bohm, David, 125–126

Bohr, Niels, 119

Bonewits, Isaac, 55, 161, 166, 285, 296

Book of Shadows, 38, 51, 63–64, 70, 91, 116, 165, 178, 192, 218, 235, 257, 270, 289, 304

Brujería, 54

brow, 101, 206, 213, 216, 218, 277

Buckland, Raymond, 52

Burning Times, 7, 28–29, 31–33, 39, 45, 48

Cabot, Laurie, 6, 10, 50, 109, 147, 166, 281, 317

candle, 67, 69–70, 94, 97–99, 162, 174–175, 195–196, 318–319

Cayce, Edgar, 36, 56

Celtic, 3, 9, 13, 16, 23–26, 28, 33, 38, 41, 46, 48, 50–55, 66, 68, 109, 165, 213, 239, 245, 261, 293–294

Ceremonial, 32, 49, 54–55, 209, 311, 314

chakra, 101, 186–187, 205–207, 209–217, 219, 228, 230–231, 270, 275–276, 279, 281, 285, 289

channeling, 256–257

Chaos magick, 55

chi, 79, 81, 136
Christianity, 25–26, 28–33, 42, 44, 50, 55, 239, 292–293, 308
clairaudience, 212, 256
clairsentience, 256
clairvoyance, 213, 256
conscious mind, 37, 73–74, 98, 104, 161, 163, 225, 228, 234, 244, 255, 261
consciousness, 12, 34, 37, 42–43, 66–67, 72, 74, 78–79, 86–88, 90–91, 96, 98, 103–105, 108, 110, 114–115, 124–126, 128, 132–133, 135, 141–142, 144, 146, 149, 153, 155, 158–159, 169, 172, 177, 181, 184, 191, 205, 207, 214, 218, 223, 226, 228, 230–231, 233–234, 241–243, 245, 256–257, 263, 265–266, 269, 271, 286, 288, 293, 295–296, 303, 306, 318
contagion, 162, 290
cord, 199, 202, 204–205, 214, 217, 231, 277, 320
core shamanism, 57, 226
correspondence, 137, 139–140, 162, 170
Crone, 12, 43, 154, 308
cross, 41, 95, 109, 122, 163–164, 173–174, 241–242, 306, 310
Crowley, Aleister, 20, 33, 35, 38, 54–55, 71, 317
crown, 46, 86, 96, 100–101, 149, 155, 182–183, 196, 214, 217–218, 231, 233, 277, 279–280

delta, 88, 317
Devil, 8, 26–30, 33–34, 44, 164, 308
Dianic, 32, 39, 50
Dirac, Paul, 119
disease, 29, 36, 212, 274–277, 280–282, 284
divine energy, 81, 86
divine mind, 74, 133–134, 136, 163, 187–188, 190, 222, 228, 239, 244, 279, 293
divine plane, 231
dream, 75, 98, 133, 182, 185, 222, 225–226, 234–235, 258, 270, 290, 304
Druid, 23, 55, 293
Dryghten, 44

Eclectic, 5, 16, 32, 40–41, 50–51, 53, 62–63, 307, 309, 316
Edict of Milan, 26, 33
Egypt, 22, 32–33, 64–65, 79, 131, 163, 239, 261, 301
Eightfold Path, 89, 91
Einstein, Albert, 119, 125
emotional body, 211, 231
emotional plane, 231
empowering, 2, 66, 174, 184, 275
energy anatomy, 5, 193–219, 274–275, 279–280
Esbat, 48
etheric body, 196, 209, 230, 280
etheric realm, 230
Europe, 7, 18, 20, 23, 25, 27, 29–33, 37, 39, 42, 51, 57, 146
evil eye, 169

first degree, 310–313
flying, 162, 221, 226
Fox, Selena, 53
Frazer, Sir James George, 33, 36

Gardner, Gerald, 33, 37–39, 49, 51, 89, 314
Gardnerian, 32, 38, 49–52, 67, 310
gates of consciousness, 265
gender, 27, 44, 153–154, 239, 244, 276
gnosis, 87, 89–90, 93, 278
Gnostic, 25–26, 291
God, 12–13, 16, 19–20, 22, 26, 29, 40, 43–44, 46–49, 51, 59–60, 62, 67, 69, 72, 74, 91, 94–95, 97, 105, 110, 112, 114, 127, 131, 133, 140, 143, 148, 153–155, 163–164, 173, 175, 188, 203, 214, 217, 226, 228, 239, 242–243, 245, 269, 308–311, 316–317, 319, 321–322
Goddess, 3, 6, 8, 11–13, 16, 20–24, 35–40, 42–44, 46–47, 49–52, 59–60, 62, 64, 67, 69, 74, 79, 90–91, 94–95, 97, 105–106, 110, 112, 114, 126–127, 133, 143, 148, 153–155, 162–163, 165, 173, 175, 185, 187–188, 191, 203, 214, 217, 226, 228, 239–240, 242–243, 245, 261, 269, 283, 308–311, 316–317, 319, 321–322

Golden Dawn, 33–35, 54, 132, 295, 315

Graves, Robert, 38

Great Spirit, 13, 44, 69, 74, 105, 114, 133, 214, 239, 283

Greek, 12–13, 26, 29, 43–44, 46, 51–52, 55, 65, 130–131, 165, 181, 247, 278

healing guide, 263

Heisenberg, Werner, 119–120

Hereditary, 37, 39, 52

heresy, 28–29, 31

Hermes, 131–132

Hermetic, 34–35, 131–132, 142, 145, 148, 155–156, 161, 165–166, 181, 222, 246

higher mind, 244

higher self, 74–75, 95, 236, 239, 244, 246, 283, 287, 289, 294, 314

Hindu, 23, 51, 57, 79, 81, 109, 124, 133, 144, 151, 206–207, 213, 293–294

hologram, 121–122, 125–127, 133, 139, 153–154, 181, 281, 293, 296

Holy Roman Empire, 28–29, 32–33

Horus, 1, 20, 35, 131, 173

hundredth monkey theory, 124–125

ida, 207

Imbolc, 46–47

incense, 67, 69, 90, 94, 115, 173–175, 178, 186, 318–319

India, 23, 66, 293–294, 301

initiation, 35, 62, 65, 68–70, 91, 147–148, 163, 247, 300, 305–322

inner temple, 1, 3–5, 16, 62, 259–271, 302–303, 319

Inquisition, 33, 36

instant magick, 5, 108, 110–114, 116, 128, 137, 160, 166, 168, 178, 187, 192, 195, 199, 218, 236, 258, 271, 290, 304

Isis, 13, 20, 34, 56, 173

Italy, 24, 35–36, 38, 53, 234

Jesus Christ, 25–26, 36

journal, 60, 62–63, 67, 70, 91, 116, 127, 166, 178, 192, 203, 218, 225–226, 235–236, 258, 260, 270, 290, 304, 310, 316

Jung, C. G., 12, 36–37, 125, 161, 244, 296

Kabalah, 28, 31, 35, 54, 223–224, 226

karma, 36, 156, 297–299

ki, 79, 81

Kraig, Donald Michael, 170

kundalini, 79, 88, 194, 206–208

Lammas, 47

laser, 121–123, 188

Law of Three, 156–157, 162, 169, 297

Leland, Charles, 33, 35–36, 38, 53

Lemuria, 22, 36

lower self, 74–75

lucid dreaming, 225–226

Lucifer, 26, 36

Mabon, 47–48

magick, 2, 4–6, 8–12, 16, 19, 22–31, 35–39, 41, 43, 45, 48–56, 59–61, 63–67, 71–77, 81, 83, 86–87, 89–90, 94, 98, 101, 104, 107–116, 119–170, 173–175, 178, 187–188, 191–192, 194–195, 198–199, 207, 209, 212, 214, 218, 221, 230, 236, 240, 244, 258, 264, 267, 270–271, 274, 290, 294, 299, 304, 307, 311, 314–315, 320–321

Maiden, 12, 43, 154

Malleus Maleficarum, 30–31, 33

mana, 79, 81

Manipura, 210

Masons, 34

Mathers, Samuel Liddel MacGregor, 34–35

meditation, 2–3, 5, 45, 49, 56, 61, 66, 70, 85, 87, 89–90, 93–117, 128, 132, 135, 143–144, 149, 154, 157, 160, 165–166, 169, 174–176, 178, 182–183, 187–188, 190, 192, 202–203, 205, 207, 214–215, 218, 223, 225, 232–234, 236, 240–243, 245, 247–248, 257–258, 262–263,

266, 270–271, 281, 285–286, 290, 304, 310, 318–319

mental body, 97, 137, 212

mental plane, 231

mentalism, 133, 246, 279, 296

Middle World, 226–228, 230, 266

Moon, 2, 8, 11–12, 43, 48–50, 57, 67, 100, 142, 150–152, 154–155, 165, 187, 191, 263, 268

morphogenetic fields, 124

Morrison, Grant, 307

Mother, 2, 11–13, 16, 19–20, 39, 41–43, 46–47, 50, 56, 79, 124, 133, 143, 148, 154, 169, 184, 197, 214, 217, 244–245, 291–292, 298, 311

Mother Earth, 11, 43, 79, 143, 148, 154, 217

Muladhara, 207

Murray, Margaret, 33, 37

muscle testing, 252–255, 258, 283, 289

Myss, Caroline, 219, 281

mystery school, 65–67

mythology, 12, 22, 25–26, 37, 42, 44, 50–51, 54, 65, 68, 98, 160, 228, 239, 261–262, 310, 315

nasties, 170, 172

neutralization, 159–160, 165, 236, 258, 271, 290, 304

New Age, 5–6, 10, 20, 34, 39, 56, 65, 136, 161, 194, 206, 295, 317–319

Norse, 12, 54, 90, 165, 245

Old Religion, 8, 11, 37, 39, 317

once born, 294

Ordo Templi Orientis, 35

Osiris, 20, 26, 56, 131, 173

Ostara, 46–47

Paleolithic era, 11

Pan, 26, 164

pantheon, 12, 56

particle, 120, 142

past lives, 156, 198, 291–294, 296, 298–299

pendulum, 20, 22, 128, 249–251, 255, 283, 289

pentacle, 163–165, 173–174, 178, 318, 321

perfect love and perfect trust, 81, 157, 170, 216, 248, 310, 320

physical realm, 222, 228

physics, 10, 119–120, 125–126, 128, 132, 143, 155–156, 165

Planck, Max, 119

polarity, 43–44, 81, 145–148, 150, 153, 239, 285

polytheistic, 11, 13, 24, 44, 57

prana, 81, 136

Pribram, Karl, 121–122, 125

priest, 4–5, 8, 15–16, 25, 27, 63, 308, 311, 314, 322

priestess, 4–5, 14–16, 25, 53, 308, 311, 314, 322

priesthood, 293, 308

protection shield, 176, 183, 198, 205, 236, 279, 283, 287, 302

protection symbols, 174

psychic attack, 168, 236

psychic body, 213

psychic diagnosis, 278–279, 282

psychic plane, 231

psychic self, 74, 98, 244

psychic travel, 222, 232, 234–235

psychometry, 290

pyramid, 64–65, 103, 261

Pythagoras, 65, 130, 163–164

quantum, 10, 119–120, 125–126, 132, 143, 165

Radical Faery, 52

Reconstructionist, 54–55

reiki, 15, 159, 281, 314

reincarnation, 26, 34, 291–295, 297, 299–300

religion, 8–11, 16, 20, 22, 25–26, 33–34, 36–40, 49–50, 56–57, 93, 130, 157, 247, 317

Roman Empire, 24–26, 28–29, 32–33

Rosicrucian, 34

Sahasrara, 214

Salem, 31, 33

Samhain, 47–48

Sanders, Alex, 39, 49, 311

Santería, 56–57

scanning, 279–281, 283

Schrödinger, Erwin, 119

science, 5–6, 10–11, 16, 31, 42, 50, 61, 71–72, 93, 119–166, 261, 281

Seax Wica, 32, 52

second degree, 312–313

self-image, 193, 210, 267, 276

self-initiation, 5, 51, 53, 62, 68, 309, 315–318, 321

sending light, 187–188, 190–191, 283, 288

shamanic journey, 226, 241, 289, 317, 319

shamanism, 3, 15, 39, 53, 56–57, 226, 281

Sheldrake, Rupert, 124

Siberia, 14, 56

sky energy, 86, 148–149, 217, 285

So mote it be, 69, 176, 205, 320–321

solar plexus, 210, 212, 217, 231, 233, 276, 285

soul group, 238–239, 295, 299

spirit guides, 5, 56, 111, 203, 212, 237–241, 244–248, 252, 254, 256–257, 261–262, 265, 269–271, 295, 297, 321

spring equinox, 46

Strega, 38, 53

subtle bodies, 194, 207, 222, 228, 241, 288, 293

Sumer, 32, 239

summer solstice, 47

Svadisthana, 209

symbolism, 72, 98, 131–132, 163–164, 173, 226

synchronicity, 37, 161

theta, 87–88

third degree, 312–313

third eye, 101, 213, 217–218, 231, 285, 320

Thoth, 35, 131

thoughtform, 199, 204, 230

throat, 100, 204, 212–213, 216–217, 231, 277, 279, 320

Tree of Life, 223, 228, 311

trigger, 108–116, 137, 187–188, 191–192, 195, 226, 251, 254, 257

Triple Goddess, 12, 43, 46, 106, 154, 162–163, 165

triplicity, 162

triskelion, 165–166

Trismegistus, Hermes, 131–132

Underworld, 12, 43, 48, 125, 160, 181, 186, 226–228, 230, 266, 293–294, 297

Upper World, 226–228, 231, 266

Valiente, Doreen, 38, 51

vampire, 170, 190

vibration, 13, 86, 94, 133, 140, 142–144, 162, 174–175, 181–182, 184, 186, 192, 198, 223, 231, 248, 252, 255, 257, 297

Vishuddi, 213

visualization, 56, 77, 89, 97–98, 100–102, 108, 110, 112, 136, 165, 177, 186, 218, 261, 283, 285, 288–289

Voudoun, 57

warlock, 8, 27

Westcott, William, 34

Wheel of the Year, 4, 46–47

Wicca, 9, 25, 30–31, 33, 35, 38–40, 44, 50, 52–54, 57, 64, 66, 72, 132, 156, 160, 170, 223, 239, 308, 310, 317

Wiccan Rede, 64–65, 157, 310

Wiccan Shamanism, 53

winter solstice, 46–47

Woodman, William Robert, 34

Woodruff, Rev. A. F. A., 35

World Tree, 226–228, 266–267, 269–270, 293, 302–303, 319

year and a day, 5, 68, 310, 316–317

Yule, 46–47